TALES FROM A NORTHWEST NATURALIST

TALES FROM A NORTHWEST NATURALIST

by

Jim Anderson

Photography by author unless otherwise noted

The CAXTON PRINTERS, Ltd.
Caldwell, Idaho
1992

Library of Congress Cataloging-in-Publication Data

Anderson, Jim.
    Tales from a Northwest Naturalist / by Jim Anderson ;
photographs by author.
        p.   cm.
    ISBN 0-87004-353-6 : $17.95
    1. Natural history--Northwest, Pacific--Outdoor books.
2. Anderson, Jim.   3. Wildlife conservationists--Connecticut--
Biography.   4. Naturalists--Connecticut--Biography.   I. Title.
QH104.5.N6A53   1992
508.795--dc20   92-13926
                                                                              CIP

The CAXTON PRINTERS, Ltd.
Caldwell, Idaho 83605
155382

CONTENTS

INTRODUCTION

by
Robert Michael Pyle

Jim Anderson grew up with the unlikely nickname "Catsfur." It had nothing to do with his own pelage, nor any particular proclivity he might have had for felines. Jim just couldn't stop asking "What's that fur?" until his uncles began replying, "Catsfur, that's what's fur." And so Jim became Catsfur. He still hasn't stopped asking what things are for, what they do, how they behave. In short, he is one curious man. This book is the celebration of Jim Anderson's curiosity, and his lifelong, ongoing, impossible attempt to satisfy it.

Yet *Tales From a Northwest Naturalist* does not simply concern itself with questions and their answers. Jim is also a conservationist of the first order. He is a man with a righteous sense of rage over the misuse of nature, as keen as his pleasure in the land and its creatures. When he witnessed a callous busdriver willfully run over a snake on one of his field trips, his indignation was such that he stormed off the bus and hitchhiked back to town, leaving the bus driver to cook in the aftermath of his wrath and the students' amazement. A love of nature so palpable as to live in the courage of its conviction runs through every one of these naturalists' tales.

One of the most prolific and admired natural history teachers in the Northwest, Jim Anderson has touched thousands with his passionate care and extensive knowledge, gently conveyed. I consider him to be among the foremost interpreters of nature beyond the city limits—sort of a one-man diplomatic corps for inter-species understanding. When I read these tales, each one drawn from his days afield among unforgettable people and other animals, I feel like one of Jim's favored students.

Another name Jim has earned from his admirers is Mr. Owl. Often accompanied on his field and lecture outings by an owl or an eagle, a snake or a crow, he has spared few measures to know nature intimately and let others know what it's like to do so. In my opinion, our pandemic state of alienation from our neighbors on earth—human and otherwise—comprises one of the greatest dangers to our future. Should it get the best of us, it won't be through Jim's doing. He is a tireless agent for close contact with nature (sometimes no farther than talon's length!), and this intimate book carries on that joyous task.

But if Jim is a curious catsfur, a wide-eyed Mr. Owl, a formidable conservationist, and a teacher *par excellence*, he is above all a family man. And Jim has many families. He has enjoyed three nuclear families as son, husband, and the best of fathers. And in a larger sense, Jim has created instant families every time he has gone afield or into the classroom or lecture-hall. That talent of melting strangers into a clan of naturalists is a rare one. None of Jim's families have escaped the orbit—or the trials—of his all-encompassing love of land and people. These special essays create that same sense of membership. Step into them and you feel a part of something you'll be reluctant to leave when the last page turns. So read them again!

Through our mutual passion for butterflies, I have come to know lepidopterist Sue Anderson and her remarkable brood. Along the way my acquaintance with her husband Jim, his unique history, and his impact on Northwest nature study, has steadily grown. I am delighted to know that those who have not been so fortunate as to meet him in person can now range afield with Jim in these pages.

A broad field it is. If the turkey vultures of Drain don't capture your fancy, you can read about a treasure-chest of jade-and-gold monarch chrysalides among the milkweed. Or, if natural history seems all posies and campfire games, read how the author deals with racism on the range and falcon-thieves in the desert, or how an owl gives back an abused child's voice.

From persecuted coyotes to beloved butterflies, from manure cures to lava caves, and all around the Northwest from Dufur to Drain and beyond, Jim gets himself and his reader into a panoply of "situations"—and out again—delightfully. Yet as far as these *Tales* range, they always come home to the congeniality of the campfire, the collegiality of naturalists.

Like Jim, my own grounding as a naturalist has brought me from Yale's Peabody Museum of Natural History to the living museum of the Pacific Northwest. Like Mr. Owl, I have known the pleasure of taking folks afield to get to know nature a little better. And, like Catsfur, I have been continually astonished by nature's resilience and ability to refresh the lives of her devout followers. Now, through his magic book, I have come to know the natural history of Jim Anderson and our shared habitat better than ever before. I thank my brother naturalist for sharing the tales of his life out-of-doors, and I know you will thank him for it too.

PREFACE

"It's not too much to a man's credit to say he does no harm. If he hasn't done any good, he has just filled up space."
(R.A. Long, *The Oregon Desert*, Caxton Printers, Ltd. 1971)

Dear readers . . .

Over the past thirty years I've presented thousands of slide programs and live animal demonstrations, hundreds of assemblies on the subject of natural history in schools all over the Northwest, and told tales around campfires from the Pacific Ocean to the Rockies. It never seemed to fail, after almost every show I would hear the comment, "You should write a book . . ."

When I was younger I couldn't see any need for a book about what I was doing with, for, and to Mother Nature, but as the years rolled on it seemed more and more like a good idea. Now that I've done it, I'm happy. This project has given me the opportunity to not only sit by the fire again with many of my old friends, it has also given me the chance to scrutinize my impact on the world of Nature; I am relieved to say that I believe it has been minuscule.

I've always believed that education is a two-way street. Information, in order to be useful, should flow in all directions. For me, osmosis has been the major way in which I gained information. I'm not a college-educated person, having taken a course or two only when it was financially possible, or when I thought I required it to understand a subject more thoroughly—like the time I signed up for a paleontology course at Portland State University. To get into the class, I needed some undergraduate work in chemistry and math, so I filled out the forms and said I was a graduate of Fort Rock

University. About a month into the class I was notified by the instructor that the office couldn't find my transcripts—in fact—they couldn't even find Fort Rock, let alone a university. (As you read this book you'll understand why.) I was fortunate to have a great instructor who just grinned at me and said, "We both know that's a mighty fine school." I completed the course and, if I remember correctly, I even passed it.

Over the years, I've soaked up a great deal of knowledge just listening to others. One evening I had the wonderful experience of sharing a PTA program with Dr. Lendon Smith, a well-known pediatrician from the Portland area, who was scheduled to speak before me. I would often draw on what the previous speaker had talked about to make a point in my talks about the conservation ethic, wildlife, or fund-raising for the Oregon Museum of Science and Industry (OMSI), in Portland, where I was employed as a Naturalist. That evening Dr. Smith said something that I will never forget, and have come to recognize over the years as a Great Truth. He was talking about events that affect a child's life and said, "You can spend forty years doing what you should have done or should not have done (with your child) in the first four." That is the most powerful statement I have ever heard regarding the raising of children. It is absolutely true. I've not only seen the evidence of this in my own children, but in hundreds of others I've shared campfires with.

Writing this book may also give me another opportunity to achieve a goal that I had when I worked for OMSI. In those days I had an almost unlimited resource of young, inquisitive minds to work with, an opportunity to cultivate natural curiosity into the power that moves—and saves—mountains. Young people from fourth grade to high school signed up for field trips and science classes, and during our adventures, we saw nature at work in many spheres. My personal goal was to handpick one hundred kids and send them out into the world with a great love for Nature. I didn't want them going into wildlife work, per se, but to maintain that love affair, no matter what they decided to do for a living.

Borden Beck, an old pal who has gone out among the stars, was that sort of person. He was a successful attorney in Portland, and maintained a personal love affair with nature all his life, helping to steer a great many people toward respect for the Wild Places and the Wild Things. Loren McKinley, OMSI's Director and Ray Barrett, the education director in those days, also helped by supporting the varied field trips and outdoor programs that I dreamed up (although Loren was less than enthusiastic about the bats I had hibernating in the lunch-room refrigerator).

Dorothy Mason, my secretary and wonderful helper at OMSI, signed up "my" kids, and when the list was filled, we'd always put on a few more, saying, "The more the merrier." I had the greatest expectations of those kids. I admit today that I manipulated parents and kids the best way I could toward my goal, but I failed.

Some of "my" kids didn't return from Vietnam, and a few who did, didn't know it. Others didn't come back from a bad trip on drugs or just stayed away too long, while others just didn't care anymore for one reason or another. It was hard for me to see these things happen as I'm an incurable red, white, and blue idealist.

One of my young nature enthusiasts, George Long, who today is in the science department of the Corvallis School System, taught me to practice what I preached, though. We had gone down to Astoria on a field trip when he was an eighth grader. About the time we arrived at the Astoria Column, it was raining like it only can in that neck of the woods. (My grandfather would have said, "it was rainin' like a cow peein' on a flat rock.") I was really out of

sorts and sat there in the bus grumping about the weather—and the rain.

George listened to it longer than I give him credit for today, and then he stopped me short. "Jim," he said, "didn't you always tell us that no matter where we were, and no matter what the circumstances, we could always find something in Nature to occupy our minds and make living worthwhile?" I grumpily admitted that I had, but failed to see anything "worthwhile" about that downpour in Astoria. Then George said, "Look out the window." I followed the direction his finger was pointing , and there was one of the most beautiful spider webs on a flower that I've ever seen before or since—a silent testimony that indeed, Mother Nature always has a treasure close by for those who seek it.

Perhaps this book will give me another chance to find one hundred people who will look at nature a little differently and read what fun I've had on this sweet Earth, and treat our home with new attitudes, new respect, and perhaps carry on a conservation ethic when I go out among the stars.

To be sure, this book is about my love affair with the World of Nature and how I inflicted this on my family and friends. It covers almost a lifetime—from the time I was a boy living, part-time, with my parents and grandparents on a small dairy farm in West Haven, Connecticut—to today, where I live near Sisters, Oregon with my lovely family. I was born the year after Lindburg flew the Atlantic, which gives me better than sixty years on this Wonderful Earth. In that amount of time, I've done a great many things in a great many places—most of the time in the Northwest.

Hal Boverman, an old friend from Portland who also knows the healing powers of Nature, pointed out a neat thing to me recently. "Did you see your license plate?" he asked, giving me a big grin. I wondered what he was talking about, because it is nothing more than a normal, older Oregon plate on my old Chevy Suburban. He poked his head in the window and squeezed my shoulder. "It says 'I'd rather be . . .'" Then he chuckled again, "That's you all over."

Even though I have hopped around like a

gadfly most of my working career, I really feel I'm a success in life. "Success," by my definition, is doing what you want to do, doing it the best you can, getting paid for it, and benefitting your fellow man.

I am deeply thankful for my childhood experiences, the love and understanding of my mother and father, my aunts and uncles, and especially my sweet grandmother and cantankerous, loving, grandfather. I can recall my first lessons in history and literature presented to me by my Uncle Ben while gathering our winter wood on the farm.

I was on the other end of a cross-cut saw with him, and as a big block of oak dropped off the log we were sawing, it revealed a lead ball that we had sawed in two. "Wow, look at that!" he exclaimed. Then he started counting the tree rings in both directions and I heard about WWI, the Revolutionary War, the French & Indian Wars, the volcanic explosions of Krakatoa and Mt. Tambora, Napoleon, Hiawatha, Uncle Tom's Cabin, and so many other events as my uncle went on and on, bringing history to life in the growth rings of an old oak tree.

My Uncle Harry taught me to pitch horseshoes and to also enjoy geography—and work—as we hoed corn and potatoes. About the time he saw I was slowing down he'd shout, "Hey, Catsfur! (the nickname Harry gave me) What's the capitol of Indiana?" And for the next three hours or more, we'd play his game of "Capitols" as we grubbed out weeds and I learned that work can be fun.

As a kid on that small farm in Connecticut, while rummaging around in my Uncle Ben's nature library, I first discovered the men who are responsible for the love I have for nature today: Herman T. Bohlman, William L. Finley, Dallas Lore Sharp, and Roger Tory Peterson. Their books and photographs on birds opened the doors to a whole new way for me to look at the world of nature.

I am so very grateful to the years of shared adventures with Dr. Matt Maberry, the man who had a great deal of influence in teaching zoo keepers how to get Asian elephants pregnant. He also introduced me to so many new friends in the natural world—from shrews to whales—what a man!

Jim Anderson and son Ross photograph and band owls in Wasco County, Oregon.

During those years another old pal, Clyde Miller, helped in ways he will never know. We shivered and coughed by many a smokey campfire with kids, and he was always ready to help, no matter what, when, or where.

Reub Long, and my mentor, Phil Brogan, true men of the Wind, Earth and Water, gave me so much of themselves. My son, Reuben Phillip, carries their names as a token of my respect for them.

Dean and Lily Hollinshead of the Timberlane Ranch in Bend were like a mom and dad to me so often. It was an honor for me to be with Dean when he left this earth for his other home. My oldest son, Dean, has his name as a token of my respect for the good times I enjoyed with Old Dean.

Carroll Peabody of Tucson, and his lovely

This baby barn owl went to the Salem legislative session with Jim as an "expert" witness against portions of a proposed falconry bill.

wife, Joan, who has since passed on, introduced me to the incredibly beautiful world of hummingbirds, and the nature of southeastern Arizona. My youngest son, Caleb Carroll, and my sweet little girl, Miriam Joan, are named for my good friends from Arizona.

This book also reflects a great deal of sacrifice on the part of my families, from my lovely daughter (who lives in Florida) and my neat, older sons, Dean and Ross (in the Air Force), to my beautiful family who lives with me at home.

My wife, Sue, is the most tolerant and sweetest person in my life. I taught her to soar in gliders, and have hiked into some wonderful worlds with her. She teaches me daily about Life, Humility, and Charity, and has shared so much of the living world with me. She also suffered through the first proofs and the rewriting of this work. Anyone who has undertaken a book with their family knows what that means . . .

My life wouldn't be near as much fun without Tim Tilton, my old glider instructor and friend, who with our departed pal, Jack Smith, taught me how to soar with eagles.

Larry Langley and his lovely wife, Theresa, crawled through a lot of lava tubes with me, and I still remember the day Larry came to my rescue and carried my backpack out of the wilderness while I hobbled out on blisters and blood-filled boots. He and I have also pulled each other out of a lot of mud holes.

To all the biologists and secretaries of the Oregon Department of Fish and Wildlife and the Game Officers of the Oregon State Police I will always be grateful. I have never been let down by any of them when I needed help to understand the complexities of nature, or to go after a hawk-killer. Gary Hayden, a longtime Game Officer in Bend is among the best of the breed, although there are many violators he met who don't share my appreciation for him.

I am also grateful to Harriet, my ex-wife, and mother of my two older boys. I have no problem matching the miracle of the emergence of an adult butterfly with that of the birth of my first son, Dean. It was a difficult birth, the first for mom and son, and as it progressed I felt the deep emotions that all fathers must (should?) have as they help their child enter the world. It was necessary for the doctor to use instruments to get Dean's head aimed in the right direction with a minimum of fuss for he and his mom, and after the birth he handed him to Harriet and said, "Now don't worry, his head will be quite normal in a short time."

In her joy, she probably didn't really hear what he was saying, she just beamed at our new baby son and said, "I don't care what he looks like to you—I just think he's the most beautiful baby I've ever seen!".

The doctor nodded in agreement and then leaned closer, carefully examining Dean's head, hair, skin, and hands, murmuring, "This is really quite a surprise; it must be some kind of a miracle".

"What?" we asked in alarm, at last conscious of his inspection.

"Well . . ." he slowly answered, grinning at us. "I don't see any scales, feathers, or

A young golden eagle complains about his new leg band.

webbed feet. Considering what you both do for a living, and the things you associate with, this looks like a normal, healthy mammal." Thanks Hat, you put up with so much during our years together with OMSI, the Portland Children's Zoo, Nature's Niche, Sunriver, and so many other adventures.

My dear friends, Connie and Joseph Jones, of OMSI's Hancock Field Station, located near Fossil, Oregon, have been a great help, not just with this work, but at any time, anyplace. Connie's gentle proof-reading, and thoughtful suggestions have helped bring this work to a reality. Joseph and I go back to the sixties, when he walked onto the OMSI science bus one day as an eighth

grader filled with questions about nature, and who today is a great naturalist. (I have often defined a naturalist as a biologist who flunked chemistry—but Joseph proved me wrong. He's working on a Master's Degree in geology, something that requires a lot of chemistry.)

I would be remiss if I didn't express my gratitude to one of the most wonderful institutions on this earth, the Public Library. What I missed in a formal education I soaked up in the Deschutes County Library, thanks to people like Marion and Ivy Grover, and their niece Mary (Grover) Berrigan who works there today. I have often said that if we spent more money on libraries, we

A "friend" drops in to sample the dead mice hors d'oeuvres always kept in the Anderson refrigerator.

"Look out the window, Jim!" says George Long.

Dr. Matt Maberry climbs out of the cockpit of his Mooney.

wouldn't have to spend so much on jails. The longer I live, the more I appreciate the social and educational benefits from our public libraries.

To all the teachers and children that "Owl," "Hawk," "Snake," "Tarantula," and I shared times with, there is no way I can say thank you adequately. Those were the best of times—weren't they? I still have boxes and boxes of those wonderful thank-you letters, drawings, and poems that I've saved all these years. I've taken the liberty of putting a few of them in this work—perhaps a few of the teachers and children (now older) will recognize their art work.

This work represents a lot of years; my hair is very grey, and when the hair gets grey, so goes the memory. In that light, I hope everyone will realize I've taken liberties with some of the, "He said . . . You said . . . They said . . . I said . . . " things. In all honesty I can't remember those statements as accurately as I would like. If I have left out a tale that someone remembers and thinks I should have, I apologize. If I have offended anyone, I apologize too for rankling your fur—but perhaps I should stick to my grandfather's advice. "Never apologize; it's a sign of weakness." Anyway, to all my friends, and (even) to those I locked horns with, I am sincerely grateful.

As you read of my lifetime love affair with Nature, I sincerely hope that the tales and experiences will provide you with the desire to go out and gently stop, look at, feel of, taste, and listen to the natural world around you. If you must tinker with Nature, please do it carefully and understand what you're doing. The Earth is our home (away from home); we should strive to leave it in better shape than it was when we arrived.

Jim Anderson
Sisters, Oregon - July, 1991

TALES FROM A NORTHWEST NATURALIST

1 | CATSFUR

A Kid on the Farm

"Quiet, Catsfur!", Horace whispered to Harry and me as we quietly descended into the darkness of the cellar. The flashlight beam swept over the stairs ahead of us, piercing the darkness like a laser, glinting off canning jars and cellar windows. "Look out for that last step, Harry," Horace whispered, "It's a squeaker . . ."

With the stealth of hunters all three of us reached the cellar floor. The beam of our flashlight continued to sweep the damp interior, when suddenly Harry exclaimed, "There's one!" Glinting back from the flashlight beam were two bright red orbs, close together.

"It's a rat, for sure! Hold the light steady . . . easy . . . steady", Horace whispered, as we held our breath.

"CRACK !" went the single-shot 22.

Just as suddenly as the sound shattered the silence of the cellar, the two beady eyes vanished. "Did you get 'em?" Harry asked. The beam swept along the floor and answered the question.

"Yep, there it is," Horace boasted, our light moving closer as we crept up to inspect our quarry.

"Careful now . . ." Harry cautioned, "sometimes they act dead and will jump right at you. They can bite like a sun-of-a-gun!"

Horace poked the huge rat lying on the cellar floor. We could see no movement as he prodded it with the gun muzzle. "He's done for," he said, proudly. "Let's see if we can get another one." We crept silently to the stairs and sat down to wait.

"Hear it?" I whispered.

"Yeah," Horace answered. You could almost see his grin in the dark.

"My turn," Harry whispered urgently.

"Okay, okay," Horace sighed, handing the

.22 over to him. We eased off the stairs and crept silently toward the scratching noises coming from somewhere near the potato bin.

"Okay, turn on the flashlight," Harry whispered. The brilliant beam slashed through the darkness, right on target.

"There it is!" Horace croaked. "Shoot!"

"CRACK!", went the 22 for the second time. A loud squeak pierced the darkness, then a frantic scurrying. The flashlight beam swept the floor, searching for the sound.

"Oh, darn!" Horace hissed, "He's headed this way!" A large, wounded rat scurried across the floor, coming straight at us, the flashlight beam showing the way.

Rattus rattus, the Barn Rat, also known as the Wharf Rat, is a stout survivor. They have been known to kill cats twice their size and cause serious wounds in dogs trained to hunt them. Like most New England farmhouses, the cellar was the storehouse for fruit, vegetables, and assorted canned goods put up earlier to help get the occupants through the coming fall, winter, and spring. Such places were attractive to rats, which in turn attracted young boys raised on stories about great hunters and marksmen in such books as *Last of the Mohicans*. Guns were, and still are, important to the growing process of young men as were the weekly rat hunts in the dark cellar. These were the highlight of the week, always taking place on Friday, the last day of school and the big night out at the movie house in town.

"Shoot him!" Horace ordered. "Shoot!"

"I can't," Harry wailed, fumbling as he tried to get another round into the chamber. "I can't see to get the shell in." Suddenly he let out a horrified scream. "He's going up my pants leg!"

Bedlam broke loose as Harry began dancing around, waving the rifle. I tried to keep him in the flashlight's beam, but his antics were too much to keep up with.

Horace kept shouting, "Give me the gun! Give me the gun!" as the rat climbed higher up Harry's pants leg. The two older boys finally bumped into each other and the rifle changed hands. "I've got it," Horace shouted, "Now hold still and I'll finish him off!"

"No!" Harry cried, grabbing at the large lump tearing at him from under his pants leg. "No!" he screamed again and then grabbed it in both hands. Loud screeching sounds came from his pants leg as he squeezed the rat, trying to keep it from climbing any higher.

"Hold him out and I'll get him!" commanded Horace.

"No!" Harry screamed, dancing away from him on one leg. The battle was on: Harry squeezed and the rat tore at him with claws and teeth trying to escape; Harry kept hopping across the cellar floor with Horace after him, trying to keep the rifle in the flashlight beam.

"Get away," Harry kept pleading, "I've got it in both hands now." Slowly, the rat's thrashings became more feeble as Harry's grip on it tightened. He was pouring it on, his leg's welfare at stake. After what seemed hours, but was probably less than three minutes, the struggle was over. The squeaking and thrashing about subsided, and Harry stood once again on his two feet.

"Turn on the cellar light, will you?" Horace asked. I fumbled about, searching for the long string hanging from the light fixture. I didn't find it, but it found me and I gave it a yank. The cellar was suddenly bathed in pale yellow light from a single 25-watt bulb suspended from the ceiling. We stood transfixed, staring at our hunting partner as he slowly released his grip on the body of the rat.

"Whew," Harry sighed. "That was a close call . . ." Shaking his leg slowly, he watched the rat slowly slide down toward the floor.

"What's going on down there?" the voice of authority inquired from the head of the stairs.

"Harry killed a rat." I called back.

"And it ran up his pants leg!" Horace added, almost laughing.

A short, bow-legged, older man descended into the pale light of the cellar, bare feet showing beneath his flannel night shirt. "My God, Harry," he exclaimed, "You're bleeding." Everyone suddenly looked at Harry's leg. Sure enough, blood was oozing from the place where the the rat had taken his last refuge. "Quick," my grandfather commanded, "take down your pants. Let's take a look at that!"

"Golly, dad," Harry muttered, as he loosened his belt and let his pants drop, exposing some nasty looking wounds on the outside of his thigh.

"Yup, he got you all right," Horace observed.

"It's all right, son," his father said. "Come on out to the barn and we'll fix you up good as new. The best thing for wounds like that is for you to pee on it—you've got to wash it clean and be sure the germs are gone— then we'll put on a good coating of Watkin's salve. You'll be okay."

Such was one event in life on the farm. Television wasn't even a dream in our lives in those days. Shucks, we didn't even have indoor plumbing. Chamber pails were a dire necessity in all the bedrooms, and trips to the outhouse were taken reluctantly, especially in dead of winter. Young boys, growing up on a small dairy farm in Connecticut, or anywhere in the early 30s, had to find their own entertainment. Thus the Great Rat Hunt was carried out in the dark of night, deep in the cellar of the great, old farmhouse along Jones Hill Road, in West Haven.

Curiosity is a Wonderful Gift

One of the earliest lessons I ever received in biology was from my grandmother as we sat by the kitchen window cleaning chickens. This was an annual ritual I was introduced to when about eight years old. As a younger part-time member of my grandparents' family that was made up of older boys and girls, I was the "natural" to be assigned to my grandmother and chicken cleaning. (I also believe she had a great deal to do with my positive attitude about the work ethic.)

"Be careful," my grandmother used to caution me, as I pulled the liver from the body cavity. "Be sure you don't pierce the gall bladder," she would point with the end of her sharp knife. "That would ruin the liver." So I was very careful, for breaded chicken liver was among my favorite foods.

I can recall the first time I removed the lungs from a chicken. My grandmother referred to those as the "lights," a name her mother used. Then she explained how lungs worked. I learned that chickens (and dinosaurs) had gizzards, and from that I assumed all birds had gizzards (this was to be corrected later on in life). We also had a great many domestic geese that we'd occasionally cook up, especially on Thanksgiving, Christmas, and other holidays, but it was the lowly chicken that introduced me to the physiology of birds.

As the cleaning process went on, my questions probably became annoying, "What's this, or that, 'fur?" My ever gracious, patient, and understanding grandmother would try her best to give me a satisfactory answer. My uncles, however, soon tired of the incessant questions and began to reply, "Catsfur, that's what's 'fur." It didn't take long before I got the name of "Catsfur," which stuck with me for longer than I care to remember, even on to high school. The curiosity that gave birth to that nickname has remained, and hopefully has been passed along to all my children. Natural curiosity, nurtured, gently directed, and

allowed to grow, is a priceless gift for any person, no matter what age, or where he happens to be growing up. Even if he gets the name, "Catsfur . . ."

My uncle Ben knew that I wouldn't pass up anything new to look at or to "ohhh", and "ahhh" over, so every time he found something that he knew I'd get excited over he'd drag it home for me.

"Hey, Catsfur!" he called out one late afternoon. "Come take a look at what I found over on Hubbard's stone wall . . .," and plunked a box down on the kitchen table.

I walked over and opened the lid—not even giving a thought that what was in there might just jump out and bite me. Inside there were two skeletons locked in the posture in which they had died. One was a bird, and the other a mammal. "What is it, Uncle Ben?" I asked, running my fingers carefully over the bones.

"Well," he began, "let's see if we can solve this mystery." He carefully opened the box the rest of the way so we could both see without getting in each other's way.

"Look at those teeth," he said, pointing to the needle-sharp, tiny fangs of the mammal. Then he asked, "Does that give you a clue what it did for a living . . .?"

I ran my finger over the fangs and was pretty sure of my answer. "Yep, I'd guess that he was a meat-eater of some kind."

"You guessed that one right," Ben answered. "I have a hunch it may have been a weasel . . . now look at those sharp talons on the bird. What do you think that was?"

I figured that was easy too. "Shucks, Ben," I said. "That's a hawk!" I was sure surprised as he stood there shaking his head, not agreeing with me at all.

"You had better take another look, Catsfur," he said as he turned the bird's skull slowly. "Look at that head. Does that look like a hawk's skull?" Before I could answer, he pointed to it. "And look at those big holes. Do you think they might be eye-sockets?" I got down for a closer look as he said, "Now, what do you think?"

"You're right, Ben," I said. "That's no hawk with eyes that big. It must be an owl." I looked up at him. "A great horned owl?"

"Now you're on the right track," he said smiling. He started to close the flaps on the box, saying, "I'll tell you what . . . I'm going into New Haven tomorrow and investigate an old house for Revolutionary War artifacts. If I can get some spare time I'll swing by

Peabody Museum and ask one of the biologists there what we have. You want to come along?"

"Peabody Museum?" I asked. "What's that?"

Ben looked at me for a moment then smiled. "I guess you've never been there, have you? Well, I'll tell you what. I'll bet after you see that place you'll never be the same again."

How right he was.

Grandfather and the Owl

Many creatures fell victim to my BB gun and single-shot .22 my aunt had given me for a birthday present. In addition to the gun and rifle, I also had access to a .22 pistol. If it flew, crawled, or crept, it was fair game to this Nimrod. If that killing business would have continued, I bet even the English sparrow might have been on the endangered species list, but fate took me by the hand . . .

Fall in Connecticut has the flavor of all New England. The maples set the stage for the colors that light up the hills everywhere. Fall migration of the birds is also marvelous. Geese and ducks fill the skies on their way

to their southern haunts. Songbirds of a fantastic variety suddenly fill the picnic grounds, heading for Florida, Mexico, and deep into South America. The bird hawks (accipiters) are not far behind, utilizing that small bird inventory to fuel their own bodies for the flights they would make. Mother Nature has so much going on in the fall not many could miss it . . . especially a twelve-year-old who was a crack shot with a .22.

So it was, on one of those brilliantly colored late afternoons, that I should be out on the hunt. "Chicken hawks" were fair game in those days, and no one bothered to differentiate among crows, falcons, hawks,

Great Horned Owl   *Artwork by Kate Hokaday*

accipiters, harriers, or vultures. If it was flying, it was a target.

Mr. Hubbard's stone wall fence was just ahead as I silently crept along the floor of the forest. The leaves of fall were beginning to lose their brilliant colors and drift toward the earth, where they would be recycled over winter. Spring peepers were already dug in, enveloped within their air supply, asleep for the winter deep under the frost line. I stopped to survey all there was about me: the old, giant elms, cedar trees scattered here and there among the hardwood forest, and the bog just over the fence, all framed in the brilliant colors of fall. Just as I lifted myself over the old glacier-worn stones atop the fence, I caught a sudden movement as something sailed out of a young maple on my left. "What the . . .?" I exclaimed, automatically raising my trusty .22 single-shot. A great horned owl, in his first year, had panicked by my close approach and bolted. With three-foot wings pumping, the young "tiger of the air" made a brave—but useless—dash to escape. Without a moment's hesitation I raised my rifle and fired from the hip.

Perhaps the machine that loaded that particular .22 cartridge at the Winchester Firearms factory had loaded a few extra grains of powder. Perhaps it was just a lucky shot for me, but the results were the same. The slug traveled faster than the sound, and went deep into the owl's body straight to the heart. All that could be heard was the crack of the rifle, then a muffled thud as the owl crashed to earth . . . to fly no more.

I was exultant! "I got him!" I leapt off the stone wall fence and over to the body of my quarry. It was a shot that would have made my Mohican heroes, Uncas or Chingachgook, proud of me. I approached the fallen owl carefully . . . you never know when they're just playing dead. Gingerly, I used the barrel of the rifle to prod it. "He's done for," I whispered, stooping to pick up the owl. "Boy, oh boy, this is a big one." I had difficulty keeping wings and body all together in my hands. The huge, yellow and black eyes stared into mine, still holding the fire of life. I turned away, having difficulty watching death replacing life. After several

attempts to use care in carrying my game, I finally took the wings by their ends and threw the rest over my left shoulder, and carrying my deadly rifle in my right hand, headed for home.

It may have been another quirk of fate that the first person I met as I arrived on the farm was my grandfather. "What do you have there, son?" he asked.

"I have an owl." I heaved the carcass off my shoulder and held it by the wing tips so he could see it better.

"Say, now," grandfather said. "That is sure a big one. Did you shoot it?"

This was no time to be coy, not when you come home with quarry as big as this. Obviously grandpa was impressed with my prowess as a hunter.

"I sure did, Grandpa, and with one shot from the hip!" As I made this boast, I didn't notice the slow change in my grandfather's face and posture.

"Why?" he asked.

That's a word I had been using all of my young life. "Why?" I was a seeker of the truth in everything I came into contact with. I had a quest for knowledge. I was never at peace until I learned all there was to know of the anatomy of chickens, pigs, cows, snakes, turtles, English sparrows—you name it. Now his questioning word had come home to roost. "Why?" That was easy to answer. "Owls eat chickens, don't they?" I replied.

"Yes, some owls will eat chickens." he said. "Was that one eating a chicken?"

The ice was getting thinner, but I didn't seem to notice. "No, it wasn't eating a chicken," I said. Still caught up in my pride, I added, "But I hit him with one shot, right from the hip!"

"Yes . . ." my grandfather answered slowly. "That was darn good shooting. But if the owl wasn't eating a chicken . . . why did you shoot it?"

That question of "Why?" again. I still didn't take the time to see where we were heading. Then the image of Mr. Hershetter's turkey farm up on the summit of Jones Hill Road came into my mind. After all, hadn't he set pole traps all over his yards in an attempt to kill all the owls who preyed on his turkeys? "Owls will kill turkeys," I answered then adding with confidence, "Mr. Hershetter sets traps for them."

"That's true. Was that one eating a turkey?" my grandfather quietly asked.

Suddenly I felt the ice crack; I knew I was in a dangerous place. (I seriously thought of lying to my grandfather at this point—but I had done that once before, only once. The horse-whipping I had received hurt my legs in a way that wasn't easy to forget. Every time I even thought about telling a lie, my legs began to hurt—even today.) "No," I answered quietly. "It was not eating a turkey."

"Then why did you shoot it?" my grandfather persisted.

A brilliant idea flashed into my mind. My grandfather was a hound dog man. He had several kinds, some for running foxes and raccoons, and others for hunting rabbits. Rabbits, I thought. That's it! With an air of confidence born out of desperation, I answered, "Owls eat rabbits, that's why I shot it."

"Now, you do have a point there, son," my grandfather said. "But tell me, do you think that one owl could make a difference in the rabbit population?" Then going on, he added, "Besides, we were just talking the other evening about how rabbits breed. Do you think that one owl could destroy all the rabbits we enjoy hunting?"

This was no time to retreat; it was the moment of truth I feared was coming. With my toe digging a small hole in the ground, and watching what I was doing, I quietly responded, "No, I don't think that one owl could make a difference in the rabbit population." Then I rushed on, trying to get it over with. "It wasn't eating a rabbit, and I don't know why I shot it; I guess I just reacted too quickly and fired before I thought what I was doing."

A look of relief came over my grandfather's face as he said, "That's what I thought, son. That sometimes happens." Then he placed his hand on my shoulder, asking, "Would you do me a favor?"

The question was an easy one to answer; there was very little that I wouldn't do for my grandfather. "Sure," I replied.

Reaching into his overalls and handing me his pocket knife, he said, "Would you take that owl out behind the barn? Near the place where the manure pile is—where we pluck all the chickens and geese. Go ahead and pluck it, like you would a chicken. Then take my pocket knife and clean him out. When you come back, tell me what he had been eating."

"What a relief," I thought. "Sure I will, Grandpa," I answered gratefully, taking the knife and heading for the back of the barn.

Plucking an owl is no easy feat for a twelve-year-old. It takes considerable strength to pull those tough primary feathers from the wing tips. It was during that part of the operation that something very distinctive caught my eye. There was sure a big difference between the owl's feathers and those of chickens and geese. Turning the primary feathers over in my hands, I said, "Well, I'll be . . . will you look at that."

The owl's feather had a long, thin ridge of curled feathers along its leading edge. Then I noticed that the trailing edge of the owl's feather was also very different than that of the others. "I wonder what that's all about?" I asked myself. "I can hardly feel some of these feathers," I thought, plucking them from the body.

Slowly, what was once a rather large-sized bird began to become smaller as the feathers stripped it of its size. The final result was a plucked bird somewhat smaller than an average chicken . . . but with unusually long legs, a big chest, and an enormous head.

At that point, my grandfather stopped by to see how I was doing. "How's it going?" he asked.

"There sure is a big difference between an owl's feathers and those chicken and goose feathers there," I answered, pointing to the various feathers scattered about. Looking up, I went on, "And look how long its legs are." Pointing to the head I added, "And look at the eyes, they're so big, and placed in front of the head, not on the sides like the chickens and geese."

Holding the owl feather in his hand, grandpa said, "I'll bet those little feathers along the front break up the air flowing over the owl's wing, making the flight very quiet, not at all like a goose or a chicken. If you're going to hunt at night, being quiet about it might be a good idea. I'll bet the placement of the eyes helps him see like we do, a great help in catching mice," he added. "Those long legs, armed with those needle-sharp talons probably help him to catch his prey." He noticed that the pocket knife was lying next to me and said, "Say, why don't you clean it out while I'm here. I'd like to see what you find."

"I can't find the gizzard," I exclaimed, searching through the viscera laid out on a piece of wood. "It's got to be here somewhere. I thought I could hear a chuckle coming from my grandfather.

"Perhaps it doesn't have one." he ventured.

"Well, here's something that resembles a stomach," I said, picking out a long, tube-like sack that seemed to have come down from the vicinity of the neck. I took a closer look and began to cut it open. "It's as tough as a gizzard," I noted out loud. That's when I spotted a small patch of fur. "Gee," I exclaimed. "There's some fur in this." As I continued to slice into what I now thought was the stomach, I found more fur, and as the contents spilled out onto the small board I was using as a table, I found three dead mice, all lined up neatly, one behind the other, head-to-tail. Beneath that there was some mushy-looking stuff that I couldn't readily identify containing bones and fur.

"Now, what do we have here?"my grandfather asked, bending over for a closer look. He then took one of the mice by the tail and held it up so we could both inspect it more closely. "What do you think this is?" he asked.

"Why, that's a mouse." I answered.

"That's right," he agreed. Then he picked up the other two mice and asked, "If the owl had these three mice in his stomach, and remains of other small animals in that mush there," pointing to the remains of the stomach contents, "what do you think that means to you and me?"

I had to think about that for a little while before answering. Images of mice running all over the feed room and rats in the cellar slowly came in to my mind. I remembered all the mice my uncles had trapped to feed their hawk. Then I could see the damages to our corn crop and stored food from rodents. It was like a whole new concept to me, almost shocking. "Golly, Grandfather," I said, "owls must eat a whole bunch of mice and rats."

"That's only part of the story, son," he responded. "Take a close look at the fur on those little mice. What else can you find?"

I laid the three mice on my work board and looked into the fur closely. Using a small stick and the point of the knife I searched through the fur. Suddenly I spotted something shiny-looking. Carefully, I pried it out from between some pieces of fur and laid in the palm of my hand. I recognized it as a flea, similar to the ones I had seen hopping off my grandfather's hounds. "This looks like a flea we can find on a dog or cat," I said.

"That's right, son," he answered. "Only that's not the same as the ones you find on the hounds or on one of the barn cats. Fleas that live on rodents are real bad news for people."

"You mean there are different kinds of fleas?" I asked.

"Yes, siree." he answered. "There are many different species of fleas that carry as many diseases. Have you studied the 'Black Death' in your school studies?" he asked. "If you have, you may recall what animal spread that horrifying disease all over Britain and Europe."

"Of course," I said, "it was the rats!"

"That's right. Now let's do some arithmetic. Let's say that owl ate three mice a night for a year. How many mice would he have eaten in a year's time?" He waited for me to do that one in my head, but laughed after a few minutes, adding, "Okay, Catsfur. I know that's a pretty big number to do in your head. Here, use my pencil and paper."

I had to scratch my head for a while, but soon the correct answer appeared on my paper. "Wow! I exclaimed, that's one thousand ninety five mice!" I looked down in astonishment at the three mice lying on the board.

"You're better at mathematics than your uncles say you are," he said. "Now, let's apply that many fleas to the mice, what do you think that means to us?"

"What do you mean?" I asked.

"Okay, we have . . . how many mice . . .? One thousand ninety five? Suppose we put ten fleas on each mouse, do you know how many that would be?" He waited for a moment, then answered his own question. "That would be ten thousand nine hundred fifty! Think of that, son!" he said.

Even a twelve-year-old boy could see the staggering implications of that. If what I had learned about the Black Death was true, and rodents were the vector for that horrifying disease, there was a good chance that owls might have something to do with the control of such diseases . . . and I said so. "Golly, Grandpa, I had no idea that owls could destroy so many mice and fleas. I will never kill another owl, not as long as I live!"

"I believe you, Jimmy," he said. Then smiling, he picked up the owl and handed it to me. "I don't think you'll ever shoot another owl. You understand how important they are to us . . . but there's something else I want you to remember: whatever you shoot . . . you eat!"

I looked down at the body of the owl in my hands, then up at his face. He's got to be joking, I said to myself. But one look and I knew he wasn't joking—he meant every word he had said.

"Why don't you finish cleaning it up and then take it in the house and ask your grandmother to cook it for you."

There was no escaping it. I was going to eat that owl! Then I thought about my beautiful grandmother . . . that sweet woman who loved her grandson more than anything! Why, there was no way she would ever make her little darling eat such a horrid thing. I was home free! "OK," I said heading for the house, skipping along the way with the owl bumping against my leg.

"Grandmother," I said, real friendly-like, smiling like someone looking for a big piece of her chocolate cake. "Grandfather says I must eat this owl. Will you cook it for me?"

She gave me that lovely look, reserved for her favorite grandson, and said, "Of course, Jimmy. Would you like me to stuff it?"

I couldn't believe my ears! Stuff it? Then the awful truth hit me. It was a conspiracy. They had teamed up to teach me this lesson. "Yes, please," I muttered, dropping the carcass on the drain board and walking back outside.

That evening, as we all sat down to eat supper, I was in the spotlight. My uncles and my aunts sat there grinning. Suddenly I remembered what my uncles had gone through about a year back. They had been forced to eat a hawk they shot. They also had tried the same lame excuses I had. It had been a "chicken hawk" . . . but hadn't been eating chickens. I should have remembered it. Then for a few moments there was a glimmer of hope as my mom showed up at the table and asked what that awful looking chicken was in the platter in front of me.

"An owl," I said forlornly.

"A what!?" she exclaimed. Then my grandfather explained why it was there and what I might be learning from this experience. She smiled at me and said, "Oh, that's different."

Over the years, people have asked me what an owl tastes like. It's difficult to express that flavor in words. To describe owl flesh to someone who has never partaken of this wildlife delicacy is nigh on to impossible; however, a dead tennis shoe, worn by one of my sons for six months, comes close. Ugh!

I often remember that owl, and the very first lecture I ever received in ecological thinking. That was also the first lesson I ever had in the science of vector control, the transmission of diseases to humans through wildlife. I have shared this story with thousands of children and adults all over the nation. I have also found myself asking the questions my grandfather asked me when I find someone who has unfortunately shot a hawk or an owl.

This happened when I was taking a group of high school students on a week-long field trip. We were traveling along a long, straight stretch of high desert road, about ten miles out of Christmas Valley, Oregon. Away up ahead of us, like a fuzzy mirage, I could see what appeared to be a motorcycle stopped on the dusty, gravel road. As we slowly rolled closer I could see a man standing alongside the motorcycle, holding a rifle. I slowed up as I started around him, then stopped the bus in its tracks. There, on the ground, right in front of the rifleman was a dead Ferruginous Hawk, one of the most beautiful and beneficial hawks found in the Northwest. I opened my window and asked politely, "Did you shoot that hawk?"

I hadn't expected the guy to confess to it, even if he had shot it . . . but he was apparently very proud of his feat and answered quickly, "Sure I did. So what?"

"So what!" I exclaimed. "Don't you know that hawks are a protected species in Oregon?"

"So what the ---- does that mean?" came the surly response. Then, to my absolute amazement, he added, "Hawks eat chickens, don't they?"

I could hardly believe my ears! I couldn't help but respond with my grandfather's great reasoning, "Sure, a hawk might eat a chicken—was that one eating a chicken?" Then I looked out across the sprawling sagebrush desert and asked, "But tell me . . . have you seen a chicken along here in the last hundred miles?"

The guy stood there, staring at me and then said, "No, I haven't." Then he added, "But hawks are no damn good. Anyway, there's no cops along here to stop me."

That was it for me. I climbed out of the bus, walked up to the guy and before he could do anything about it, snatched his rifle from his hands, opened the breech and then with all I had, slammed it against the power pole. There was a good solid "Crack!" as the rifle and stock parted company. Then I threw the gun down next to the hawk. "OK—now you've got a dead gun and I have a dead hawk. What do you want to do about it?"

His face turned red and he balled up his fists, all ready to have a go at me (which I really didn't blame him), but before he could start swinging I stepped back and said. "OK,

you've proved that you can hit a hawk on the top of a power pole. Big Deal! And you may also be able to lick me, but before you start, take a look in that bus. There's twenty-two high school kids in there that all want a piece of your hide. All you have to do is start it and I can promise you, they'll finish it." Then I remembered Ernie, a big farm boy from Canby, Oregon who could chew nails and spit rust. "Ernie!" I called. "Come out here a minute, will you!"

As Ernie came ambling out the door, I watched the expression on the hawk shooter's face. He began to slouch a little, looking less hostile. Ernie walked up to him, and I could see I had done the right thing. There was an enormous weight and size difference between the two. Ernie had at least six inches on him and close to sixty pounds. Before anything rash developed I stood next to Ernie, acting as though I was holding him back, and asked, "Get my point?" then added, "there's also one more very important factor in the hawk's favor. I have your description, the license number of your motorcycle and your confession before twenty-two kids that you killed that hawk. As soon as I can get to a telephone, guess who I'm going to call?"

The guy glared at me, than Ernie. Then he turned, grabbed up what was left of his rifle and stuck it into the scabbard on the side of his machine, giving all of us an awful look, then gave his motorcycle a vicious kick and with a roar went screeching down the road behind us.

The first phone we came to I did just as I said I would and made sure he got into the state police files. For the next thirty miles or more, the topic of conversation throughout the bus focused on the emotionally charged incident and the Ferruginous Hawk's natural history and ecological interactions. If those students weren't zealots before the trip started, they were when it ended.

Ducks Can Drown, You Know

'Dad!" My Aunt Dutchie shouted, "The poor little ducklings are dying! Hurry!" My grandfather came rushing out of the two-holer, suspenders snapping over his shoulders.

"What's wrong?" he called, hitching up his pants, as he ran through the pouring rain. As he rounded the corner of the barn he saw my aunt, Dutch. "What do you want, Dutchie?" my grandfather asked, looking at the little ducklings in her hands.

"Something has happened to the ducklings," she exclaimed, holding them up.

"They're soaking wet," my grandfather observed. "And look, isn't that water running from their nostrils? Now where are the rest of them, and where is that momma duck?" he muttered, as we all went in search of the others. Rounding the garage attached to the barn, Grandpa suddenly stopped. "There she is," he said, heading for the back of the garage. He slowly walked up to the old duck, huddled over with bills and tails of ducklings sticking out from all sides. "Steady, steady old girl," he said, snatching her up. Ducklings scattered in all directions. Dutchie snatched them up, looked them over and turned to Puffy, my grandfather.

"Some of these are really wet," she observed and then exclaimed, "Look! These three have water running out of their nostrils, too."

"OK. Put the dry ones under the hen duck and we'll take the others in the house," Grandpa said. Then we headed for the house.

After a big discussion on how to dry them out quickly and make them warm, we took Dutchie's suggestion: put them in the wood stove oven with the door open. The ducklings were placed on a towel in a pie pan with their heads lower than their bodies so the water would run out of their lungs and then placed inside the warm oven.

In a few minutes a tiny peeping came from the oven. Dutchie looked inside and found four little ducklings standing on the towel, looking like they had never been near the jaws of death. "Well, I'll be . . ." my grandfather muttered.

At that moment my grandmother happened to look out the window. "Look, Ben. There's a few more of the other ducklings. Why . . . they're standing out there . . . and their little bills are pointing straight up into the driving rain!"

We all ran to the window. Sure enough the fluffy, little ducklings were just standing there, heads held high and the cold rain soaking in their down like a blotter. "Where in the h--- is that hen?" my grandfather exclaimed angrily, heading for the back porch door.

As we ran up to the little ducklings, they made no attempt to scatter or escape. They just stood there, slowly drowning as the rain poured down their nostrils and into their lungs. "Never seen anything like this in my life," Dutchie said, exasperated. She grabbed up ducklings, putting them inside her pockets, inside her shirt, and other places she wouldn't like me to mention.

Standing around the oven drying ducks is not a very exciting project, at best. Dutchie suggested we all play a game of pinochle. When we started to play she suddenly snapped her fingers and said, laughingly, "Say, do you remember the time Francis and I got the ducks drunk?"

"Oh, my gosh. I sure do," Puffy answered. "You had better not be thinking of doing that to these little guys!"

"Oh, no!" Dutchie said. "I just happened to remember that time . . ."

"I'd like to hear about it," I said quickly.

"It's not funny." My grandmother scowled at Dutchie.

"How did it happen?" I insisted.

"Oh, all right Flossie," Grandpa said. "Go ahead and tell him. He won't be happy 'til he hears about it, now that you've opened your big mouth."

She began her story as she was dealing out the pinochle cards:

"Well, my sister Francis and I were wandering around the silo over on Grampa Cooper's old farm and found some corn whisky dripping out from under the corn silage. You remember how his hired men used to get into that stuff and go off on a bender? Well, we decided to get some in a jar and see who else we could get drunk. We soaked bread in the stuff and then tossed it out to the ducks. It didn't take long before those silly things were staggering all over the place. And you should have seen their necks! I had no idea they were that long! They stuck them out and tilted their heads to the side, trying to see the ground more clearly, or get their balance I guess. Then they would let out with a silly quacking noise and slowly pass out."

"That was a mean thing to do," my grandmother said, shaking her head at Dutch.

"Oh, I guess it was . . ." Dutchie started to say, but Puffy cut her off.

"Yes, and you would have had everything on the farm drunk if I hadn't stopped you! I should have taken that ---- jar of white lightning away from you. What did you do with it after I chased you away from the ducks?"

My aunt started to laugh so hard she had to lay her pinochle hand on the table and wipe her eyes. As she got control of herself she said, "Frannie and I took it out to the picnic grounds, along with the rest of the bread. We poured the rest of it on the bread and left it on the picnic table for the crows." She started laughing again. "Oh, you should have seen those silly crows as they started flopping around. They ran into each other, crashing into everything as they tried to take off from the picnic table. Finally, some of them were staggering off into the forest, looking for a place to sober up . . ." A loud peeping interrupted her story and we all scrambled to the oven to make sure we didn't have baked ducklings.

Everyone was still laughing when my grandmother quietly said, "I'll bid 350."

The Cow Manure Cure

I often tell people that I spent the first sixteen years of my life without cold hands or a cold forehead. (Unless you've milked cows by hand, you haven't had that pleasure.) My grandfather was a short, stout man who demanded performance from his children and from his cows. He was a postman, up early to milk, do other chores, and be on his way to deliver the mail. He would often leave notes dangling from the light switch cord in the kitchen. "Harry—do this," "Horace—do that," "Catsfur—do this," "Ben—do that." Those were our instructions for the day, and woe to him who did not carry them out.

We had a small dairy farm, milking three cows. The aroma of fresh cut hay, sweet manure in the trough behind the cows, and the taste of fresh milk, right from the cow are still vivid, pleasant memories. We used to keep a cup hanging on a nail within easy reach of the milking stall; it was delightful to drink the warm milk as you stripped the cow of her last drop. There is also something very peaceful about the rumbling noises you can hear coming from a cow's stomachs as you sat on the milking stool, keeping your balance by leaning your forehead into the flanks of old Bessy, as she quietly chewed her cud, submitting to this ancient ritual.

As age crept up on my grandfather, he slowly began to suffer from the onslaught of arthritis in his knees. For as long as I can remember he consulted Dr. Rogers, our family doctor, the man who brought me into this world. They made attempts to check the effects of this crippling problem, but nothing seemed to help. My grandfather was a pretty tough guy and not prone to having much patience. After almost a year of no progress from Dr. Roger's medicines, "Puffy" (the nickname our family gave to grandfather) thought it was time to take this arthritis problem on himself. It was only natural he would find the solution in the organic raw materials we had all around us, and quite literally, under our very feet.

He got to looking at cow manure one day as the possible solution. "After all," he said as we were shoveling out the trough in the milking barn, "if we use cow manure to cure sore joints on our work horse, why won't it work on me?" The more he thought about it, the more he was convinced it would work.

Little did I know that some of his favorite radio shows would be also part of his cure. Not having television and entertainment scarce, we had to take what we could get. Radio was an important focal point for all of us. "The Shadow," "Jack Armstrong-The Great American Boy," "Red Skelton," "Fibber McGee and Molly," "The Lone Ranger," and many others were highlights. Two programs were paramount in my grandfather's list of things worthwhile on the radio: "Gabriel Heater," for news and "The Lone Ranger" for entertainment. These two shows were an important part of his cure for arthritis.

The first thing he did was to ask my grandmother for some old pieces of sheet, which he cut into wide strips and hung them near the cow stalls. Then he got two chairs: one an old, overstuffed monstrosity that had been stored in the back of the barn for as long as I could remember, and the other smaller, but padded for comfort. "Catsfur," he said to me. "How would you like to help me show Dr. Rogers how to cure this ------ arthritis?"

We went to work and dug into the bottom of our manure pile and laid out about six inches of it on the long strips of old sheet. Then we carried the strips on long planks over to the place where he had placed the two chairs. He pulled his pants up over his knees and sat down while I helped him wrap the cow manure poultices around his knees. Then we'd sit there and listen to Gabriel Heater and the news, then "The Lone Ranger" and "Fibber McGee and Molly." This took an hour and a half. The process went on for several months.

I can remember the day Puffy was sure the cow manure cure was working. "Jimmy," he said, "I think we're making some progress. Watch this." He got up from his big chair, removed the poultices and with only a trace of stiffness, he began to dance a jig! That was something I couldn't believe . . . but he wasn't ready to share this with Dr. Rogers, not quite yet.

Gramp kept at the cow manure cure for another good six weeks and then one day he climbed into the old Model T and took his knees to town to show Dr. Rogers. We thought he might make medical history. Dr. Rogers said that it was wonderful that Puffy had done such a good job, happy that he was able to get around again, and, don't call me, I'll call you.

That would have been that, if grandfather hadn't got that terrible sore throat. He got up one morning suffering from a terrible cold, sure he was going to die. He tried skunk's grease and molasses, one of his favorite cures for any problem. (He tried that on me when I had rheumatic fever while serving in the Navy.) That didn't do it. After several days of this awful pain he decided it was time to see Dr. Rogers. House calls were a normal part of a doctor's life back then, and Dr. Rogers always enjoyed coming to the Rockefeller Farm, as my grandmother made the best pies in New Haven County. He showed up one evening, just in time for dinner—and pie—then looked at my grandfather. I'll never forget the cure he suggested.

After gazing into Puffy's throat for a while, humming away as he did, old "Doc" put away his tools and the sample he had taken from my grandfather's throat. He leaned back with his cup of coffee and said, "Well, Ben (my grandfather's full name was Benjamin Franklin Rockefeller), seeing as you had such good luck with that cow manure of yours, why don't you try gargling with it. I'll bet that would cure you."

Puffy's face turned all shades of purple, and he looked as though he was about to explode. Then Dr. Rogers slapped his leg and started to laugh, and everyone enjoyed the joke. However, if I ever have a serious problem with arthritis, I'm going to find a dairy farm and get myself a good selection of that cow manure cure; I think it worked pretty well . . .

The Pond

It was an accident, or perhaps curiosity, that led to my discovery of Allspaugh's Pond. I found it one late afternoon while out looking for spring peepers, those lovely spring choristers of New England that proclaim the official end of winter.

It was a warm evening, milking had been completed, and I had some free time with no homework or chores. The peepers were calling me and it was irresistible. I was walking slowly through the old bog at the far end of the cow pasture when I came to the old stone wall fence that separated our land from Mr. Heanie's fields and decided to keep going. As I stepped on the top of the long line of glacier-polished stones I thought I heard a new sound. I cupped my hands behind my ears, a trick I had learned in my earlier explorations. Sure enough, that was a new sound, a low "kerrruuum, kerrruuum" way off on the other side of Mr. Heanie's hay field. There was still light in the sky so I could see my way across the field, and off I went.

The farther I went across the field, the louder the "kerrruuums" seemed to get. As the noise became clearer, I picked up my pace to almost running. I was on to something, I knew it! I could see a tall line of maple trees concealing another stone wall fence as I approached the far side of the field. Slowly I crept up to the trees and peeked through the spaces between them.

About twenty feet away was a small body of water, and from all around it, the evening air was filled with the loud chorus of "Kerrrrummm! Kerrrrumm!" I eased over the wall and crept closer to the pond. When I was about four feet from the water's edge the din suddenly stopped. It was such a shock that I stopped dead in my stride. I couldn't understand what had happened.

I eased myself slowly to the ground and stretched out on my stomach. As I did, I could feel the dampness of the earth slowly coming through the knees of my corduroy knickers. I was going to wait until something

happened, that was that, dampness or no. (If I had known the consequences of what I had just done, I would have got to my feet immediately and headed back home for more appropriate clothing for lying in the mud . . .)

In about ten minutes, a subdued "kerrrrum . . ." sounded very close to me. It was followed by another, then another and another. In a few minutes the din was on again. I was so close to it all that I can remember how the noise filled my head. I slowly raised myself so I could see better, and as I did I could see huge, greenish-yellow orbs appearing and vanishing, in beat with the sounds. I had a guess that the sound might be coming from some kind of frog or toad, but what I saw was astonishing, especially for a ten-year-old on a nature hunt! I eased a little higher for a better look. Sure enough, these were some kind of frog, but the size of them! The yellow, balloon-like orbs were throat pouches of the male frogs, filling with air as they bellowed out the "Kerrruuuum!" "Kerruuuuum!" I skidded along, belly-down on the muddy ground, inching closer and closer. In a moment I was at the edge of the pond where I raised my head slowly and looked, face-to-face with the largest frog I had ever seen!

I don't know how I did it. It was probably a stroke of sheer luck. I made a grab for it and was probably as shocked as it was when my two hands closed tight around its huge body. I had it! I had caught it! I couldn't believe my eyes as I raised up to look it in the eye. "Oh, Boy!" I exclaimed aloud, standing erect. "Wait 'til Harry sees this!" I didn't hesitate for a moment, but turned and headed for home, eager to show my prize to everyone. I didn't for a moment think about all that mud I had slithered through, having no idea of what I looked like, from the neck down. My only concern was that enormous frog and what everyone would say when I got home with it.

As I got closer to the house I began to

shout, "Hey, Harry! Come see what I've got! Come see!"

Harry stepped from the little room attached to the barn that was the outhouse. "What'cha got, Catsfur?" he called back.

"You wont believe it!" I blurted. "Look at this . . ." I raised my hands right in front of his face so he could see the frog better.

"So you found the pond, eh?" he said, taking my hands and turning the frog so he could see better. The he called out, "Hey, Horace. Catsfur has found the frog pond. There goes our frogs' legs!"

I could hear Horace's muffled response coming from the shop next to the barn. "He has, has he . . ?" Then he stepped out to join us. "Okay, Catsfur," he said. "You can have some of the frog legs too, but you can't tell anyone else about the pond. Promise?"

Both of the boys were bigger than I was, and in addition to that, anything they told me was "Gospel," so I nodded my head in agreement. Then their remark about "frogs' legs" struck home.

"Do you guys eat the legs?" I asked, holding the frog higher.

"You bet!" Harry answered. "They're great fried in butter. That's a bull frog. It's the biggest frog in these parts." He grinned at me. "Wait 'til you see how those breaded frogs' legs taste."

I looked at my prize again. Then looked at my two uncles. "Not this one, you're not!" I said, clutching the frog tighter. Harry was about to say something else when suddenly he was cut off by a shout at the back door of the farm house.

"Come for supper!"

All three of us headed for the back door at a run. I stopped at the stairs and looked about me for something to stick my frog into, spotted a pail standing by the well, grabbed it up and ran for the shop door, looking for a cover. I found a board, stuffed the frog into the pail and quickly covered it, placing a rock on top.

"Coming!" I shouted, and ran into the back porch.

Unfortunately, my dad was standing at the door when I came running through, into the light. "Hold it!" he ordered, taking my arm. "What have you been doing?" he asked,

then turned me to the light and added, "Look at your clothes . . .!"

My mother soon joined my dad, then my grandmother and the rest of the house. "Hey," Aunt Dutchie called out. "Take a look at Catsfur. Looks like he's been playing around with Mr. Latella's pigs!" Then she let out a laugh.

Neither my dad or mom thought it was very funny, especially my dad. He took a look at me from head to toe, then stared at my shoes. "I just bought you those shoes,—" he grumbled, pointing to my feet. "—And look at them . . ." I did, not knowing what to say. They were so muddy I couldn't tell what the original color had been. I knew I was in big trouble. My dad took me aside, sat me down in the kitchen chair, and, while everyone else was at supper, I was told that if I ever came home looking like that again, especially the shoes, he would never buy me another pair.

Well, as anyone in my family might guess, I did come back home looking that way frequently, and true to his word, my dad never bought me another pair of shoes. I had to get a paper route to get enough money for shoes and other such things from then on.

The pond was relatively untouched and as wild as any old glacial pond could be. All spring, summer, and fall, I was a constant visitor to this wonderful place. I watched the newts and salamanders lay their eggs, then hatch and grow into adults when they left the water. It was a tribute to my stalking ability when I could crawl and slither close enough to the mud turtles and catch one before it slipped off a rock to the safety of the muddy bottom of the pond.

After a few years of prowling this unique place I developed the notion it was "my" pond and would get pretty upset when I found other kids prowling around it. On one occasion I came upon three boys there doing something I couldn't believe . . .

I heard them long before I saw them. I could tell by their whooping and laughing they weren't up to anything good. I hurried along through the grass and peeked over the stone wall fence to see what was going on. I couldn't believe me eyes! Two of them were holding the beautiful meadow frogs by their hind legs and blowing them up with straws stuck into their anal vents! I was like a madman!

I let out my crazed Tarzan cry and leaped over the fence, catching them completely by surprise. They jerked up and stared wide-eyed at me screaming at them with arms waving. The two closer to me threw their frogs into the air and started to run. I headed right for the one at the edge of the pond, catching him off guard and off balance. With a thud and then a big splash we went sailing into the pond. He was under me when we hit the water and although the water wasn't more than a foot deep, it was enough to put a scare into him. With arms and legs thrashing, he got his head above water and sputtered "Stop!" I just pushed him under again.

He was gasping for air, covered with mud, and might have even been in shock, but I didn't care. He and his buddies had been injuring "my" frogs, and that was something no one did!

"What do you think you're doing!" I shouted at him. Then I looked at the dead frogs floating around us and got mad all over again. "I jerked him up by his hair, dragging him across the water to the closest frog. Snatching it from the water, I tried to shove it in his mouth, shouting, "What you kill, you eat!" (A phrase I was going to hear again, under different circumstances.)

That was all that kid could take. He suddenly jerked free and went thrashing through the mud and water, scrambled out on the bank, and ran for home. I stood in the water shouting at him, warning him and all that could hear that, if anyone ever came back here and did something like that again, I'd sic my uncles or the law on them. I guess it worked. I noticed that the kids gave me a wide berth as I walked to school the next day.

The snapping turtle from Allspaugh's Pond was another unforgettable event. I had been frequenting the pond for several years, finding only the mud sliders and an occasional box turtle nearby. I was shocked one sunny summer day when I saw an enormous head poking above the water. As I

approached, it quietly disappeared under the surface. I thought it was something big, but had no idea how big as I sat down to quietly wait for it to reappear. It took over an hour before the huge head silently eased above the surface. This time I was close enough to see the bright red eye and the powerful hooked jaws.

"My gosh!" I whispered, aloud. "It's a snapping turtle!" I rushed home to tell my uncles about it. Ben came back with me; he wanted to catch it for turtle soup. I just wanted to see it caught so I could get a better look at it. (I thought I could talk my uncle out of making the soup.)

Ben got a piece of liver and placed it on a stout fish hook, then he tossed it out into the vicinity of where we last saw the turtle's head above the surface. It seemed to take only a short time when a series of jerks came up the line. I watched in amazement as a prehistoric-looking reptile exploded to the surface, jaws gaping and snapping. It was as big as a bushel basket!

Ben hauled in on the line, ignoring the deep gash it was causing in his hand. The pond was beat into a muddy mess as the snapping turtle and Ben battled it out. He hauled in the line, so tight it was cutting into his hands, and the turtle would haul it back out again, clawing at the muddy bottom. The turtle was tiring as Ben kept hauling it closer and closer to the bank. The closer it got the more I feared those cruel-looking jaws and tearing claws. It was almost like seeing something from the age of dinosaurs suddenly appear in the twentieth century.

He hauled the huge turtle to the edge of the water and shouted, "Grab a stick, quick!" I went over to the maple trees and picked a dead branch, about an inch in thickness, and handed it to him. "Now, Catsfur," he said. "As I get him out of the water, you take that stick and try to get it into his mouth while I grab a hind leg." I did as instructed and cautiously poked the stick at its enormous jaws.

"Crunch!" The snapper's jaws smashed shut on the end of the stick. "He bit it clear off, Ben!" I said, showing him the sharp cut end of the maple stick.

"Get a bigger one then!" he shouted, trying to keep the turtle on its back.

Ben was sweating and blood was running from his injured hands where the line had cut into his flesh. I knew he wasn't going to hold on much longer and I shoved a thicker stick into the jaws again.

This one was big enough to hold this time. The snapper clamped down on it and held tight. Ben quickly released the line and grabbed a thick, back leg, hauling the turtle into the air. He stood there, waving the enraged beast, trying to avoid the jaws that were snapping at him now, having let the maple branch drop. Blood was running down his hand in rivulets, perhaps giving the turtle a taste what was to come if Ben became careless.

"Have you got a good look at him, Catsfur?" Ben shouted, dancing away from me.

"Yeah, Ben!" I shouted back. "I've seen him as close as I want to."

Without another word, Ben started into a spin like a discus thrower, and with a loud grunt, sent the snapper sailing into the air, right out into the middle of the pond where it landed with a gigantic splash! Ben stood there, chest heaving. Then he gasped, "I didn't want turtle soup that bad . . ." then he looked at me and grinned, "Did you, Catsfur?" I quickly admitted that I didn't!

The alligator was quite a shock too. I was in high school at the time and had been studying enough biology to know that an alligator in Allspaugh's Pond was, well, impossible! My friends insisted that it wasn't . . . "I tell you, Jim," one said. "It is an alligator. I'm sure of it! We saw it!"

"OK, OK," I kept saying, heading out for the pond. As we silently crept to the water's edge, we could see what appeared to be about an eighteen inch alligator stretched out on the board I had placed for turtles and newts to sun themselves on. "Well, I'll be . . ." I muttered to myself as we eased up for a closer look.

"See it . . .?" hissed one of the boys. "I saw it dive in this morning. It's alive!"

"I see it, but I don't believe it!" I said to the others. This even beat the snapping turtle! Suddenly the alligator raised its head,

took a quick look at us and glided off the board, vanishing silently into the pond.

I can still recall the three of us stretched out on the bank of that lovely little pond waiting for the alligator to resurface. Our backs were to the sun, the warm rays of summer cooking the warmth deep into our bodies—probably not unlike a feeling that I believe reptiles must have when they soak up the heat of the sun, so vital for their survival. I can't remember how long we waited, but it was suddenly there, with only its eyes and nostrils above water, quietly inspecting us. I do remember seeing those eyes though, causing me to shudder as I whispered, "There he is . . ." The other two boys, who had been half asleep, opened their eyes and moved for a better look. As they did, the alligator quietly dropped out of sight, not to be seen again for the rest of the day.

We spent three days trying to get another look at our "impossible" discovery. We carried our binoculars with us, knowing we'd never get close enough again for a really good look. Finally, in the late afternoon of the third day, our vigil was rewarded. The alligator slowly crept up on its sunning board for a short stay in the late afternoon heat. Sitting there, watching him with our binoculars we whispered back and forth, extolling its beautiful scales, texture, color, and the fierceness of its eyes.

After almost an hour, we saw the alligator slowly raise itself up, then slide off the board and into the water with only its eyes showing above the surface. It stopped about three feet from the bank, motionless in the water, apparently watching something at the edge of the pond. We held our breath as a yellow-legged frog drifted out into the open water. With practiced stealth the alligator propelled itself toward the hapless victim, then jaws opening wide, it snapped up the frog and was gone in an instant. It was as though the frog had never been there at all.

We sat stunned, hardly believing our eyes, witnesses to what is an everyday thing in nature, but rare for kids from the country. I was beside myself—imagine, an alligator in my own Connecticut farm pond, and seeing it make a kill! "Wow!" I whispered for us all.

As we slowly walked back toward our respective homes, we all took an oath that we would never tell anyone about "our" alligator. In some way we hoped it would survive the coming winter. Although I looked, I never found a trace of that beautiful, little reptile the next spring. We all speculated on how it actually arrived in the pond. The only plausible answer was that someone had it as a pet then, tired of feeding it, had dumped it. As I think about that experience today, I can't help but wonder what a paleontologist will think, perhaps millions of years from now, if he finds that alligator in the fossil mud of Allspaugh's Pond.

I didn't see my pond for a good many years after leaving for the Navy. Had I known that someday someone might see the pond as nothing more than an interference for a construction project, I would have gone back to see it every opportunity I had, and make every attempt I could to save it—but Allspaugh's Pond is already well on its way to becoming fossilized, buried under tons of land fill, concrete, and steel. There's a high school football bleacher section right on top of what was once a thriving ecosystem that gave a young boy the thrill of knowing nature by her first name. Progress had taken its toll again, leaving behind another biological void in its wake. Land is becoming more scarce every day, and as I mull over the fate of that lovely little pond, I experience a great sense of loss for this tiny treasure of nature. It's times like these that I am grateful for my membership to The Nature Conservancy and the Audubon Society, just two of our most effective insurance policies against the complete and utter destruction of ponds, native plants, habitat, and ecosystems that will be of incalculable biological wealth in the time to come.

Things That Go Bump in the Night

Sometimes, a ten-year old kid can get into trouble if he gets too curious about what his older uncles have hidden around the house. I was always going up the stairs that led to the treasure room of our farm, the attic. There were Civil War guns and clothing up there, books of ancient works, family treasures, old Erector sets, and piles of boxes. One box I found contained a wonderful variety of eggs, all sizes, shapes, and colors, and every one of them empty. I asked my Uncle Ben about that one day and got scolded for even looking at them.

"You keep your nose out of things, Catsfur," he ordered, pointing his finger at the place I thought he might stick an arrow! "Those boxes contain eggs from just about all the birds that nest around here." He added, "I'm taking them to the museum soon to show to Professor Bent when he comes through." I didn't know who that guy was (at the time) but I respected my uncle's wishes and left the eggs alone. But the rattling sounds coming from a cigar box in his top bureau drawer were a mystery . . .

Spring had sprung on the farm. The scent of summer was in the air and nights were getting warmer. Dreaming about school ending for summer was often the way I drifted off to sleep. That's just what I was doing that warm spring evening when I was slowly forced awake by a soft, thudding noise against the outside window of the bedroom.

I lay quietly in my bed for a while just listening. Finally I woke my uncle, sleeping beside me. "Harry," I whispered. "Wake up. Listen, there's something outside bumping against the window. Listen . . ."

Harry stirred, then he heard it too. "Yeah, I hear it, Catsfur," he whispered. We both lay there, wondering what to do next. Harry finally made up his mind. "Where's the flashlight?" he asked, groping around on the bedstand.

I remembered we had placed it on Benny's bureau after the last rat hunt. "I'll get it," I whispered, sliding out of bed as quietly as a ghost—looking like one too, I suppose, with my long, white nightshirt. The flashlight was right where it was supposed to be and I lifted it up without a sound and tip-toed back to the bed, handing it to Harry.

"You stay quiet," he said, easing out of bed and crawling over to the big window that looked out onto the farm from our upstairs bedroom. He sat directly under the window, waiting. In a moment the soft, thudding noises began again. "Bump," "bump." We could make out at least four sets of "bumping" all over the outside window. Harry slowly raised himself off the floor and turned on the powerful light.

At first we couldn't make out what we were looking at. It appeared there were leaves, or something like that, bumping against the window pane. Then Harry placed the light at an angle and exclaimed, "They're moths!" I hopped out of bed and trotted to the window for a better look.

Sure enough, there were four, huge moths bumping against our window. "Well, I'll be . . ." Harry muttered. "What's that all about?" We stood there watching as the moths repeatedly bumped against the window. "You know . . ." Harry said, slowly, "I think those moths are trying to get into the house. But why?" We looked at each other and hadn't the slightest idea why.

Our voices finally woke the rest of the upstairs bedrooms' occupants. My grandfather came plodding out of his room, nightshirt flopping around his ankles as he scratched here and there. Then Uncle Ben ambled into the room, "What's all the racket?" he mumbled, giving Harry and me a sleepy look.

"Look, Ben," Harry exclaimed, pointing the light at the window. "There's a bunch of moths knocking on the window out there. Looks like they're trying to get into the house. But why?"

Ben walked over to the window, rubbing his eyes. He took the flashlight from Harry and pointed at the moths, studying them through the glass. "They look like cecropia moths, Harry," he said. He turned the light at different angles to the glass for a better view. After a few moments he said, "Yep, that's what they are, cecropias, all right. It sure looks like they're trying to get past

that . . ." He suddenly snapped his fingers, exclaiming, "I'll bet I know why!" He turned to Harry and me, "Give me a hand with this window, will you?"

As we walked over next to the window, Ben handed me the flashlight. "Hold this, Catsfur," he said, then turned to Harry. "OK, you take that side, I'll take this side, but be careful, we don't want to injure them as the window opens." Slowly, the window eased open , squeaking along the old, weather-beaten track. The moths kept bumping against the glass, oblivious to the movement. As the window passed the first moth it swiftly flew directly into the house, followed quickly by the other three. It was though they had been here before, and knew directly where they were going—straight to Ben's bureau, especially the top, right-hand drawer. "I thought so," Ben said, heading for the bureau himself.

The moths fluttered against the drawer of the bureau in a frenzy, frantically bouncing against the closed drawer, apparently trying to get inside. Ben stopped in front of the drawer, turned to us and said, "Turn on the light." I pulled the cord and light flooded into the room. "Now," Ben said. "Watch this . . ." He slowly pulled the drawer open and opened the cigar box. Suddenly the room was filled with six Cecropia moths zooming around each other in a wild, aerial dance. It was a wonder to watch.

Ben stood there, grinning like someone who had really discovered a great secret. He turned to us and explained, "Isn't that wonderful? The moths that were outside are the males. They knew the females were here in the house, somewhere, and were frantic to get in. See how they flutter around each other! Soon the female will come to rest, they'll mate, and she will lay hundreds of eggs, right on the plant that the tiny caterpillars must have when they hatch. The males will mate with other females, then die, and after the females lay their eggs they too will die." Then he added, "Why don't you turn off the light, Catsfur . . ." I pulled cord again and darkness blotted out the fluttering moths.

Ben walked to the window and placed the flashlight on the window sill where the moths slowly fluttered toward it and out into the night. As we were closing the window, Ben turned to us and asked, "Catsfur, do you know how those male moths knew there were females in the house?" I had no idea and said so. Ben was about to reply when Harry spoke up.

"I think I know, Ben. I remember reading about how female moths put off a strong perfume, a scent, that the males are able to detect, sometimes from a long distance." Then he looked at Ben and added, "Do you mean those moths were able to detect that perfume coming out of the cigar box in the drawer, out of the drawer, and then out through the glass?"

Ben confirmed it. "Did you notice when they came into the room, how they went straight as an arrow, right to the bureau?"

"That's right!" I chipped in, "I thought they had been here before. They knew exactly where they were going."

Ben laughed, "You bet they did, Jimmy. The perfume the females were emitting was like a road map to the males." (We know the "perfume" as pheromones today.) He went over to the bureau and pulled the drawer open, then removed the cigar box. "Look here," he said, pointing to the empty silk sacks inside, "See those? They're cocoons I picked up last fall and placed in this box. Remember? You asked about what was inside and I told you I would show you someday. Well, now you know." The mystery of the cigar box was solved . . .

As we all started back to bed, Harry walked to the window and cupped his hands behind his ears. I was puzzled, so I walked over to listen too. As I was standing there with my hands cupped behind my ears he turned, and I could see his grin in the dark. "Listen," he said. "I can hear them singing . . ."

The Red-Tail Caper

It was natural curiosity that always took me out to an area in back of the farm fields, at the edge of a big patch of old-growth elm, oak, and sassafras trees that we knew fondly as the "Picnic Grounds." Woodpeckers were abundant throughout the old-growth forest, brilliant butterflies flashed in the summer sunlight, small frogs—our "spring peepers"—sang from late February to April and a host of natural wonders could be found in the woods.

In one of the old, tall, dead sassafras trees, my uncles created the "Tarzan Tree." Tarzan, in the form of Johnny Weismuller, was one of our greatest heroes. He sailed from tree to tree, seemingly oblivious to the fact that what went up, according to Newton, must come down. It was only natural that we would be inspired to practice Tarzan's art.

Rope, to be used as "vines," began to disappear from the stall where the work horses were kept. Then ropes used to haul hay into the back of the barn quietly moved to the Picnic Grounds. In the short span of one day, vines were hanging throughout the old sassafras, transforming it into the Tarzan Tree .

To add authenticity, Horace and Harry cut up an old cow hide to fit like Tarzan's. I watched how they were swinging from rope to rope, seemingly as effortless as Tarzan himself, and thought, "That sure looks like fun." I was eleven at the time, and yearning to get up there and swing in the ropes as the big guy Tarzan did.

One afternoon after school, my uncles were off doing the chores my grandfather had assigned them. No one was at the Tarzan Tree—my big chance. I had secretly taken one of my grandmother's old blankets and cut it up to resemble the loin cloth Tarzan wore, and, taking it with me, I sneaked out to the Tarzan Tree. I can't remember all the details, except that I had very sore muscles, at first, but after about an hour of grabbing ropes, sailing to the next one, and then to the next, I perfected my Tarzan-like performances pretty quickly and felt that I had become one with the older guys. While I was sitting on this high perch, enjoying my wonderful achievement, I noticed a large pile of sticks in the fork of some limbs in a large elm, not too far away.

I climbed higher in the Tarzan Tree to get a better view. I can still remember the excitement of reaching the top of that great, old tree and at last being able to see into what turned out to be a nest. At first I thought it was unoccupied, but as I perched in the swaying branches, I finally made out the form of something brown, huddled over the nest. At that moment a large bird zoomed by; it was a Red-tailed Hawk, known to us as the chicken hawk. Shaking with excitement, I climbed down to the first of the high ropes, took a stout hold, and with the wild Tarzan cry , sailed through the air, rope-by-rope to the ground. I had discovered something the big boys hadn't seen. I couldn't run fast enough back to the farm to spread the news.

It was my Uncle Ben who was the intellectual of the group. He had read more books, was the oldest, and the one who made most of—if not all—the important decisions. "Let's get the hawk," he said. "We'll train it like the sheiks do in the Middle East." Then with a faraway look he added, "We can hunt rabbits and ask Mom to can them for winter, like they did long ago, in the castles of Britain. Come on Catsfur," he ordered. "Show us that nest."

More ropes were needed, but by now the farm was ropeless. Everything we had was already hanging in the Tarzan Tree.

"I know who has some," Harry said, snapping his fingers. "Barney Luttenburger."

"I'll call him," Horace volunteered.

We didn't have indoor plumbing, but we did have a telephone. My aunt was a pioneer in the Southern New England Telephone Company, and a telephone was hooked into the farmhouse long before water or a toilet were.

Soon, Barney came riding down Jones Hill Road with ropes wrapped all around the handle bars of his bike. "Here they are," he proudly said, dumping the long ropes on the ground. "What do you want them for?"

"You'll have to promise not to tell anyone," Harry answered, making Barney raise

his right hand as a promise to never tell anyone the special secret he was about to receive. "Catsfur here has found a hawk's nest. We're going to climb the tree and get a hawk to hunt with, and we need your ropes to climb with."

"You guys have plenty of ropes around the farm," Barney said. "Why don't you use them?"

"Uh, well, we've already got them used in another place, Barney." Harry replied.

"Oh yeah, where?" Barney asked.

"Umm, we got a secret place that we used them . . ." replied Horace, then he added, "Oh, rats, Barney, you're going to see the tree anyway, come on, we'll show you."

Now five people knew the secret, but Barney couldn't believe it. "Holy cats!" he exclaimed. "Do you guys really fly on those ropes like Tarzan?"

"You bet we do!" Harry replied proudly, then added, "Even little Catsfur here, can do it. That's how he found the hawk's nest."

"Golly," said Barney, looking up at the ropes swaying in the breeze. "I'd sure like to try that."

Horace was the first to speak up, "Now, I don't know Barney . . . ummm . . . you're not as strong as we are, you know. You may not be able to hang onto the ropes. You might fall."

Well, that was the wrong thing to say! You can't tell a fifteen-year-old that he's not as strong as you are: That's a serious slap in the face—a challenge even.

"I can so!" blurted Barney. He looked at me and remarked with disdain, "If Catsfur can do it, I know I can!"

"OK . . . OK, Barney," Horace said, quickly. "But let me show you how this works before you try it."

"Not now," Ben said. "We've got a hawk to go after."

It took a long time to climb that huge, old elm tree. Hands were sore and everyone was exhausted by the time Horace was high enough to look into the nest to see what was going on. The adult hawks were soaring about us continually, crying out in their high pitched whistle, telling us to leave them alone, but young boys intent on getting a hawk are not easily discouraged.

Horace balanced himself on a comfortable

limb then shouted down, "Send up the burlap sack!" His climbing rope was used as a messenger line and the sack went up to receive the prize.

"Let's see the hawk!" I shouted, and Horace lifted the young hawk from the nest for all to see.

"Be sure to get the largest one!" Ben shouted, "They make the best hunters!"

In a few moments the young hawk was slowly being lowered to earth, leaving its sanctuary and headed for a life that was going to be less than ideal. "Oh boy!" all said as the sack was opened, revealing the young red-tail. It was about the size of a young chicken. Its downy fuzz had been replaced by juvenile feathers, something that Ben obviously knew something about.

"That's just the right age to train," he said, carefully grasping the hawk in such a way as to avoid the clutching feet. He wasn't fast enough. Without warning, and as swift as a bullet, the hawk twisted over on its back and lashed out with both legs. The needle-sharp talons on its strong feet went deep into Ben's hands as he attempted to drop it. Howls of pain and shock could be heard all over the Picnic Grounds, probably clear back to the farm. Ben couldn't get loose of the bird. He raised his hands in an effort to shake it off, but the hawk just went along for the ride, upside down and grasping even tighter.

"Yeoowww!" Ben yelled, swinging the hawk around in a circle, trying to shake him off.

Red-tails are tough—they make a living by grasping their prey and either piercing a vital organ with those needle-sharp talons—or by squeezing the life out of their prey with powerful feet, suffocating them. This hawk was no exception; it wasn't about to let go.

"Hold still, Ben," Harry said, trying to stop him from spinning around in a circle. "I'll pry him off, if you'll stop jumping around." Ben obeyed, and with help from Harry and everyone else, the hawk was slowly pried off of his bleeding hands.

What had begun as a noble attempt to train a hawk to provide meat for the table was already off to a poor beginning, and it wasn't going to get any better. The hawk was confined to a cage, not quite big enough to fly in. No falconer's hood was made that would cover its eyes to help quiet him down. No fancy leather jesses were made to tether the hawk to a long line and allow it to fly, and then be trained to hunt. His food was assorted meat scraps from the kitchen, mice caught in the feed room and barn, and an occasional cotton-tail. My grandfather said to my uncles over and over, "You've got to do something with that bird."

"We will," they always responded. But the hawk grew and the cage got smaller . . .

Meanwhile, Barney couldn't get the Tarzan Tree out of his mind. It was a great afternoon in late June, warm and with a light breeze, just right for swinging in the Tarzan Tree. Ben, Horace, and I were playing out the roles so well known to us . . ."Saving the White Hunter . . . Finding the lost gold mine deep in the jungle . . . Keeping thoughts of Jane at bay . . . Calling all the elephants for help" . . . and all of this requiring a great deal of aerial expertise: arm waving, Tarzan grunts, imitation African wildlife sounds, and the screams of dying bad guys.

"Hey, you guys!" Harry shouted. "Here comes Barney."

Everyone looked out toward the farm, and sure enough, there he was ambling along on those enormously long legs, long arms swinging from his side, and his big adam's apple, bouncing up and down. "Hi, guys!" he shouted.

Barney was a nice enough guy. We all got along pretty well, except the time I hit him smack in the middle of his forehead with a green apple, pitched from the end of a throwing stick (my marksmanship had been uncanny). It had taken Barney a month to get over his mad. One talent he did not posses was the cat-like climbing ability of my uncles, nor did he have a trace of their coordination. It was those two factors that prompted Horace to try and talk Barney out of using the Tarzan Tree . . . but his efforts were all in vain.

"Hey guys!" Barney shouted again. "I want to try the ropes today. How about it?"

"Sure, Barney," Horace muttered, "Why not . . ."

"Oh, boy! That's great." Barney shouted,

grinning like a bullfrog, and heading right for the first rope, grasping it in his giant hands.

"Now wait a minute, Barney!" Harry called to him. "Maybe we should give you some instructions before you try it."

"OK, but hurry down," Barney grumbled.

All three of us looked at each other. Horace was the one who shrugged his shoulders and sailed down. "Okay, Barney," Horace began, pointing to the ropes about them, "Here's the way you have to do it. First, you climb up this rope here, then step onto that limb over there and grab the rope real tight in both hands and give yourself a push as you swing over to that rope, over there."

Barney nodded his head, "OK, I've got it. Here I go!"

"No! Not yet!" Harry shouted, grabbing Barney. "What you've got to do is be sure you hold onto the first rope just long enough to grab the other one, in case you miss . . ."

"I got it," Barney grinned. And up he went.

Barney wasn't too good at giving the Tarzan cry either; he just sort of let out a shrill scream. It was awesome to watch Barney's long legs dangling down, and to hear that ear-shattering scream as he left the first limb, suspended from the rope. We all held our breath as he arrived at the next rope and watched as he reached out with his left hand to grab it, while holding tight on the other with his right hand.

"Oh, no . . ." Horace groaned.

We all watched horrified as Barney swung to center, still holding on to the two ropes, one in each hand. Then, letting out a blood-curdling wail, he began to slide down the ropes, his poor hands fairly smoking, and headed straight for us.

"Get out of the way!" Horace shouted and we all jumped to the side.

"Wham!" Poor Barney landed flat on his back, right at our feet in the soft forest duff. We all bent down to get a closer look.

Horace asked the question that was on all our minds: "Is he alive?"

Barney was just lying there, trying to suck air into his lungs, but he couldn't get going. The signal between inhale and exhale seemed to be confused, and he was slowly turning a peculiar shade of blue.

"Do something!" Harry yelled, and Horace did. He grabbed Barney's belt and began to pump up and down, all the time saying, over and over, "Damn it, Barney, you shouldn't have done it . . ."

This wasn't prescribed first-aid treatment for anyone, but then what did kids on the farm know about the book art of first aid? You just tried something and if it worked, all the better. Luckily, it did for Barney. Slowly the color began to seep back into his face and his breathing got stronger with every minute.

"I know what I did wrong," he muttered. He sat up slowly and looked at his hands. We all gasped; they looked a little like raw hamburger, but he didn't seem to notice. He got to his feet and turned toward the climbing rope.

"No, Barney," Ben pleaded. "You can't."

With a withering look, Barney rubbed his sore hands on his pants, took hold of the rope, and began to climb. As he went up he looked down and said, "Don't worry. I know what I did wrong. This time I'll let go."

We all watched anxiously as Barney crept out on the limb, grasped the rope, let out that terrifying imitation of the Tarzan call, and went swinging out toward the next rope. He did just as he said he would do. He did let go . . . but he didn't bother to grab the next rope first.

With that same, bloodcurdling howl, he came hurtling down towards us again, crashing right at our feet again, almost in the exact spot as the first time. The same thing happened as before—confusion in the breathing department. Horace watched the shade of blue coming and decided it was time to pump him up again. It worked better the second time. Barney's face quickly lost the blue tint and his breathing became normal.

His eyes seemed glazed, and it was this symptom that gave Ben the opportunity to get him away from the tree. "You just take it easy, Barney," he said soothingly. "We'll take you over to the house. Mom has some nice cold cider she's saving for you." Barney didn't argue, he never did when someone offered free cider. Without looking back, Barney and all of us slowly walked back to the farm.

It was July 4, a day off for my grandfather, when the red-tail situation came to a head. He had been watching the poor bird grow up in the small cage, and seeing the mess, he put his foot down. He also had some feelings about the bird that I wasn't to understand until later on. My uncles were preparing for the big swimming and picnic day always held on the 4th at Lake Phipps, and they had no thoughts for the poor hawk, stooped over in his cage, looking out angrily at the world about him. My grandfather had watched the bird suffer long enough, and without a thought of caution he just opened the door of the cage and grabbed the hawk, dragging it toward him, feet first.

"Yeoww!" he yelled, as the hawk grabbed at my grandfather's rather robust belly, all eight talons sinking in deep. Everyone on the farm heard him—you couldn't help it! We all ran out behind the barn to see what had got hold of him. It was Ben who got there first.

"Oh, no!" he groaned, watching his father trying to pry the bird off of his belly.

"Oh, no!" repeated Harry as he came sliding around the barn from the other direction.

"Get this thing off of me!!" my grandfather yelled, arms waving, pieces of torn shirt flapping as he leaped about. "Get him off of me!!"

I'm not sure who let go of whom first, but as Ben and Harry attempted to get the hawk off of grandpa's ample stomach, the bird suddenly dashed out from under their legs, wings flapping, but unable to fly. It was probably an accident, but the hawk headed in the only safe direction he could go and get away, straight toward the old forest behind the Picnic Grounds—where it had come from. Ben started out after the hawk, Harry close behind when the air was split by a thunderous shout.

"Leave that bird go!" my grandfather bellowed.

There must have been something in his voice that day that none of the boys had ever heard before; they stopped dead in their tracks. The hawk didn't. The last I saw of that red-tail was his brown back and barred tail, running and flapping for all he was worth across the pasture, heading directly for the trees that had been his home many months, and many mice before.

I have an indelible image of that whole hawk experience embedded in my memory. Each time I hear about anyone taking a hawk to hunt with or as a pet, I worry about its fate, remembering that poor red-tail my uncles "raised" on the farm.

In the mid-1970s, after I had moved to Oregon, the issue of whether to license falconers in Oregon was hot in the Salem legislature. I testified against the proposed bill, using a pathetic, young barn owl, fed hot dogs, that had been taken from its nest by two aspiring "falconers."

Time after time I have been asked to rescue hawks, owls, and eagles that had been taken from a nest with the same intentions as my uncles, and suffering the same fate. I can remember the time when Chuck Trainer, a biologist on The Sauvies Island Wildlife Management Area, near Portland, Oregon, called me about an immature Red-tail that chased his wife each time she came out to hang up her laundry. Chuck was going to shoot it, but I suggested we try to capture it and see if we couldn't just transplant it.

It was easy to catch, we just used his wife for bait. As we were inspecting the bird we could see the marks where someone had tied jesses (leather straps) on its legs, and we noticed marks on its wings from being caged. I did some checking on the "grapevine" and sure enough, a young man at Grant High School in Portland, had owned the bird, and, tired of working with it had turned its care over to his mother. After the bird was released, it had no idea of how or what to hunt.

It ended up in Chuck's back yard thinking it had spotted the woman who used to care for it (the two women looked remarkably alike). It was necessary to keep that hawk for another two months, training it to catch its own prey, before it could be safely released into the wild—and even then I wonder if it made it.

Oregon has a falconry law today, but it's a

tough one that requires would-be falconers to pass a rigid, written test. Applicants must also demonstrate a full knowledge of raptors and have the proper housing before they're allowed to take a bird from a nest. Something my uncles and I never thought of . . .

Joe the Crow

There is one bird that humanity has been persecuting for more years than anyone can remember: the common crow. Their nests, and roosting areas have been blasted out of trees with high explosives. The birds themselves have been sprayed with detergents in an attempt to break down their natural oils, thus making them vulnerable to the cold rain of winter. Young men and adults have shot them out of trees with every conceivable type of firearm: shotguns, .22s, high-powered rifles, pistols, revolvers, and even crossbows. They have been poisoned, clubbed, and killed in an attempt to control their numbers. Nothing has been successful.

In my lifetime, the common crow has expanded its range throughout North America, from east to west and north to south. We have to face it; they know how to succeed in the face of extreme adversity. I've often said that when the smoke clears from a world-wide explosion, there will be four warm-blooded organisms left on this earth: the coyote, the raccoon, the Australian aborigine, and the common crow.

My uncle Harry had great aspirations toward having a bird that could "talk." He had read about parrots that could talk, but they were beyond our financial capabilities. Then we heard that the common crow was known to be quite a talker when you got it young enough and kept it close to people. This became the topic of breakfast, lunch, and supper on the Rockefeller Farm.

"What do you think, Ben?" Harry was anxiously asking his brother while dessert was being polished off one evening.

"Well, I guess you won't be happy until we get a crow, will you?" Ben answered, looking toward his father for confirmation. As he did, he noticed that my grandfather had spilled what appeared to be gravy on his shirt. "Hey, dad," he said, pointing to the shirt, and kicking Horace on the shin at the same time.

"What is it, son?" Grandfather answered.

As Ben was about to answer, Horace leaned over and whispered to him, "That was on his shirt when he came in. I think it's sparrow poop." Then Horace smiled at grandad and said, "I think Ben was going to tell you about the gravy you spilled on your shirt," he pointed to the spot. "Right there."

Gramp looked down, took his knife and saying, "So I did," he scooped the deposit off his shirt and licked it off his knife. A peculiar expression slowly crossed his face as he licked his lips. Then he jumped up, grabbed a glass of water, gulped in a mouthful and dashed for the kitchen sink. We could hear him out there gurgling and spluttering. As he thundered back into the dining room we all sat straight as pins on our seats, not a trace of a grin on a face.

"That was a mean, rotten, trick!" he growled. "Anyone who would do that to their own father should be horse-whipped!"

No one said a word; we just sat there, rigid.

At times like this my grandmother was even more saintly; she looked at him and smiled, "Is there something wrong, dear?" she asked sweetly.

"Something *wrong*," he shouted, "Something *wrong*? No, I just ate something that tasted like bird poop, that's all." Then he glared at my uncle Ben. "Was this your idea?"

Poor Ben didn't know what to say. He just sat there, stunned. Then something like a titter started somewhere, and it began to grow. The tiny wave of tittering slowly grew into a crescendo of laughter that enveloped everyone at the table, including my grandfather. He sat there with tears in his eyes, trying to stay mad but failing miserably.

Horace was the one who almost brought the house down when he asked, "How did it taste, Dad?" Above all the commotion I could hear my poor grandmother trying to quiet it all down. "Now, children," she was saying over and over.

As some degree of order began to settle again at the table Harry asked his question again. "What do you think, Ben, can we get a crow and teach it to talk?"

Ben had trouble drying his eyes and keeping a straight face, but managed to send along his usual, good advice. "Yes, Harry, I think this is probably a good time of the year to get a young crow. I saw some nests over near Allspaugh's hill the other day and the adult crows were feeding nestlings. Perhaps we can get into one of the nests. How about tomorrow?"

The stage was set. Evening the next day Harry was the proud owner of an absolutely ugly creature, a beast I thought couldn't possibly grow into a crow. It was a lump of dark purple flesh with black pin feathers sticking out all over, and about the size of a tennis ball. It had a head, eyes, legs, and feet sticking out beneath the bulbous dark purple body, and short, ugly appendages poking out from the sides that would probably be wings. If someone waved his hand over its head, the ugly looking bill would open, revealing a bright red lining. The smell coming from its gullet was enough to gag a maggot. "Oh, boy," was all Harry could say as he wrapped his precious bundle in a soft linen diaper.

Well, the ugly thing grew fast, fed on a diet of worms, bread soaked in milk, raw and cooked eggs, mice, hamburger, spaghetti, lettuce, cookies, cheese, and anything else Harry could find to poke down its bottomless gullet.

As it is with anyone who has an animal for a pet, it has to have a name. At times the name addresses some quality or physical appearance of the animal. If I had been picking a name for that crow it would have been "Ugly," but Harry couldn't see even a trace of ugliness in his new pet. Then someone suggested we give it a name that rhymes with "Crow," and wouldn't you know it . . . Joe went with crow. Harry

thought that was an appropriate name: "Joe the Crow" or "Joe" for short. We had no idea of what a dramatic error that was until almost two years later . . .

My grandfather had set down the rules for the welfare of this bird, right from the beginning. Even before the boys climbed the tree they knew what was expected of them. Even if this was a crow, it was not going to be treated like the hawk had been. The penalties for not taking the best of care of the crow were going to be very severe. Harry had seen the handwriting on the wall and was more than willing to see that everything was done correctly.

It wasn't long until word traveled around the neighborhood that Harry had a crow and was going to teach it to talk. Of all the people who came by to see the bird, one, in particular, wasn't greeted by the crow as a friend: poor Barney. For some reason I have never quite understood, that crow hated Barney at first sight. As Barney came into the shed where Joe was kept, it raised straight out of the nest box and gave a harsh, hissing sound. Barney didn't understand bird talk and just kept right on coming. As he reached out to pet it, the crow drove its long, thick bill straight into Barney's hand.

"Yeoooouch!" Barney yelled, shaking his fingers.

"What happened?" Harry asked, looking at Barney shaking his bloody hand, then at the crow perched on the edge of its box, glaring at Barney.

"That @#$%()! crow bit my hand! Look!" Barney bellowed, holding out his hand for us to see. Blood dripped from two puncture wounds.

Harry said, "Gee, I'm sorry Barney. Joe never did that before. You'd better go outside and do what Dad says to do when you're hurt like that."

Barney stepped outside and you could hear the excess water hitting the rocks in front of the shop door.

"Gee whiz, Barney!" Harry shouted, "Not there!"

The crow grew and its hatred for Barney grew right along with it. Harry kept trying to teach it to speak its name; we all took turns trying to get it to say something. We told it who we were and took special pains to pronounce our names clearly, about three inches from the crow's bill. We all took turns feeding it, telling it what its name was, thinking that food was the key to friendship, and ultimately, speech. But nothing happened. All we got were some strange squawks and the usual crow noises.

Someone suggested that we split its tongue to get it to talk. After a very serious discussion we all agreed that none of us had the guts to do that. Harry was the one who put it more eloquently, "If we have to split my crow's tongue to get him to talk, I don't care if he never says anything!" That was that.

The crow did become quite a watchdog, however. No one could come through our driveway without that crow sounding the alarm. Of all the people who came and went on foot or bicycle, Barney bore the brunt of most of the crow's police activities. We didn't understand how the crow could either see or sense Barney's arrival, but he could almost always tell when he was coming. Joe would run and hide behind the tall hedge at the edge of the main road, then dash out, most times on foot, and hammer at his ankles, drawing blood every time. Then if the ankle attack didn't work out, Joe would fly up and start on his head. The oaths Barney uttered at these times amazed us all. I didn't know such language existed . . .

By September, school was back in session. We attended Colonial Park School, about a two mile walk from the farm. The Great Depression had a firm grip on the economy, money was scarce, especially on the farm, and bicycles were out of our financial reach at the time, so we all walked—Harry, Horace, and me. It was after school had begun, perhaps a month or more, when we suddenly were shocked to hear our names being called early one morning.

"Oh, Har-ry! Oh, Hor-ace! Oh, Jim-my!" came the cry, just about dawn. Then our names were followed by one more, also repeated several times. "Joe! Joe!" I sat straight up in bed.

All three of us used to sleep in the same bed, a big featherbed my grandmother made.

(One night my Uncle Harry rolled over and kissed my Uncle Horace, calling him "Carol." What a battle that developed into! I can still see Horace standing astraddle of poor Harry, who was still sound asleep. Gritting my teeth, I watched Horace raise his clenched fist, grumbling, "Carol! You @#$%()!," and slugged poor Harry, smack on the nose! The blood flew and one of the most exciting battles I've ever witnessed developed . . . but that's another story . . .) We all ran to the window to see who or what was calling our names. There, standing on the top of the grape arbor, was Joe the Crow. As we watched, he looked up toward our bedroom window and let go again with our names, clear as a bell.

Harry was beside himself. "He did it!" he shouted over and over.

"Who did what?" came a mumbled question from my grandparents' room.

"It's the crow, Dad," Harry exclaimed. "It can talk. It knows all our names. It's calling us!" Right on cue, Joe called us again. "He knows his own name too!" Harry added.

For over three years Joe called us every morning, rain or shine, snow or heat. You couldn't stop him. In fact, we couldn't stop him from doing other things that weren't so amusing. One was taking the parts of a carburetor or distributor Horace had lined up as he overhauled his car. Even spark plugs vanished! Anything that was shiny was fair game for Joe. Spoons, forks, jewelry vanished, along with buttons from clothing my mother or grandmother hung on the clothesline. If it was shiny, and attractive, that crow would haul it away, and it would disappear forever. I know that when the old buildings on the farm are torn down, a treasure will be found that will put a packrat to shame, made up of the stuff that crow hauled off.

It was his habit of following us to school that almost got Joe killed. We had clipped his wings on several occasions, but the feathers just kept coming back and soon he was flying again. There was no way to keep him at home, aside from putting him in a cage, and that was out of the question . . . Grandfather's orders. We tried to tie him up like a falcon, but he almost hung himself a couple of times. About twice a week that silly crow would follow us to school. Then one day, quiet, shy, blameless Harry was called into the school principal's office, something that scared the poor guy half to death. The principal laid down the law; no more crows at school. Period!

Joe didn't understand school law, and just before recess time he would suddenly appear at one of the school windows, calling, "Oh, Jim-my. Oh, Har-ry. Oh, Hor-ace!" If he had just come directly to one of the rooms we were in it probably wouldn't have been so bad, but he insisted on experimenting, going from window to window, causing bedlam in the room and terrible problems for the teacher trying to conduct class. Then of course, there were the girls that were deathly afraid of him and when the crow lit on the window sill and began to call us, they would scream, run around the room, cover their heads and make more commotion than the crow. When he suddenly found one of us, Joe would pound on the glass with his beak, trying to get in and get a 'goodie' we always had for him. That was the only way we could get him to come home with us, waving his favorite food in front of him, like a lump of sugar leading a stubborn mule.

I took many trips back home and missed some pretty important classes because it was my turn to take Joe back to the farm. (Some of those trips I took home were also caused by a classmate of mine I remember as "Bob." He sat right behind me, and every time the teacher called on him he would throw up. After the first time he got me, I would jump up each time the teacher called on him; I didn't have to go home so often and change clothes if I jumped up first.)

Joe's vocabulary slowly got better. He knew everyone on the farm. He stayed clear of most of the adults, except my old Uncle Joe. The crow would speak to him any time. One night Joe the Crow almost caused poor Uncle Joe to have heart failure when my uncle was going out to use the outhouse. The crow always slept in the huge grape arbor, a thick, leafy canopy over the walkway that linked the house to the barn (where the two-holer was located). One dark night, Uncle Joe was ambling along the walkway beneath the arbor when he must have awakened Joe the Crow. The crow knew who it was and probably feeling friendly, he just called him by name, "Hello, Joe." My poor old uncle almost didn't make it the rest of the way . . .

Joe the Crow became a well-known attraction all over West Haven. Curious neighbors placed the farm on their itinerary for the Sunday drive. Once in a while, the trouble-making kids in the neighborhood would try to sneak onto the farm, bent on doing some kind of mischief to Joe, but that crow was tuned into those kind of people somehow (perhaps their body language) and would use the same tactics on them that he used on Barney.

When Joe reached his third year, almost to the day, we received another lesson in avian biology. Harry lost Joe and couldn't find him anywhere. "Catsfur," he asked anxiously. "Have you seen Joe? I've looked all over the farm and can't find him." That started the big crow hunt.

Soon, we were all looking for Joe. We peeked into every crook-and-cranny on the farm: up along the roof of the barn and sheds, into the old chicken coops, all around the sides of the hay, up in the rafters, and all throughout the grape arbor. It was my Aunt Dutchie, the telephone operator, who finally found him. We heard Joe let out a shrill squawk of alarm then we heard Dutchie shout, "Hey!" somewhere outside the horse barn. As we ran around behind the horse barn we could see Joe zooming around and cawing like mad, but there was no sign of Dutch.

"Hey!" she shouted between Joe's cawing. We all looked up and spotted her standing on a ladder between the horse barn roof and the hay barn, and she was holding something in her hand. "Look what I found!" she said laughing.

Harry was closer to her than anyone else and I could see him shading his eyes from the sun, trying to get a better look at what his sister was holding in her hand. "Is that an egg?" he shouted to her.

"Looks like one to me, daddy," she laughed again. Then she did something we didn't expect. "Here!" she shouted. "Catch!" and tossed the egg underhand, straight to Harry.

Harry was a pretty quick guy who excelled at sports. No one could beat him at horseshoes, and at catching eggs he was an expert. We used to save all the rotten duck eggs and keep them in a cool place. When one of our city kin came to visit us or we wanted to give someone else an awful surprise, we'd get them into a game of "Who-Can-Catch-The-Egg." A rotten egg will explode if you even look at it wrong, and we sent a lot of kids home smelling like a dead cow. Once in a while we'd get wild and throw them at each other, and Harry was the only one who could catch one without it exploding. He caught the egg Dutch threw to him with ease. We all crowded around to see it. I got there just in time to hear him exclaim, "That sure doesn't look like a chicken egg." Then he held it out for Ben to look at for he was the egg expert.

Ben looked at it for only a moment and then looked up at Dutchie who was pointing to a small bunch of sticks under the eaves of the horse barn. Looking back at Harry, he laughed, and said, "Here, daddy, I think this is yours." Then he laughed all the harder as he added, "Joe has just changed her name to *Josephine* . . ."

Harry stood there, staring at the egg, then at the crow sailing around us, squawking her head off at us for interfering with some-

thing we obviously knew nothing about. Dutch put the egg back into the nest, but we must have upset Josephine pretty badly. She left it and didn't try to nest again.

It was a very cold morning that following winter when I suddenly awoke to silence— our names hadn't been called! I jumped up, shook Harry and Horace and told them I hadn't heard Joe calling us. We all sat there, a question on our faces. Suddenly Harry leaped out of bed, muttered, "Oh, no" and with his nightshirt flapping in the breeze, he dashed down the stairs, jumped into his boots, and ran outside into the snowy, cold morning.

I can still see him, slowly trudging into the kitchen, tears streaming down his face, carrying the stiff body of old Joe. The cold, or perhaps age, had sent her out among the stars.

Harry and I were a long time getting over it. Even Barney had a few nice things to say as we prepared Joe for her last rites. With tenderness that boys seldom demonstrate, we all stood by the small grave, hats in our hands, as Harry held his friend in her special casket made from my mom's best shoe box. Then we laid our friend into the special place we made for her under the big cherry tree in the front yard. We often talked about getting another crow, but we knew that we never would. Nothing could take the place of Josephine. She was special, one-of-a-kind.

2 | BLAZING NEW TRAILS

Owls in the Dog House

Back in the late '50s, while I was conducting field studies to determine what effects poisoned bait might have on eagles, I followed the government trapper and discovered where and how he was putting out poisoned horse meat to kill coyotes (and, as a consequence, any other predators who happened to eat the stuff). At times I became pretty vocal about the slipshod methods I thought they used back in those days, especially when the trapper was setting out too much bait, too close to civilization. I got a reputation for being a "nature-lover," an environmental busy-body, and a big pain to the sheep growers.

This reputation often got me into trouble: like the time I presented a paper on government predator control in Central Oregon at an Audubon Annual Convention and the feds were there taping it, looking for "evidence" to put me in the slammer for tampering with government property. More often than not, the encounters led to new friends, broader horizons, and a better understanding of the natural world for me.

I had been sleeping for well over an hour, down and out as a fellow can be when he's had a hard ten hours out in the woods, sneaking up on logs at 4 am, setting chokers, herding a cat around slippery slopes, and just trying to stay alive while making a living. The jangling of the phone reached into my unconscious and I fumbled for the receiver . . .

"This the Jim Anderson who likes coyotes?" came the gruff question.

I wasn't in too good of a mood to carry on a casual conversation about my likes or dislikes of coyotes at that moment, so I just grunted, "I guess so . . ."

"Well," the man continued. "I raise Pekinese dogs out here near Sisters, and I'm having a hell of a problem with these damn coyotes! They're about to put me out of business, running off with my puppies. If you want to save those @#$%()! coyotes, you'd better get up here and get the ones that are getting my pups or I'm going to kill every coyote in the country!"

After he gave me his phone number and address, I assured him I'd get out to his place just as soon as I could, then managed to replace the receiver and fall back into the bed.

Three days later I drove into a yard that had a sign hanging by the road, "Pekinese Dogs For Sale." I was really impressed with the layout. There were several concrete pens laid out in neat rows, each with a six-foot-high, woven fence around it. It might have been possible for a small predator, like a spotted skunk, weasel, or small cat to fit through the mesh, but from what I could see from first sight, it was probably impossible for a coyote to get through—unless it could fly.

While giving me the tour, my host stopped in front of a small empty pen and exclaimed, "See! Two of the pups are gone! Those damn coyotes did it again!" I glanced at the ground, inspected the wire mesh of the fence and even looked at the jagged wires on top, but for the life of me, I couldn't see hide nor hair of coyote sign.

I thanked him for showing me around and then asked if he'd let me give the place another look, on my own. I was pretty sure his problem wasn't coyotes—but you could never tell, they could do some pretty unbelievable things. Like any good naturalist, I began slowly walking in circles, first around the pens, then his outbuildings, then fences, and finally out onto the adjacent BLM land that ran off to the east. I was about a quarter mile from the house when I thought I spotted the answer to his dilemma. Well, I actually heard it first.

"Whoo, whoo, who, whoooo," came the faint hooting from the junipers about 100 yards ahead. I recognized the call immediately as a great horned owl. Within seconds, another hooting began from a partner. Yep, I said to myself, it's a pair all right. They kept hooting as I walked closer, each call sounding more aggressive the closer I approached. Up ahead, I could see an old hawk's nest in the top of a juniper snag, and in it I spotted the ear-tufts of the female owl hunkered down on the nest.

As I got to within about 100 feet of the tree, the two owls began to hoot louder, then clack their beaks and make sounds similar to a dog barking. (I had been knocked about by these "tigers of the air," and had a great deal of respect for their ability to protect the home place; at times they could be meaner than a junk yard dog.) I stopped when the female stood up on the nest and put the evil eye on me. Suddenly she launched herself from the nest, diving right at me, hooting as she came.

At the last moment I ducked as she went zooming over my head, missing my face by inches. I ran to the base of the nest tree, and as I crouched under the branches for protection I discovered the reason for the vanishing pups at my feet. The sandy surface beneath the tree was littered with pup parts. Listening to the owls hooting above me, I grinned with admiration for their ingenuity . But now what do I do . . .

Gritting my teeth, I began to climb the nest tree, crunching my way through the brittle limbs. Each foot I gained up the tree would bring a renewed attack from the parents. The male owl was mostly bluff, but what he lacked in courage, the female made up with persistence. Once she slammed into my back with both feet, leaving gashes in the back of my leather jacket. If I didn't have a good hunch what had to be done to stop the pup-pillaging, I would have given it up right there, but I continued to the top, and as I carefully peeked over the rim of the nest my suspicions were confirmed. Blinking back at me were two, fat, young owls, stuffed to

the lid with Pekinese puppies. They were the healthiest looking great horned owl nestlings I had seen in many a moon.

I couldn't tell the dog rancher—he would probably shoot every owl in the country and undoubtedly set out pole traps all around his place, if not clear out on the public lands. I looked back toward the ranch house and figured I was far enough away that no one could see or hear me, so I scooped up the two owls as quickly as I could, opened my jacket, and stuffed them under my shirt. It was a tight fit, and I received additional scratches for my efforts, but I was able to zip the jacket up and carefully ease down through the branches without injuries to myself or my passengers—all the time looking over my shoulder at the two adults who were still hooting and clacking their beaks at me. When I reached the ground and started to walk away, the adult owls got into a frenzy again and swooped over me. This time I was leaving, however, and with each foot that separated me from their nest, the attacks became less aggressive.

In a few minutes I was out of their territory and both owls quit, almost as though they had turned off a switch. I took the long way around to my pickup, avoiding the house completely.

Making sure no one was watching, I carefully placed the two young owls into the big, wooden tool box in the bed of the truck, quietly closed the lid, and then eased through the trees toward the back of the house. As I approached the yard from the back I began to whistle loudly.

"Well," the dog man inquired, coming out to the porch. "How'd you do?"

"I think I've solved your problem," I answered, going to my pickup for my thermos. He watched me as I poured myself a cup of spiced tea, and leaned on the front bumper, smiling at him.

"Well . . ." he inquired again, "Wha'ja do?"

I knew I had to go easy with my answer— I couldn't give away the real reason the poor guy had been losing puppies. After all, I thought to myself, he was the one who moved into the countryside, wasn't he? He was the one who had placed this fantastic

Jim's librarian friend looked at these three baby owls in the old golden eagle's nest when the golden eagle came swooping by.

feast before the owls, wasn't he? He was the newcomer, wasn't he? Shucks, I said to myself, those owls had "grandfather rights."

"Well, I'll tell you what I did. Coyotes are very territorial, so I walked all around your place and looked for bushes and trees, about 100 yards apart that would make good scent posts. Then I walked from tree-to-tree, and peed on each one. I don't think a coyote will ever bother your puppies again."

He just stood there, looking at me like I was nuts. Then he shook his head, took another look and said, "I'll be damned," walking back toward the house. He stopped once more and said, "Uhhhh, thanks for coming out anyway," and went into the house without another word.

Well, I took the owls home and switched them over to jackrabbits. (In those days it was possible to drive a circular route around

Bend and scoop up at least twenty jack-rabbits and cottontails off the road—but not any longer.) I figured the jackrabbits would be healthier, and a darn sight easier to come by than pekinese puppies . . . I was also pretty sure the parent owls would give up the site as soon as there were no babies to feed and the pressure would be off the dog rancher's livelihood. In fact, I felt very good about the whole project—until I got a phone call about two weeks later.

"Hi, Jim," my caller said, real friendly-like. I recognized the voice immediately; it was the dog rancher. I held my breath, beginning to sweat a little. "I sure owe you an apology," he said. "I thought you were just pulling my leg about that business of peeing on the trees and that territorial stuff, but by golly, it worked! I haven't lost a pup since you left. I haven't even heard a damn

Jim walked up to this adult great horned owl that was holding a road-killed dead jackrabbit and refused to fly. He walked closer and finally got this photo on his old 4 X 5 Graflex. You can see Jim's reflection in the owl's left eye.

coyote." Then after a long pause, he asked, "Incidentally, what were you drinking when you staked out those scent posts?"

Like any poor liar, you're bound to get caught; Abraham Lincoln was right—no one does have a memory good enough to make a successful liar. I looked around the house in a panic, searching desperately for an answer. Then I spotted the thermos on the kitchen counter. "It was spiced tea!" I blurted out. Then sounding very serious, I added, "But remember, you'll have to keep those scent posts fresh, especially after a rain storm . . ."

"Thanks! I'll get some of that tea tomorrow," he said. "I sure want to thank you again. You're a damn good naturalist!"

Just as I was hanging up the phone, I heard one of the young owls begin squawking for its food. I went to the refrigerator and got out a nice, fresh, hind leg of a jackrabbit (I always keep jackrabbits and other good food on hand for friends whoooo drop in).

Timing is Everything

Raising great horned owls is no casual chore—they're messy, always hungry, and not convenient to take travelling. Just keeping them fed is a full time job in itself. I often have cages upon cages of rats and mice stacked up in my shop, barn, and garage trying to maintain a population sufficient to keep abreast of an owl's voracious appetite. In addition, I rarely pass up a good-looking rabbit road-kill, stopping to scoop it off the road and dump into the back of my rig. People driving by would shake their heads in sympathy for my destitute situation.

It was spring and I was raising two young great horned owls again. Every evening I stepped out on the back porch and shouted, "Hey owls!" holding a piece of delicious-looking mashed jackrabbit in each hand. The two owls would come out of the darkness, one swooping in from the barn roof and the other squawking as he hopped and ran from the woodshed. One would land on my hand while the other would run around my legs, begging for food like a puppy.

The two owls were just starting to fly pretty well when I got a phone call that was really good news.

"Mr. Anderson," my caller said. "I'm looking for some wildlife photos for a book I'm writing, and I understand you have some of the wildlife from around here. May I come over and review your work?"

I was logging at the time and doing some wildlife work on the side, and this sounded like it might be my ship coming in—I needed a new 400 mm lens. "Do you want to buy photos, or just look at them?" I inquired.

"Oh, I want to purchase some photos, of course," the woman replied.

"Well then, come on over!" I said cheerfully, and started cleaning up the house.

In about fifteen minutes, a car slowly drove down the lane to the ranch house I was living in on the northwest side of Pilot Butte in Bend, Oregon. I walked to the porch and watched as the car stopped and a very attractive young lady walked up to the house. We passed pleasantries for a while, then she came inside to look at my photos. In a short time, she had an expensive pile of black & white prints stacked up on the kitchen table. Her favorite was a porcupine on the top of an old fence post.

Then she asked, "How do you find these animals to photograph? It must be very difficult."

Her question was innocent enough and sincere. I should have let it go at that, but I had just returned from a couple of weeks with Reub Long, a philosophical old horseman from the Fort Rock country who was known for his quick wit which always seemed to fit into a situation just right. As the young lady's question went through my mind, I thought this was going to be my chance to emulate my old desert pal.

"Oh, shucks," I began, with a straight face. "It's not too difficult to find an animal to photograph. All you have to do is make up your mind what you want and then go outside and shout for it."

The young women looked at me , startled. "What do you mean?" she asked seriously.

"All you have to do is get your camera ready, shout for the animal you want, and shoot. It's really very easy," I stated matter-of-factly.

"You are joking, Mr. Anderson," she declared, giving me a very suspicious look.

"No!" I insisted, warming to my artful deceit. "You came here to get photos of wildlife, didn't you?" I continued. When she nodded her head slowly, I went on, "Well, I see you have your camera with you—how would you like to take a photo of a great horned owl?"

"Really?" she asked.

"Really," I replied. "Now, you get your camera and stand right here by this big window and I'll go out on the porch and call up an owl for you." I took her to what I thought would be the best place to see the owls when they came in for their evening meal and then asked, "Ready?" She stood there, looking at me very suspiciously, but was pointing her camera in the right direction, so I went out onto the porch, cupped my hands around my mouth and shouted, "Hey! Owl!"

It was fantastic. This was the first time I had ever seen the woodshed owl even care about flying (he must have been very hungry), as he came flapping out of the woodshed toward me, skimming along over the grass like a glider. The other owl also responded, swooping down from his favorite perch on the barn roof. I didn't have their usual jackrabbit in my hand, so I didn't know what was going to happen.

To my utter surprise and delight, the

Some people call dogs; Jim Anderson calls owls!

woodshed owl sailed in to land right on my foot, and the owl from the barn roof sailed right up and landed on my hand! It was really wonderful and would make a fantastic photo. Really pleased with myself, I looked back through the window—but no one was there! I quickly eased the owl off my hand onto the porch railing and dashed back into the house.

There was my photo buyer, slumped down in a chair, her face as white as a ghost, repeating over and over, "I don't believe it, I don't believe it." I suppose I should have let it go at that, but I was feeling pretty guilty about the trick I had played on her, so I proceeded to tell her the truth. Embarrassed for being so gullible she got up from the

chair, brushed her hair into place, straightened her skirt, then looking at me with an icy stare, she said "Thank you, Mr. Anderson," and walked out of the house— without any of my wildlife photographs. Watching her car leave the driveway was like watching my ship sinking—along with my hopes for a new 400 mm lens. Reub Long would have handled that one better.

As she was driving out of the yard, another car was coming in, an insurance salesman. Oh, no . . . I groaned to myself— as if things weren't bad enough already . . .

In those days I was a sucker for any new policy that came down the pike. I just couldn't say no, and those guys knew it. I think they must have had some kind of weekly get-together where they discussed likely prey for their business and I came out on the top of the heap. After a while though, the constant calls got to be overwhelming and very annoying. I had to find some way to stop it. Then I had an idea . . .

The next night I placed two juicy pieces of jackrabbit into an old briefcase, went out on the back porch, and sat down. When young owls are hungry and don't get stuffed with something in a short time, they begin to let out the most awful squawks, screams, and caterwauling you can imagine. I know deer hunters who have been spooked out of their campsites by the screeching of young owls.

My two were no different. They had seen me come out to the porch with something, and not spotting any food, they began making their awful ruckus. Then owl number one silently swooped down and landed at my feet. Owl number two came hopping and leaping out of the woodshed and he too stopped in front of me. Both of them began to bob their heads back and forth, looking at me from every angle, trying to see where I had hid that rabbit.

After about three minutes of these gyrations, I placed the briefcase in front of them and opened it. Both of them leaped backwards, pulled their heads way back and stared at the contents. Recognition soon hit them like a bolt of lightening, and they leaped on the pieces of rabbit, tearing at them and each other, trying to get them away from the case and off to their favorite feeding places.

After just three days of this, they were conditioned. When I walked out on the back porch with the briefcase, instead of flying right to me as they did in the past, they dropped at my feet and waited for me to open the briefcase.

I relented and agreed to see the next insistent insurance salesman who ignored my polite telephone refusal.

At precisely 6 pm the next evening, a car slowly drove into the yard. I watched out the bedroom window as a light came on inside the car, and I observed my eager caller stuffing things into a briefcase. I was elated and a little apprehensive; I didn't know how far the owls might go with a stranger. The light went out, the door opened, and the insurance man started for the house. He got to about no-man's-land, midway between house and car, when the first owl suddenly swooped out of the dusk, heading straight for the briefcase.

It caught the man completely by surprise! He jumped back in shock as the owl swooped by and turned to make another pass. Swinging the briefcase, he flailed at the owl as it flew toward him again. All the activity got owl number two's attention, especially the briefcase, and he came squawking and hopping from the woodshed. With two owls assaulting him now the astonished man let out a "Yeeeeohhhhwww!" and dashed back to his car, jerked the door open, and scrambled in.

I was in hysterics. Tears were running out my eyes—I was so weak I could hardly stand up. Both owls were now on the car roof, walking back and forth, peering over the edge. It was a scene right out of a Buster Keaton movie.

I dried my eyes and walked out onto the porch. Waiting for a lull between horns blasts, I waved to my quarry trapped in his car, looking wildly about him. As I put my arms and shoulders up in the "What's the matter?" posture, he rolled his window down and shouted, "Some big birds tried to get me! They were eagles . . . or something!"

I shouted back, "Oh, I think they were owls, because there's two of them walking around on the roof of your car!" He cranked the window up with a thud, and stared at me, probably wondering what to do next.

I couldn't stand it any longer, and neither could the owls. They saw me standing on the porch and came flying over, one landing on my hand and the other at my feet. I tried to look innocent, but the jig was up. In a cloud of dust, my new policy vanished up the driveway. Funny, but I never had any more calls after that . . .

Lavacicle Cave

Lavacicle Cave is a very unique lava tube. It's about a mile in length and like most lava tubes, it begins and ends with lava pinching ceiling and floor. The opening to the Lavacicle, located about midway, is so restricted that a person going into it must slide down, over, and around huge lava boulders that almost block the entrance. Then he must crawl on hands and knees through ankle-deep sand with his back bumping against the sharp lava ceiling.

After about one hundred feet, the tube widens and a person can stand upright and walk through a tunnel large enough to park two railroad locomotives, side-by-side. The walls are spattered with the remains of at least four other lava flows that sloshed through the tunnel after it had been formed, painting the walls a mosaic of rusty red, purple, orange, tan, and faded yellow. Poking up through mud and sand on the floor are various pillars formed by lava that dripped from the ceiling after hot gases had been forced into the cave time after time. There used to be several, child-sized lava stalagmites that had been formed on the floor of the cave by the remelting lava, but they have all been stolen by vandals.

A stalagmite is a formation that rests on the floor of a cave. Stalactites are attached to the ceiling. I keep them separated by the *g* in stalagmite: *G* for *ground*; and the *C* in stalactite stands for ceiling. Also, stalactites have to hold on *tight* to keep from falling, another way many people remember the terms.

I had the pleasure of taking Phil Brogan, a noted author and geologist from Bend, into the lava tube shortly after Phil Coyner and I had explored it fully. Mr. Brogan was so impressed with the abundant lava formations throughout the cave that he coined the name "Lavacicle."

As Phil Coyner and I continued to explore Lavacicle, we found additional lava stalagmites and other geological formations that later investigations found to be unique in Central Oregon and the nation.

For a long time we thought the cave ended at a massive breakdown, about two thirds of the way into the tube. One evening when we had more time, Phil started poking around the lava boulders and debris, looking for another way around. As I watched him squeezing around the mud and wet rocks I heard him shout.

"Hey, Jim! I found a way through . . ." and his light slowly vanished in a cleft between some enormous boulders. (As it should always be when you're spelunking, you always stay alert as your partner begins to explore a new route.) I listened as Phil continued giving an account of his progress as he squeezed around the slippery, muddy boulders. I wanted to join him, but waited until I got the signal that he was in the clear again. After what seemed like a half hour I heard him shout, "I'm through!"

Then after a moment he shouted again, "Come on. You've got to see this!" That was all I needed. I began to squeeze through the cleft I had seen him use, around the muddy boulders, down to the floor of the cave, then around more breakdown and suddenly, there he was, grinning like a cheshire cat.

"How do you like that!" he exclaimed, pointing to the floor of the cave.

The floor of the tube was covered with a layer of fine, silica mud, and as we got down for a closer look we could see hundreds of water-soaked, tan-colored bones, as far as we could see into the darkness ahead. Jackrabbit bones made up the bulk of the skeletal remains, but we also found bobcat, coyote, small rodents, packrat, and unidentified remains. As we slowly walked toward what we knew would be an end—somewhere—we noticed the tube was slowly getting smaller, and the ceiling getting lower. In about 600 yards we found the end where the ceiling slanted to the floor.

As we reached the positive end (spelunkers always have to get to the end of a cave . . .) I saw another skeleton, lying in a muddy trough of the wave patterned lava floor. Most of the smaller bones had been

The formations shown in these first photographs ever made in Lavacicle Cave have been destroyed by vandals. Jim took these pictures in the mid-60s to capture the beauty of the waist-high lavacicle. The formations were so fragile that a slight vibration on the floor of the cave would shatter them.

destroyed by fungi, or the dampness and the minerals in the mud, but the skull was somewhat solid and all the teeth were in the upper portion.

"Looks like a badger . . ." I said to Phil as I carefully picked up the skull and placed it into tissue and then into my collecting pack. I gave the skull to the University of Oregon Natural History Museum where Dr. James Shotwell gave me a more accurate identification. It was not a badger after all, but a river otter, which left Phil Coyner and I shaking our heads in disbelief. Lavacicle Cave is at least thirty miles from any body of water capable of supporting such an animal. The additional information supplied by Dr. Shotwell left us bewildered; the skull was approximately 6,000 years old! This prompted Phil Brogan to write an interesting article about the river otter that was migrating across the high desert with a canteen on its back . . .

After some deliberation between the US Forest Service (FS) and The Sierra Club, a steel gate was installed at the entrance to

Phil Coyner and his three children (Margaret, John, and Joe) join Jim and his daughter Kristin in Skeleton Cave, near Bend.

Lavacicle and only those who were guided by FS personnel were allowed to enter the cave. For about two years this was a working solution to protect the unique geological formations of the cave. Then the first "crazy" hit.

Someone apparently thought no one had the right to bar he/she from the cave and proceeded to jerk the steel door off the entrance with what appeared to be a powerful winch. I think I was the first person to go into the cave after this had happened. I was shocked to find several of the large lavacicles had been stolen and over twenty of the others had been knocked over. It was a sad sight.

Each time the FS put a new, locked gate on the entrance it would last for about three months and then some crazy would jerk it out or cut it up with a torch. Each time this happened another treasure from the cave would disappear, or the cave was vandalized. It finally got to the point where it was no longer possible to protect the lava tube. What had once been a treasure house of geological, and biological wonders was

OMSI science students look at the formations of Lavacicle Cave (1962).

becoming just another vandalized lava tube. Oh, a scattering of the artifacts that made it unique remained, but the great Horse-head Lavacicle, and others of its stature are gone.

Phil and I guided several groups into the cave for the FS in the late '50s and early '60s, and each time we slithered down the entrance we would look longingly at the lava boulders blocking the upper part of the lava tube. We couldn't stand it.

We contacted Joe Stenkamp, who was then the Fire Officer for the Fort Rock District. He asked his brother to join us, and the four of us took on the southern part of the lava tube. It took several hours to find a route that would allow us past the labyrinth of boulders, clefts, and dead ends. Phil Coyner was the one who could always find a way to get around, if there was one. I used

to kid him about having a nose like a mole, who could locate anything underground.

He soon shouted to us that he had found the way through, but it was a tight crawl-way. I was behind him and could hear him grunting as he inched along, squirming past the sharp boulders that snatched at his coveralls, and were only inches from his face.

"You're going to have to roll over at this next bend," I heard Phil's muffled voice shouting. I looked up ahead and watched as his feet twisted 180 degrees. I could also see that he was up against the wall of the tube and rocks at almost every point in his body—and Phil was skinnier than I was. Soon, his scratching and struggling noises were muffled in the distance and I began to squeeze into the hole I had seen him go through. As I began to roll over to make the tight bend I felt my coveralls begin to snag on the sharp lava around me. Anyone who has been in that predicament knows what happens next—you suddenly swell up, like a puffer fish. "Kerumph!" I was jammed tight into the lava rock around me.

"I'm stuck . . ." I mumbled, and began squirming a little to see if I could get loose. I shifted my weight, tried to move my arm, tried to move my leg, but it was all to no avail. "Better hold it up, Joe!" I shouted, as I heard him coming up behind me, "I'm stuck . . ."

Joe Stenkamp is a good man to have around when something goes wrong. He doesn't get rattled about anything. I felt him press against the bottom of my boots and then he asked, "Do you want a push?" I didn't think that was going to do anything but get me in tighter, and I told him exactly that (Joe says I had more panic in my voice than I can remember).

Then we started this interesting dialogue:
"How tight are you stuck?"
"Very tight, Joe . . ."
"Where?"
"All over."
"Really?"
"Yeah, really!"
"What do you think we should do?"
"Get me out of here!"
"How?"
"How should I know! You're the guy that runs this place! Think of something!"
"Be right back . . ."

I could hear him slowly inching his way backwards toward the exit, a direction I would have loved to have gone. Soon it was all quiet. Very quiet . . . too quiet. I was beginning to get the heebie-jeebies and I could feel myself sticking even tighter as I expanded with the panic I was trying to swallow. Then, as quickly as the panic began, it suddenly vanished, with one word . . .

"Hi," Phil said. I twisted my head as far as I could and saw the light from his head lamp casting erie shadows on the walls of my prison. "Be there momentarily . . ." he said quietly. In another few moments I could feel the heat from his head-lamp and smell the acetylene gas from the flame. "You stuck?" he asked.

I couldn't help but chuckle, in spite of my rising panic. "I won't be in a minute, Phil," I said. "You'll roast the fat out of me with that gas light of yours, then I'll just dribble out of here."

He began to chuckle too, removed his hard hat, and then reached out to feel around my shoulders with his one free hand. "Yep, you're stuck tighter than a bull's tail in fly time," he said, really laughing. After fumbling around a few minutes he waved something in my face and laughed, "Don't worry, I know I can get out of here . . . I just found my pocket knife!"

I was about to tell him how humorous he was when I heard a clanking sound coming behind me. "You still there?" Joe asked.

"Yeah, I'm still here."

"OK," he replied. "Hold still . . . I'm going to peel away the lava rock from around you with this bar and make the hole bigger." Then he chuckled. "I'm surprised you didn't get your head stuck in there first." I could feel the rock bar slowly inching along my thigh and up to my waist. "Let me know when I hit rock, or whether it's you," he instructed. As the bar hit a sharp piece of lava I told him where he was and I heard the slam of his single jack hammer striking the end of the bar. "Clank!"

A tiny piece of lava rock chipped off and into the space below me; and I could feel freedom as the chunk dropped away. "Clank!" went the hammer again, another piece of lava chipped off, and I shrunk another eighth of an inch. "Clank!" went the hammer again, and I gained another eighth of an inch as less air in my body and less rock against me made the hole larger. I could move my leg, then my arm, then my shoulders.

"I'm free!" I shouted and began to squirm toward Phil who was already backing away, grinning as he put his pocket knife in his coveralls. In a few more minutes I was free of the crawlway and into a huge cavern.

"You made it!" Phil said, slapping me on the back.

I began to look about me, and discovered literally thousands of tan colored bones. The floor of this portion of the cave wasn't the rough, ribbed surface of cooled lava, but a

The only way anyone can get into Lavacicle Cave is to crawl down the entrance hole, and onto the sandy floor to the larger portion of the lava tube where it was then large enough to park two railroad locomotives side-by-side.

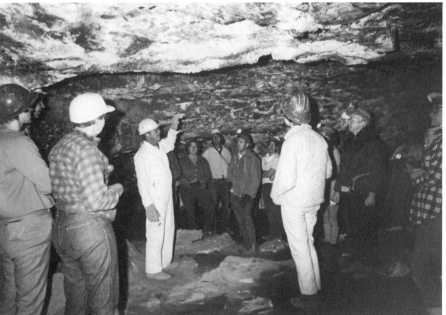

Jim teaches at the first place it was possible to stand after crawling through the sand in Lavacicle Cave.

thick coating of silica mud. As I stomped my foot, the resulting sound was like that of a huge, bass drum. Soon Joe and his brother joined us and we all began to slowly inspect the amazing variety of bones around us. Most of the bones were the same as we found in the lower portion of the lava tube, but Jackrabbit made up the bulk of the bones, with coyote, bobcat, packrat, and

small rodents all mixed in. We all wondered about them. Had they been transported here? By water? Or was this a gigantic graveyard for these animals of the desert? Perhaps we'll never know.

As we began to slowly walk toward the source of the tube, I discovered a true cave animal: an inch-long, blind centipede, a specialized animal of the realm of absolute darkness. What lived in this part of the underground labyrinth of absolute darkness had no need for eyes. I have often wanted to go back and look for other blind arthropods, and perhaps I will some day.

Breakdown after breakdown of huge lava boulders slowed our progress toward the source of the ancient lava tube. After about a quarter of a mile of tortuous struggling we encountered a huge breakdown that completely blocked the passage. Phil was about to search out a route around—or under it—when we heard a voice call out . . .

"Time to head home," Joe said. "I told the guys at Cabin Lake Ranger Station I'd be there by 3 pm, and it's getting close." Then he came over and slapped me on the back, "I'm going out before you do, Jim, old scout; I don't want to be the one to cut you up into little pieces after you get stuck again!"

Several years later, in the early '70s, Mike Houck, a naturalist with OMSI, and I got together with a bus-load of high-school students and spent two days in Lavacicle Cave repairing the damage done by the vandals. We used cement and plaster-of-paris to glue the lavacicles back where they had been broken off, and ceramic coloring to try and match up the color of the lavas. It was a noble attempt to restore the remaining formations to a state that resembled what it was before it had been vandalized. Even that was in vain. Within a year the gate was jerked off again and havoc spread throughout the lava tube, not only destroying what we had repaired, but also many of the features that had survived the previous onslaughts. How unfortunate it is that some people treat the beautiful treasures of Nature this way.

Coyotes and Bats Have Rights Too

It wasn't a very big newspaper story, just a few lines in the Bend Bulletin, the daily paper that served Central Oregon where I was living in the '50s. It was a story about a coyote that was frothing at the mouth and had run into the school yard in the tiny town of Brothers east of Bend. Everyone who saw the coyote thought the animal was rabid, and it was put out of its misery. To be on the safe side, the coyote's head had been shipped to the Oregon State Board of Health where the Vector Control staff would inspect it. As a health precaution, the Brothers school was closed and the kids kept home for a few days. That was that.

Well, that's no surprise, I thought to myself. I had read a great deal about the problems rabid coyotes and skunks caused in the West. Having one show up in Brothers was interesting. I had never seen a rabid animal, but I was logging at the time and didn't have time to drive thirty miles to see it; at least I thought it was going to be that way. I didn't know it at the time, but the ringing of my phone was going to bring me

closer than I knew to a great deal of the Oregon high desert wildlife.

"Jim," the caller said. "This is Phil. I just got a call from the guys in Vector Control at the Oregon State Board of Health. They want to know if we're finding any rabid bats in the lava tubes we've been investigating."

Phil Coyner and I had been crawling through the local lava tubes scattered about the Bend area for several years. Apparently, we were the first ones to really look into the "caves" to gain more knowledge of geological aspects of the lava tubes, as well as the wildlife inhabiting them. Phil was into geology and really enjoyed spelunking, while I was interested mainly in the wildlife, above and below the ground. During the winter we had discovered small colonies of bats using the caves as hibernating chambers. Our good friend, Phil Brogan, a well-known geologist and writer, had written several articles about Phil Coyner and me and our discoveries in the lava tubes. It may have been the result of those stories that provided Vector Control with a bat contact in Central Oregon.

"Gee, Phil," I replied. "I can't remember finding anything that resembled a rabid bat. Can you?"

We discussed it at length and decided that the next time we went spelunking we'd watch more carefully for any unusual actions of bats, or dead ones in the lava tubes. Then Phil announced that an epidemiologist was going to be in town the next day and would we like to get together. I thought that would be a great opportunity to absorb new information, especially from a field man from Vector Control, since their specialty was the mechanism that spread diseases from wildlife to the human society.

As it turned out, I was able to get the next day off. The small gang mill I was helping to feed lodgepole to in LaPine was shut down for a few days. While I was sitting on the back porch trying to train a juvenile turkey vulture to fly, a state pickup drove down the lane to my house. A friendly-looking cuss stepped out and walked over to where the vulture and I were perched and offered his hand.

"Hi, I'm Dr. Munroe Holms, of Vector Control." We shook, and I poured him a cup of coffee and we got down to talking about lava tubes, bats, rabies, and wildlife diseases communicable to man. As we got into the rabies discussion, I remembered the coyote from the Brothers school yard and asked him what he had found when the brain was inspected.

"Oh," he replied with a shrug of his shoulders, "that animal didn't die of rabies. It was poisoned." We stood there, looking at each other; he probably didn't think it was worth further discussion, but I did.

"What do you mean, poisoned?" I asked.

"Sure, poisoned," he replied again. "It was probably the stuff the government trapper uses. No big deal. It's the first time I've seen anything that died of the stuff, but they've been using it for a few years now and I guess it knocks ---- out of the coyote population. It just looks like rabies, that's all."

I was immediately interested in a poison that made an animal appear to have rabies, and to die in that way. My gut feeling was I didn't like it; it didn't sound good at all.

Questions went racing through my mind: Was the poison that close to the school yard? Did the animal travel a long distance after ingesting the poison before it died? Was there a threat to humans? How was the poison put out? On baited meat? What kind of bait? How much poison was there on the ground?

"What can you tell me about the poison?" I asked him.

We sat down next to the saw horse the vulture was perched on as Dr. Holms explained what he knew about the poison. "I think the stuff they're using is a material known as 1080, monofloroacete. It was developed during World War Two and is pretty lethal. It's particularly effective on carnivores, especially coyotes. I don't know how much the animal has to ingest to kill it, but I understand it's a residual type of poison that will build up as the animal feeds on additional bait. When it gets enough, the poison will cause the digestive system to react and the animal will try to regurgitate the stomach contents, then blood carries the poison throughout the body. I believe death is usually a long and drawn out process. I guess that's how that coyote got into the school yard. I doubt if the poison station was close by."

Then he said something that shocked me out of my shoes, "I don't think anyone has ever come up with an antidote for the stuff."

"What!" I exclaimed. "You mean the US government is using a poison that has no antidote?"

This was incredible. Then I thought about the animal that had run into the school yard, frothing at the mouth, regurgitating the poison into the place where the kids were playing. "Is there a chance of secondary poisoning?" I asked.

"You bet," he said. Then he cut me off as I was about to ask about the Brothers school. "Oh, the one that died in school yard at Brothers. Yes, we sent a man out to clean up anything he could find near the school or in the yard. Funny," he added. "The only stuff he found was right at the base of the flag pole, where it died."

That seemed like some kind of an omen to me, but I kept it to myself. I commented that

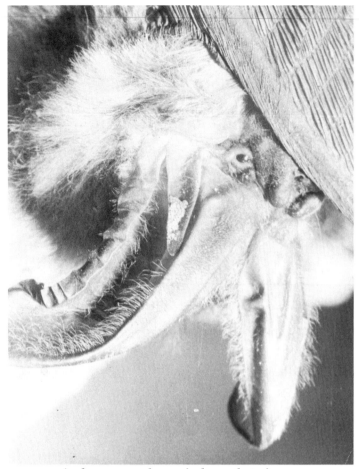

A lump-nosed or jackass bat is a common resident of the lava tubes around central Oregon.

I thought his department had handled everything pretty well, but I was still curious about the poison.

"How did you dispose of the stuff," I asked, " What about the old bait that's not used up? What about the carcasses of the animals that have died from the stuff? How do they find them and dispose of them?"

Before he could answer I thought about eagles and my blood ran cold. "I've been spending a lot of time out on the desert since I moved here three years ago, and I've seen golden and bald eagles out there feeding on road-killed jack rabbits and other critters. What happens if they find a dead coyote, or some other carnivore? Will they get enough of the stuff to kill them?"

I almost knew what the answer might be to that one, and he confirmed it. "Boy, I just

don't know, Jim," he answered. "It may be possible to kill an eagle with the 1080, if they eat enough."

Suddenly the vision of two juvenile golden eagles feeding on a dead coyote just last winter along the Silver Lake Highway near the Horse Ranch flashed into my mind. At the time I thought the animal had been killed by a motor vehicle; now I wasn't so sure. The eagles had been quarreling over the kill, and both of them had ingested so much their crops stuck out like boxing gloves. In fact, one had eaten so much of the coyote that when a truck went zooming by it had trouble getting into the air.

"I think it's very possible for an eagle to ingest enough 1080 to kill him," I said, telling him about the eagles near the Horse Ranch. Then pointing to the turkey vulture perched next to us I added, ". . . and what about them?"

"That's a good question," he said. Dr. Holms gave me a very hard look and added, "Why don't you try to find the answers to those questions . . ." Then he slapped me on the knee and said, "Hey, I didn't come over here to talk about 1080 and coyotes. I want to know how many bats you and Phil Coyner have found in the lava tubes, and whether you've found any that have been rabid."

"Okay, doc, but I'll tell you something. I'm going to investigate this business of killing coyotes with poison with no known antidote, and see if the same stuff might be killing eagles. That's a pretty strange thing: the US government protects eagles on one hand, and on the other they pay a guy to go out and possibly poison them . . ."

"Yes, I agree," he said. "But you can look into that business when I'm back in Portland. How about the bats?"

I grunted, "Okay, but to be frank with you, I wouldn't know a rabid bat from a healthy one. Most of the bats we find in the lava tubes are there during winter, and they're all hibernating."

I told him how the bats would occasionally awaken if we got our gas lantern too close to them, or if we touched a bat hanging from the ceiling. Otherwise they didn't seem to be too active. When I mentioned that we had found small groups of ten to thirty in various caves he seemed pleased.

"There is a possibility that we can take some of the bats that are hibernating. We'll sacrifice them in the lab and check the brain tissue for the rabies virus." Standing, he added, "What do you say we take a run out to the cave with the most bats and we'll take a look . . ."

"No dice!" I said, rather abruptly. "Phil and I have been prowling around the lava tubes now for over three years, and we've yet to find a sick bat. I don't think it's necessary to take any of the ones that are sleeping and sacrifice them. Besides," I pointed out, "we have such small population groups. If you take enough to satisfy a large sampling, you'll decimate the populations. No, I don't think I want a hand in that."

I thought I had made a strong point, but he insisted, and didn't want to go back to Portland without at least a "couple bats" to check, and after a great deal of haggling we finally settled on a very small, random sampling from each group we found. As we were about to get the spelunking gear together, my brother Don came driving into the yard.

"Hello. all," he shouted, walking to the house. "What's cooking?"

"Hi, Don," I answered, introducing Dr. Holms, and then explained why he was here and where we were heading.

"Hey, that sounds like a lot of fun," he exclaimed. "Can I come along?"

I looked at Munroe who shrugged his shoulders and said it was OK with him, so we got one more set of lights, hard hat and gloves and headed out for the lava tubes.

The closest group of lava tubes to Bend is near the area where the county operates the Knott Landfill today, near the site of Bend's first airport. Unfortunately, many of the tubes have been filled with refuse, or have been backfilled, or broken down to keep the public out of them. In the '50s this was a great spot to find bats and other wildlife. We unloaded our gear at the first cave, one with an old, broken down davenport in the opening and empty beer cans scattered about. Putting our hard hats and coveralls on, we headed for the entrance. "This is a

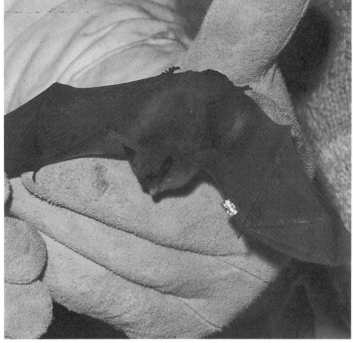

This lump-nosed bat returned to the same cave for eleven years.

short one," I said, as we climbed over the big lava boulders scattered about the opening.

"How do lava tubes form, Jim?" Don asked, shining his light inside the cave.

As we slowly picked our way along the rock-strewn floor, and low ceiling,I explained the theory of the formation of lava tubes, whereby hot lava remained fluid beneath the cooling surface and surged ahead, sometimes leaving a tube as it emptied out down slope. We were still in a faint amount of light as we came to a wall of lava boulders, what I thought was the end of the cave. "This is it," I announced. "End of the line."

Don had a powerful flashlight with him, and as he was swinging it about the low ceiling of the cave he suddenly stopped in one area. "Hey, Jim," he said. "That looks like a crawl space over there."

Munroe and I crawled over to where Don's light was shining, between some large lava rocks, and spotted the small space. "Yeah, Don, I think we can get through here. Might be a good place to find bats," Dr.

Dean Anderson views a group of hibernating lump-nosed bats. In 1991, one of these lump-nosed bats banded by Jim was discovered by researchers to have returned to the same cave for over twenty years.

Holms said, dropping to his hands and knees, then to his belly. Slowly, he inched himself through the small space and crawled out of sight. "It's . . . a . . . low . . . ceiling . . ." we heard his muffled voice say, from within the tube. "Come on in . . ."

Don gave me his big grin and dropped down onto his belly and crawled into the hole, and I went through behind him. The space was tight all right, and my stomach was not nearly as big in those days as it is today, but I still had trouble squeezing through the tiny space.

After a short distance I could feel the tube getting larger and then I heard Don's voice ahead of me, "Hey! Isn't that a bat?"

"Looks like one," Munroe was saying, as I stood up to look about me. I was in a lava ball-room, about thirty feet wide and fifteen feet high, and as I looked, I could see another small crawl space ahead of me. He pointed out the bat hanging from the ceiling.

"What species do you think it is?" he asked, pinpointing the small mammal in the bright light of Don's flashlight.

I found a large rock, rolled it beneath the bat and stood up as high as I could for a closer inspection. "Looks like a little brown bat," I said, trying to keep my balance. Then we searched the small room for more, but that was apparently the only one. "Let's leave it," I said, hoping the suggestion would be heeded.

"OK," Munroe said. "But let's keep going. I'll bet there's more up ahead."

"I don't know . . ." Don said as he slowly crouched down for a look into the space between the ceiling and floor. He shined his light around the small space for a few moments and then eased down and started to squirm into the space, only this time he was doing it on his back. "I think it's easier this way," he said. In a moment all we could see was his big feet, then he was gone from sight.

"I guess I'm next," Munroe said, sliding into the space on his back.

I waited for a minute or two then dropped down and began to inch along through the breakdown with the two ahead of me. After only a few feet I bumped into someone's feet. "That you, doc?" I asked.

"Yeah, it's me," he replied. "Don told me to wait, he's gone ahead to see if it opens up. Then he hissed, "Shhh, I think I hear him."

From somewhere up ahead we could hear Don's faint voice calling us, "Hey, come on . . . it's . . ." but we could not make out what he was trying to say.

"I hope he hasn't bumped into a big bunch of porcupines," I said to Munroe. "I ran into about fifteen of them in one of these lava tubes last winter, and I don't mind telling you, that was a tight squeeze. As I was going in, they came ambling out. It sounded like a bunch of brooms marching across the lava rock. I was afraid I'd get smacked in the face by their tails and end up with a bunch of quills, but they were as polite as I was . . ."

"Porcupines in lava tubes are a surprise," he muttered.

"I guess we'd better get going," I said, pushing him a little. In a short time we were up to where I could see Don's light casting shadows on the rocks around my face. After some additional crawling we were all lying side-by-side, our faces very close to the rocks above us. "This is tight enough for me, doc," I announced.

"Yeah, me too." he replied.

Suddenly I had a vision of Phil Coyner's lovely wife, Ardith, on the first time we all went into a cave together. She had a very serious case of claustrophobia, but Phil didn't really know how bad it was. She did a wonderful job of masking it . . . But one day she couldn't hold it any longer, and as we were crawling into a tight spot in Wind Cave she suddenly came unglued. She scared me to death. Phil and I had all we could do to keep her from hurting herself as she screamed and thrashed about, blindly trying to escape the terrifying feelings she had succumbed to.

I eased closer to Munroe and asked, "how you feeling?"

He laughed as he replied, "Oh, I'm feeling a little spooky—but if you're worried about claustrophobia, don't let it bother you—I'm OK."

Don was just out of earshot and he squirmed closer to us, muttering, "What are you guys whispering about?" He stopped very close to me, with his nose up against the ceiling of our tiny crawlspace. "What did you say?" he repeated.

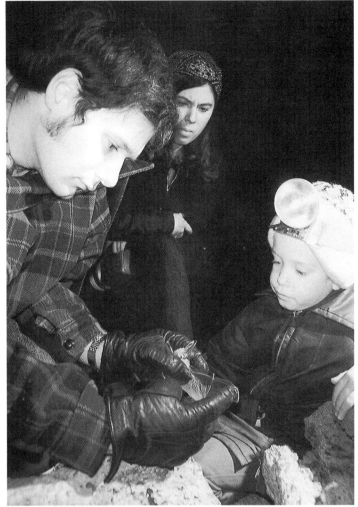

George Long shows Ross Anderson a banded bat while Theresa Langley watches.

"Oh," I said. "Doc and I were talking about claustrophobia."

"What's 'claustrophobia'?" Don asked, rubbing his nose on the roof of the tube as he turned his face to ask me the question.

Munroe chuckled and asked, "How you feeling, Don?"

"Oh, I'm feeling OK." he replied. "Why?"

"Don't worry about claustrophobia, Don," he chuckled again. "Let's just get the heck out of here!"

"OK," I quickly agreed, scrambling back toward the comfort and warmth of the spring sunlight. "We'll head for Skeleton Cave. There are more bats there."

Central Oregon was still locked in a cold

spring, so I knew the bats would be in the caves, but as we inspected the ceilings and walls of Skeleton Cave, about twenty miles southeast of Bend on the Deschutes National Forest, I was surprised to find that quite a few had apparently already left.

"There's one!" Don exclaimed, pointing his flashlight beam to a tiny lump of fur on the ceiling thirty feet above our heads. I inspected it for a moment, watching for any sign of movement. There was none, so I assembled my portable bat pole, which I called my "Little Acme Bat Snatcher," a twenty foot piece of thin-walled, half-inch, electrical conduit with a padded loop on the end made from a coat hanger. While Don and Dr. Holms held their flashlight beams on the bat I slowly eased the padded loop beneath the claws clinging to the lava rock ceiling, and then lowered the bat to the sandy floor.

"This is a Myotis bat, the little brown bat," I said, carefully removing the tiny animal from the padding.

Don and Monroe walked over for a closer look. The bat was moving very slowly, in a vain attempt to escape from whatever had jolted it out of its deep winter sleep. As we watched, the bat slowly opened its mouth, uttering sounds that were higher than we could hear.

"I can't believe that little guy has rabies," I said, trying to talk Dr. Holms from taking it.

"Well, we'll know when I get it back to the lab," he said, grimacing at me as he placed it into a small box he had for transporting the bats.

As we slowly walked along the rock-strewn sandy floor of the lava tube I could see that several of the bats I had seen on the ceiling a week before were gone. I was under the opinion that they had moved out during the short "false spring" we had in the tail-end of February. I was to find out differently very shortly.

"Hey, Jim!" Don called out. "Here's a bat!"

We walked over to where he was standing and followed the beam of his light to where a bat was lying on the sand. I stopped to pick it up and almost had my hands on it when suddenly Dr. Holms shouted. "Don't touch it!" Then he asked me to move and

using a set of tongs he had in his field kit, he picked the animal up. As he turned it in the lantern light he said, "I don't think this one died of rabies."

I looked at the bat closely and could see a gaping wound in the animal's body and where the wing had been shattered by something. "Looks like someone shot it" I said, turning my light to look around the cave.

"Yes. It does appear that it was shot." Monroe agreed.

"Now who in the hell would do a thing like that!" Don exclaimed angrily.

I shrugged my shoulders and started walking slowly, swinging my light along the sandy floor. It was only a few moments before we had recovered twelve dead bats, apparently shot by what we thought was a .22. Don became more angry as we picked up each bat, muttering about the type of person who would do such a thing, and how he would like to get his hands on them. I felt the same way, but the memories of all the sparrows I had plinked as a kid on the farm kept getting in the way of my anger. Meaningless killing, I thought to myself, is still with us, and still unexplained.

"Well, I think we've got a good sampling." Dr. Holms said. "We've only got two species: Myotis, the little brown bat, and Plecotus, the Lump-nosed bats. I don't think these have been dead very long; perhaps they will not have died in vain and we can detect rabies if it's there."

As it turned out, the hibernating bats found in the lava tubes of Central Oregon were apparently free of rabies. Dr. Holms called from Vector Control to report that they couldn't find any trace of rabies in the bats from our lava tubes. After some serious deliberation we all decided it was unnecessary to take additional specimens from the small groups we had in the caves. I was happy to hear that.

Unfortunately, the indiscriminate shooting of bats in the lava tubes still goes on to this day. I haven't found a way to educate people fast enough to halt the shooting of such a harmless, beautiful creature.

Several, years later, while working at the Oregon Museum of Science and Industry

Jim shows Kirk Horn, USFS, and a group of OMSI science students a banded lump-nosed bat in Boyd Cave near Bend. Inset is a lump-nosed bat wearing his new gold-colored anodized band.
Courtesy of Clyde Miller

(OMSI), I received permission to band bats in the lava tubes around Bend. I obtained the tiny, aluminum bands from the US Fish & Wildlife Service (USF&WL) banding lab and then had them anodized to a gold color. The anodizing made them stand out more clearly for visual inspection, plus the bats couldn't bite into the aluminum, making the numbers illegible as they did on plain aluminum bands. Also, anodizing prevented the band from tearing the wing tissue and causing the bat serious, if not fatal, infection. The gold color also gave me a code to use for the year banded.

I took a busload of OMSI science students with me on each banding expedition, which had a two-fold purpose. I thought I could spread the word about the ecological values of these beneficial members of our wildlife community, and it was very beneficial to have twenty-five sets of eyeballs all looking for the same thing at the same time. That way we found a higher percentage of bats and had a better idea of how many actually used the caves for hibernating chambers.

I discovered several things from the banding project. First we found that most of the bats moved around the lava tube at least three times during the season they were hibernating. (I managed to find and keep secret a lava tube that no one visited where the bats were unmolested.) Further investigation demonstrated that the reason for the movement was logical. The bats were just running out of oxygen as they dropped their respiration and heart rate, which is so necessary to conserve energy during hibernation. Lactic acid would build up in the blood, which in turn would trigger an alarm in the brain, waking them up. They would fly about the cave, pumping up their bodies with oxygen, then find a new place to hang up and go back to sleep for another three to six weeks.

Second we found various parasites moving about on the bats as they slept, including a fly that crawled about beneath the folded wing skin, probably feeding on blood. I often wish I had pursued these interesting parasites further, and perhaps will some day . . .

Third was the longevity of the bats we banded. It was exciting to return to caves each winter and find old friends hanging from the ceiling. One lump-nosed bat (*Plecotus townsendii*) came back to the same cave for twelve years. I had banded it as a juvenile in 1958 and while on a trip to Boyd Cave with a group from Sunriver in 1970 we found the old timer hanging from the ceiling, all alone, apparently the only one in the cave. The following year there were no bats found in that cave, which was also the first cave visitors came to as they left Bend for a day of recreation, adventure and spelunking. (In spring of 1991, a group of Forest Service biologists found another Plecotus that I had banded in 1964, in the same cave, and almost on the same lava ledge—talk about longevity!)

Another factor that concerned me was the lack of returns of bands from the more than 300 bats we banded. I had expected at least one to come in, especially in the Newberry Crater area, a popular recreation area with two "crater" lakes, only ten miles south of the lava tubes. During the summer plecotus and myotis bats are regular visitors to that area, swooping over the campgrounds and the surface of East and Paulina Lakes, feeding on the myriad insects that fill the night air. But to this day, I have never received a band from one of the banded bats.

We did find that several bats often settled into lava tubes other than the ones we banded them in. Some plecotus bats were in caves five miles from the one where we had been banding them. The next winter we'd find them in a different cave. I guess there's no place like home to a bat . . .

Unfortunately, we continued to find bats that had been shot. My "secret" cave eventually was discovered, and was named "Bat Cave," probably because it was the only one where bats could be found in any quantity after spelunking became a favorite form of recreation for more and more people.

Eventually the Forest Service published a guide to the lava tubes around Bend, and I stopped banding. The word has spread as to the unique features of the lava tubes, and, while the majority of people who visit the tubes respect the life they discover there, it only takes one dingaling with a .22 to destroy what Mother Nature has been working on for untold ages.

The Lava Bear, Reub Long, and Other Good Stories

There's a fable that's been drifting around Central Oregon ever since the white man first set foot on the land: the Lava Bear. It is supposed to be a dwarfed, sub-species of the black bear (Ursus americanus), but I can't give you the scientific name for this mysterious, little member of the Family, Ursidae. To

my knowledge, no one has ever had the opportunity to inspect the animal from a scientific point of view.

When Bud and Helen Parks, pioneers of the Fort Rock Valley in Oregon, were putting together the Fort Rock Valley Historical Society book, *Portraits: Fort Rock*

Valley Homestead Years, they called me to ask about Lava Bears. In all honesty, I couldn't tell them any more today then I could in the '50s when I talked to Dr. Kenneth Gordon at Oregon State University, about the lava bear stories that I had been hearing in the central Oregon country. He just sat there and smiled at me, without saying a word, and that was the extent of his answer about lava bears: a smile.

According to the research Bud and Helen did on this supposed pygmy bear, there are two specimens in the Smithsonian collection. Both had been shot in the Fort Rock Valley in 1922, but they were identified as young black bears, one a female and the other a male.

The lava bear story isn't the only tale that has come from the rimrock country of Oregon. There's the fable of the Blue Bucket Mine, that illusive piece of real estate somewhere between Bend and the Snake River where there is supposed to be a fabulous treasure of gold. Then there's Crystal Cave, another place no one can seem to find, said to be located between Bend and Silver Lake, where a couple of buckaroos who were crossing the desert with a herd of cows at the turn of the century said they discovered a cave with clear crystals in it as long as a man's finger.

I think I've got the answer to that one. There is a 'crystal cave' all right. It's located between Bend and LaPine, on the south end of the Fort Rock District of the Deschutes National Forest, where the towering yellow pine meet the sagebrush of the high desert. It's known today as South Ice Cave. In early spring, beautiful, six-inch crystals of ice can be found hanging from the ceiling of the cave. On the floor, ice stalagmites have built up as water seeped through the lava ceiling from the surface, and froze on the floor into child-sized pillars of ice. I think those ice crystals in South Ice Cave could trigger anyone's imagination, and open doors to some wonderful stories.

Perhaps like the lava bear, another illusive form of wildlife in the rimrock country is the Side-hill Gouger. This is an animal that apparently walks along the hillside on four legs, one set shorter than the other, leaving

Reub Long, the well-loved man of the Oregon desert.

its trail behind it. There are supposed to be two species, one with the two left legs shorter, and the other with the two right legs shorter. They graze the hillsides, one species going clockwise, while the other travels counter-clockwise. In addition, they're nocturnal—no one has ever seen one out in the daytime. Unfortunately, no one (to my knowledge) has ever seen a side-hill gouger at all, but the trails of these creature are very well preserved in the country where sheep and cattle have grazed on the steep, side-hills of north slopes for a century.

In the '30s, radio had a difficult time getting through to the Fort Rock Valley. It was a long time into the '50s before television arrived, and electricity wasn't used on many of the ranches until the '60s. Entertainment was something that required imagination and self-service. A buckaroo or sheepman, left to tend their livestock had to be able to read or have a vivid imagination, to keep himself entertained on long winter nights.

That may be why Reub Long had such a wonderful philosophy on life, and was as good as he was at spinning yarns. His brain wasn't cluttered by a lot of the stuff we put up with today, plus he was a natural born story-teller.

I first met Reub when he called Dean Hollinshead in Bend on Christmas Day. I was living with Dean and Lily on their small ranch in Bend, a public park today. Reub had called asking if we wanted to come down and help him do his haying.

"What the hell are you doing hayin' this time of the year?" Dean asked, looking out the window at snow falling. I don't know what Reub said, but Dean laughed and said, "OK, I've got Jimmy Anderson here. He just moved out here from Connecticut. He and I will be down tonight." Thanks to Reub and Dean, that trip was another milestone for me: a new and wonderful way to look at this business of living.

Several years later, Reub's place became a natural spot for me to land my Cub when I was out conducting my annual aerial census of golden eagle nests in Jefferson, Crook, Deschutes, and northern Lake Counties. I kept a drum of aviation fuel there, and would often use the old rye field out behind his house to land in.

Back in the '60s, I stopped at Reub's ranch quite often with busloads of young people, teachers on In-service workshops, show-me tours, and with family members out for a weekend trip to the desert. He would explain what a horseman does to improve his range, show his beautiful desert horses, share his wonderful philosophy on living, and talk about his extensive collection of Indian artifacts he had picked up in the sixty plus years he had been riding across the Oregon desert.

During one of these trips with a busload of teenagers, while he was showing his collection to them, I observed Reub do something that lives with me today. He had just laid down a huge, twelve inch, beautifully made obsidian tool from his collection when I heard one of the boys say, "Boy! I'd

sure like to have that! If he would turn and look the other way I'd steal it!"

I wasn't the only one that heard that remark; Reub did too. He snapped around, spotting the young man in an instant. He picked the knife back up and stood directly in front of the boy. "I heard what you said and would like to do," Reub said, holding the huge knife-like tool in front of the boy. "I'll tell you what I'm going to do," he continued. "I'm going to lay this thing right down here in front of you, and then I'm going to walk away." Reub set the knife down on the table in front of the boy and turned, saying. "Now you go right ahead and pick it up. Do you know what will happen? In a short time I'll wonder what I did with that piece of obsidian. I'll think I gave it to someone or lost it in the house, or just dropped it on the ground or just plain lost it. But eventually I'll just forget it." Then he turned back and looked right into that boy's eyes, almost boring holes into his head. "But you know what? Every time you pick it up and look at it, you'll know you're living with a thief . . ." And he walked off.

On one particular trip to the ranch with a busload of teachers, it was raining like a cow peeing on a flat rock everywhere else on the desert except on Reub's place. The town of Fort Rock was almost swamped by the downpour, but his place was out in the sunshine. That's the way those desert rains operate at times.

One of the teachers on the bus asked, "Mr. Long, I noticed that as we came out here it was raining everywhere except here on your ranch. Is there a reason for this?"

"Why yes," he immediately replied, holding his hands in front of him, fingers splayed in the typical fashion of a horseman holding the reins of a team of horses. "The good Lord looks down on all us here in the Fort Rock Valley and says, 'I guess I'd better give them folks some water, they look thirsty—but I won't give none to old Reub Long, he don't need it . . . He's tough!'" The teacher just stood there looking at Reub, probably expecting something else, but he winked at me and picked up one of the obsidian Indian tools from his collection to show to another teacher.

One day, Reub dropped by the Oregon

Phil Coyner stands in the skylight of Derrick Cave, east of Fort Rock.

Museum of Science and Industry in Portland where I was working in the '60s as a naturalist. He was working on a book with Mr. E.R. Jackman, a retired professor from Oregon State University. He and Jackman wanted to look at a bunch of photos of mine for their book, *The Oregon Desert.* That day I was in the museum auditorium giving a talk to a school group, and he came in and sat down to listen. While he was waiting he must have turned on that entertainment center in his head because when I walked over to shake hands, he got up looking at me with deep concern, put his arm around my shoulder and asked, "How are you feeling now, Jimmy?"

I looked at him, wondering what was coming next. He and I had been around each other long enough that I could tell when something was going to make a story.

"Fine . . ." I said, then with a sudden touch of inspiration, I added, ". . . thanks to you."

Reub grinned at me, then turned to the audience of school kids and teachers and started this story . . .

"I'm Reub Long, a horseman from the Fort Rock Valley. You probably don't know where that is, so I'll give you a lesson in Oregon geography. It's between Lakeview and Bend, out on the sagebrush and sandy desert. It's a very pretty part of Oregon, but if you 'ain't ever seen it, you'll have to take my word for that. However, to give you an idea how pretty it is there, I'll tell you a story about a buckaroo that died and went to heaven.

He was standin' outside the Pearly Gate when old Saint Peter come up to him and asked, 'Who are you?' 'I'm recent dead,' the buckaroo said, 'and I want to come into Heaven.' 'Where you from?' Pete asked. 'Fort Rock.' the old cowpuncher answered. 'Well, you can come on in if you want to,' Pete said, frowning, 'but this place 'ain't near as pretty as Fort Rock.'" He waited for the

Jim parked his Piper Cub J-3 next to Fort Rock to take a lunch break.

Phil Brogan (left) and Reub Long talk with OMSI students at Reub's ranch.

Reub Long holds an obsidian spear point crafted by early Indian residents. OMSI students eagerly question him.

laughter to settle down then turned to them and continued.

"Anyway, Jimmy and I have been pals for a long time, and as you know he used to live in Bend, over there on the east side of the big white mountains." (He waved his arms to show which way was East.) "When he first come here to live in Portland he had a hard time adjusting to all this rain you folks seem to order up over here. About two weeks ago I come over to see Jimmy about some pictures Mr. Jackman and I are looking for to put in a book we're writin'. He wasn't at home, and I was astonished to find him in the hospital in a coma." (All the kids, and teachers stared at me with sad expressions of sympathy on their faces.) "Well, I dashed

up to the hospital to see him. Bustin' through the door to his room I found him layin' on his back, face white as snow, and hardly breathin'. 'Do you know what's wrong with him?' I asked the doctors. 'Nope!' they said. So I looked at him real close and then touched his skin. Right then and there I knew what was wrong with Jimmy. (He placed his hand on my shoulder and gave it a shake.) So I run out of there, jumped into my pickup and went back to Fort Rock, hell-bent-for-leather. I got me a bucket when I got back to the ranch, scooped up what I needed and headed right back to the hospital. I ran up them stairs, into his room and told the nurse that was standing close by to look the other way, and

Alan Hannawalt views at close range the ice crystals on the ceiling of South Ice Cave near Fort Rock.
Courtesy of Barry Lewis

threw a whole bucket of Fort Rock sand and dust right in his face! You know what happened? He came right to!! You see, he had just got water-logged, and needed some of that good old desert dust to dry him out."

The kids got it long before the adults did. They howled with delight. If you want the truth of what I felt, I was delighted too. I loved Reuben very much, and to be the focus of one of his wonderful stories gave me a great sense of belonging in his world. But once I thought he might have gone too far . . .

Reub was often guiding college groups and range people throughout Central Oregon, and on this occasion had accepted the job of leading a small group of rangeland people on a tour of the Fort Rock and Christmas Valley basins. He called me to ask if I would come along to give him a hand on the wildlife and geology part. I thought that would be a lot of fun, so I accepted and drove from Portland to his ranch on the allotted day.

As I drove into the ranch yard, Reub had all his artifacts laid out on a couple of long tables, and was telling the small group about the various pieces. After a few minutes he introduced me to the group, and told them I

A four inch long ice crystal found on the ceiling of South Ice Cave.

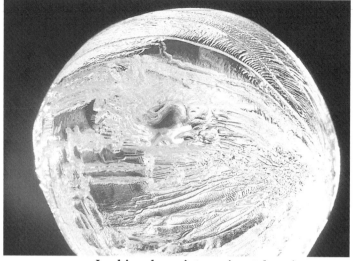
Looking down into an ice stalagmite.

"Could be a lava bear all right, Reub," I said loud enough to be heard clearly. "Could be . . ." I should have looked at the tracks.

Derrick Cave has a hole in the ceiling not far from the entrance which provides light to anyone starting down the lava tube. Then light fades to darkness quickly as one walks along the lava gutters, on smooth sandy surface, and around the large, lava boulders that are strewn all over the floor. (The only way to safely go into the lava tube (or any cave) is with at least three good lights. We had only one, a Coleman gasoline lantern that I had brought with me from Portland. I had wrapped aluminum foil around half of the chimney so the light was directed forward and those following didn't have the full blast from the burner right in their eyes.)

As we walked carefully into the darkness of the cave I thought I heard something stumbling in the rocks ahead of us, and looked down at the sandy floor of the cave. I could see fresh tracks that had stirred up the wet sand beneath the surface. "There's something ahead of us," I said to Reuben, quietly.

"What!" he exclaimed, just loud enough so the folks close behind could hear, then raised his voice. "There's something ahead of us! Do you think it might be a lava bear??" he added with crystal-clear pronunciation.

I wanted to turn around and see what was going on when the people following heard him, but I was afraid to. I tried to change the subject by explaining the geology of lava tubes to the group as we proceeded. When we got to the questions about what kinds of wildlife use lava tubes I mentioned insects, bats, pack-rats, skunks, weasels, porcupines, mice, and even the ravens that nest at the entrance of some caves. But you can guess what animal came out on top.

"Yep! That's why they're called lava bears. They were always found near the lavas and probably hibernate in these caves," Reub and I explained.

At that moment an unmistakable clatter came from the pile of rocks just outside the range of my light. "What's that?" one of the members of the group asked warily.

We were standing among a bunch of big boulders, in the area of the cave that was in

was an expert on 'bullet hawks', what he called the Prairie falcons that nested on Fort Rock itself, just east of his ranch. I don't know to this day how the subject got started, perhaps someone asked the right question, but we got onto the trail of the lava bear.

"Oh, he was a dainty little cuss. About the size of a sheep dog," he explained when asked about its size.

Not to be outdone, I said "Could eat your leg off in a second," when asked about its temperament.

"Yep. Might still be some around," Reub answered when asked about its whereabouts.

From that moment up to the time we drove into the Devil's Garden, the lava flow that surrounded Derrick Cave, it was lava bear-this, and lava bear-that. As we parked the pickups and cars near the entrance to the cave, Reub really had those folks cranked up on lava bears. I couldn't help but get in on it as he embellished on each comment. We left no question that the lava bear, as small as it was, when hungry or cornered, was meaner than a junkyard dog. As we walked down the narrow trail through the pile of lava boulders marking the entrance to Derrick Cave, Reub looked down at the ground and said, "Say, Jimmy. What kind of sign is that . . ."? Think it might be a lava bear . . .?"

I choked back a laugh and smiled at him,

Reub Long would display his Indian artifacts along the side of his old bunk house, and then talk for hours about the days when he picked up these beautiful pieces as he rode horseback across the Oregon desert.

complete darkness, so I asked the group to sit down—or stand still—as I went ahead with light to see what was making all the clatter. Reub came along, following closely behind. I slowly walked ahead, swinging the lantern from side to side, and hadn't gone more than twenty-five or thirty yards when I heard something moving on the loose stones ahead and stopped. Holding my lantern as high as I could, I suddenly spotted a set of red eyes glinting back at me from the darkness, then another, and another. Peering into the darkness we tried to see what they were, then I began to make out an image. "I think they're deer, Reub," I said, holding the light as steady as possible. At that moment the frightened deer must have had enough. They suddenly made an end run, towards the entrance of the cave. Over the boulders they came, clattering and knocking rocks helter-skelter. It sounded like a whole herd was trying to make it past us to freedom.

"It's a lava bear!" someone shouted back in the darkness. Then all hell broke loose! Those poor people panicked, and started running back toward the entrance to the cave—in the dark!!

Oh, no! I thought to myself. I shouted "Stop! They're only deer!" but it was too

Fort Rock on a beautiful summer day.

late. All I could hear were those poor people scrambling in the darkness as they ran back toward the entrance.

"Oh!" "Owh-which!" "Aaagh!" "Damn!" were just the few epitaphs that I can repeat that floated back to me as the group crashed along. Then I noticed that Reub was standing right behind me.

"You think I might have overdone it?" he whispered.

I had to laugh as I put my arm around him. "I've got a hunch we did, pardner," I said. "But I'll tell you something—if those folks survive and get to the entrance—and see those deer go by, we're both in a heap of trouble."

We had no choice but to follow the trail back to the entrance of the cave. As we walked along I found a pair of binoculars that had fallen in the sandy floor, then came across a small notebook, and on a rock was a part of someone's pants leg. Reub called a halt when he stopped to pick up a hat. As we came around the last turn in the trail we spotted the group ahead of us. Some were sitting on lava boulders. Two men were on the sandy floor, while others were limping about holding a knee or a hip or an arm. It was awful.

As we approached them, one member of the group looked up and saw us coming. He hobbled to his feet, limping toward us with a grave look on his face. "Oh, Mr. Long . . ." he stammered, ". . . we're the worst kind of cowards there are . . . why, we ran off leaving you and Jim alone to face the lava bear!" Then he looked down and mumbled, "Will you ever forgive us . . ."

Reuben walked up to the man, put his hand on his arm to help him back to the rock, looked all about at him at the assembly of groaning people and said, "You have no need to apologize . . . not a one of you . . . without a doubt; you are the bravest people I have ever met! There is nothing on this earth that would ever get me to try and run through a lava cave in the dark . . . why . . . it's a testimony to your bravery and great strength that you made it alive!"

Each member of the party slowly looked at each other and then a titter began that grew into a crescendo of laughter. Reub and I just stood there and grinned at each other. He took my arm and said, "'Ain't life wonderful!"

In the late '60s, Reuben went out among the stars, but he left us with his wonderful legacy that Life is indeed, wonderful. Of all the people I've ever known in my lifetime, I think Reub Long will always be on the top of my list as a person who lived his life the way he wanted to, had a good time doing it, made some money now and then, and left a great deal behind for people like you and me to enjoy. He was a complete success and a true gentleman.

Did You Get 'Em?

Jack Shumway raised sheep on his land out near Powell Buttes, Oregon, and ran them on the public lands of the Deschutes National Forest and BLM. He was a good sheep man with a lambing area out behind his home place, and watched over his ewes at lambing time to insure as much lamb survival as possible. However, he had a problem one spring back in the late '50s that he couldn't handle.

A big dog (male) coyote had learned where to wait for its supper out behind the lambing pens. Apparently neither Jack's hired hands, or the government trapper could get that clever old rascal, so he called me one night and asked if I'd get my airplane and come out and try to shoot the animal. Like most of the critters that get into the habit of stealing livestock, this coyote was getting too expensive to have around. I couldn't turn my back on a sheepman with coyote trouble, anymore than a lawman would turn his back on a person who had someone trying to break into his house. I thanked Jack for the opportunity to help.

I'm a pretty good aviator, but to try and fly an airplane twenty feet over the junipers and shoot a coyote at the same time is more than I can handle. As far as I'm concerned, that old saying, "There are old pilots, and there are bold pilots—but there are no old, bold pilots," is true. I was out looking for a shooter when I bumped into Ernie Beaver.

"Why, shucks, Jim," he said, laughing. "You can fly pretty good, but not as good as I can. You shoot and I'll do the flying."

I knew Ernie was right, he was a better aviator that I was, but after all it was my airplane, and that made a difference to me.

"Nope, you shoot, and I'll fly." I said, puffing up.

Ernie outweighed me by ten pounds, and he also knew I knew he was a better flier, but he was gentle about it.

"Now don't get all in a huff," he said, grinning. "Let's talk about this first, before we make up your mind."

We haggled for about twenty minutes, which was a lot of fun, but got us nowhere. Then he made a suggestion.

"OK, we'll draw straws to see who flies and who shoots."

I agreed; it was a good way to make the decision without anyone getting pushed out of joint. I got the long one, so I got to fly, and Ernie got to shoot.

Early the next morning I cranked up the old, WWII surplus, 90HP Piper Cub and we took off for the Shumway Ranch. The shadows were still long as we zoomed over the lambing pens. I had looked the ground over the day before and found the coyote's tracks coming down from the juniper and crested wheat fields above the lambing pens. I banked over and made a run over the trail, and found him on the first try. As I banked over the trees Ernie slapped my shoulder and pointed toward the coyote making a dash toward another juniper.

"I see him!" I shouted back and made a sharp turn to cut him off. Well, we played cat-and-mouse with that coyote for almost an hour, slowly hazing him up the hill toward a big, open, crested wheat field. He went, but reluctantly. He had been chased by airplanes before and knew many of the tricks that coyotes can learn so well and so quickly. Each time I thought he was on his way toward the fields, he'd double back and we'd have to play it over again. However, I could see from where I was that every time I moved him toward the field we got a little closer each time.

As I made a turn I shouted, "OK, Ernie! This time he'll be out in the open! When he starts to run for it I'll slip right down on top of him. You get him!" Ernie grinned at me and poked my big, 10 gauge single shot out the side doors.

The Piper Cub has the best door of any airplane flying for shooting out of. The top half folds up and locks into a catch (and occasionally stays there) on the under surface of the right wing. The bottom half drops down against the fuselage and locks in place. The result is a big door in the side of the cockpit, giving ample room for movement and weapons. As I dove on the coyote, he made break for the open field. I went in low, reversed the controls and put the cub into a side-slip that brought the slipstream slamming into the cockpit. I glanced over my shoulder and saw Ernie raise the shotgun, and I held the slip, closing in on the hapless coyote. I knew we would get him for sure.

"Boom!" went the old 10 gauge. I straightened up, poured on the coal, and gently pulled up as the wheels were almost into the crested wheat. I turned to look over my right shoulder, as we were climbing and banked so I could spot the coyote below. As I did I could see Ernie's face. He was laughing so hard there were tears streaming from his eyes.

"What the . . .?" I said searching ahead to see if we had got the coyote.

As I started to dive I noticed the top door was riding the slipstream, free of its lock. I glanced around at Ernie who was still laughing. I thought he was pointing toward the ground ahead of us, but when I looked over the side I couldn't believe my eyes. The right tire was flopping around, slowly revolving in the slipstream, and each time it rolled over, I could see a gaping hole where Ernie had blasted it away with the shotgun. I pulled up level, turned in my seat and glared at him.

Ernie pointed to the upper door and shouted, "The door came loose and ruined my shot!" Then he choked, pointed to the tire slowly revolving in the wind and shouted, "Did I get him?" I sat there, wondering what to do next when I suddenly thought of his statement, "I'm a better aviator than you are." I decided that he was absolutely correct . . . "You shot the tire!" I shouted, "You land the airplane . . ."

I'll never forget that landing, it was a beauty. We lined up on the upwind side of the runway at Bend, and Ernie just let the Cub slowly settle onto the pavement with the right wheel just off the ground. We rolled along just like any normal landing, while I sat there holding both support posts behind the windshield in a grip that should have left dents in the tubing. The airplane slowed down as we rolled along and pretty soon the right wheel began to settle on the runway. Loud, ker-plopping sounds announced the tire's arrival as it bounced along on the blown away portion.

I fully expected a violent ground loop as the tire started to drag against the pavement, but Ernie's superb aviator talents had anticipated that. With left brake and a lot of left rudder we slowly flopped to a halt with both wheels still on the runway. Ernie was out before I was and had the tail raised. I picked up the horizontal stabilizer on the other side and we hauled the little Cub clear of the runway and gently lowered it into the sagebrush and sand. Then Ernie turned to me and said, "Sorry about your tire" We both looked at it, and started laughing as we headed for the airport office. As we walked into the airport office, the fixed base operator, Pat Gibson, looked up and asked, "Did you get him?" Ernie and I looked at each other and headed for the Pepsi machine grinning.

About three days later Jack Shumway called to say he hadn't seen that old dog coyote since we'd been there. I was sure

Ernie hadn't put a piece of buckshot into him, it had all gone into the tire. We probably just scared him to death. I didn't tell Jack that though, I just said I was happy to hear that his problems were solved—then I shelled out the twenty-five bucks for the new tire. After all, it was my airplane.

Skunked

The old Jones Place on George A. Jones Road, located near the north slopes of Pilot Butte in Bend, Oregon, was an experimental orchard that went back into the early 1900s. It was eventually purchased by Dean and Lily Hollinshead in the late '40s, who named the place Timberlane Ranch. It's a public park today, with a big community garden and other restored buildings, wagons, and other pioneer equipment, thanks to the generosity of Dean and Lily, who left it in perpetuity for the people of the area to enjoy.

Back in the '50s it was a working ranch, with big hayfields, and one of the best dairy farms in the area. I had the pleasure of living there in those days, right in the old Jones House. This is one of those typical western ranch houses that started out with one room, then grew as needed for additional children or more storage space. The pipes froze every winter and I had to crawl under the house to hook a welding lead on the frozen pipe, and the other lead on the shut-off of the supply pipe. Then I'd crank up the old, WWII surplus electric welder and pump heat, in the form of electrical energy, through the pipes until they thawed. That doesn't work anymore today, what with all the plastic pipe strewn all over the country-side and in the new houses. The pipes just freeze and bust.

One winter Dean and Lily went to visit relatives in Minnesota and I watched over the place while they were gone. I fed horses, made sure the hired man took care of the cows, thawed pipes and troughs, and generally made sure all was well at Timberlane Ranch, and it didn't winter kill.

Anyone who has struggled through snow, and hacked ice out of the horse trough knows how winter can often gnaw at a person's insides. Over the years I've come to almost hate winter. If it weren't for the beautiful sights of winter, I'd really find it intolerable. I was in that "I hate winter!" frame of mind one evening as I struggled through the snow and into the chicken house to collect the eggs and give the poor old hens some warm water.

As I started pounding the snow off my boots inside the door I was suddenly startled by a small, black and white, furry animal as it scurried by. "It's a skunk!" I thought, jumping back. Sure enough, it was a skunk, a little western spotted skunk, known to the scientific folks as *Spilogale gracilis*. Some people call it a Civet Cat, but it's not a cat—and the real "Civet" is found half a world away in Africa.

The little western spotted skunk is the smallest member of the family, *Mustelidae*, which are animals that possess glands capable of sending their scent great distances—with very remarkable results. As a kid on the farm in Connecticut, I had trapped the larger stripped skunk and sold their pelts for spending money, so I had a very personal relationship with the defensive weapons they possess. When that little guy went skittering by, I just held my breath, but nothing happened. I have a hunch they don't like the smell of that stuff any more than we do.

As I looked around the chicken house I was suddenly conscious of a great deal of straw on the floor that had been in the laying boxes. As I bent to scoop it up and place it back, I found broken eggs shells. "Now what's going on?" I thought to myself, inspecting the shells. Egg yoke, still fresh and unfrozen, was plastered on the shell. Under the window I found another broken egg, this one only half consumed.

Then the truth suddenly dawned. I remembered the havoc the big striped skunks wreaked in the hen house back on the farm in Connecticut. They not only got eggs, they ate chickens too. I quickly searched the room for dead chickens, but aside from the straw and egg shells scattered about, things didn't look too out of place. There were about a dozen eggs in other laying boxes, so I didn't get too excited, scooped them up and went out to finish my chores.

Next day was almost a repeat of the day before as I stomped into the chicken house. Wham! Wham! my snow-laden boots stomped on the old pine floor. Away skittered the little skunk. This time I didn't jump too high, but watched as it disappeared through a small hole under the roost. "Ah, ha," I said to myself, thinking I'd better plug the hole. But I forgot to . . .

For about a week that little skunk and I competed for eggs. Once I caught him right in the act, egg all over his face as I stomped into the house. By this time we had both gotten used to each other and darned if that little guy didn't just sit there and stare me down with his black and white warning flag erect, lapping away at the broken egg.

I've come to accept the unexpected consequences of interacting with a variety of wildlife over the years. If I got pounded badly by an adult great horned owl while banding their young, I figure I had it coming for disturbing them in the first place. I fell out of a tree once while banding red-tails, and that left me pretty humble—and sore. I also fell out of a tree and into the water while banding Osprey, and that leaves you wet and humble—especially if you're wearing your climbing irons like I was.

Anyway, I got to enjoying that little skunk and began to think of him as family. I knew he couldn't hurt the egg production and was too small to pose a threat to those big Rhode Island Reds. If he tried to take one of them

on, they'd stomp his poor little hide into the floor. So I got to talking to him.

"Hi Skunk," I'd say aloud as I entered the chicken house each evening. He was usually in the midst of his egg feast and would sometimes raise his head and look at me, but more often than not he'd just keep right on slurping, hardly giving me the time of day—or evening.

Well, winter began to wane, the days got longer, and Dean and Lily returned. Dean said he'd be happy if I continued to collect eggs. I was happy about that too; he didn't have near the tolerance I had for the variety of wildlife that can come indoors during winter. I remembered how he flew into a rage one day when a porcupine went ambling through the horse barn. I guess he was afraid of quills in a horse's nose. Which reminds me of the time Dean, Lily, and I went camping with the Rim Rock Riders at Todd Lake (nestled in the eastern foothills of the High Cascades of Central Oregon).

It was a dark night and we were all snuggled down in our sleeping bags under the stars when suddenly I heard Lily call Dean in a hoarse, but loud whisper. "Dean!" No answer, just snoring from beside me. "Dean!" This time a little louder. Still no answer. "Dean!" Lily hissed. "Dean! Wake up! There's someone sitting on me!"

That's when I sat up. I looked over to where I could just make Lily out as a faint shape lying on the ground. I thought I could see something faintly outlined against the stars, and it did appear as though it was sitting on top of her.

"What is it, woman?" Dean asked, like any man who was suddenly awakened in the middle of the night.

"Someone's sitting on me," she repeated.

"What are you talking about, woman?" Dean grunted, at the same time groping for his flashlight.

I watched as his arm slowly aimed in Lily's direction. With a faint click, a beam of light suddenly stabbed into the darkness. Two small red orbs flashed back and then as my eyes adjusted to the light, I couldn't believe what I was seeing.

"Oh, it's only an old porcupine!" Dean said, and shut off the light.

"Get him off!" Lily pleaded with a hoarse whisper. "Get him off!"

"How'll I do that?" Dean muttered, already sliding back into his sleeping bag.

"I don't know," Lily almost shouted. "But get him off!"

I started to get out of my bag at this point, but I heard Dean sigh as he again started to back out his long frame from the bag. It takes a little while for a guy who was his size, over six feet, to get himself unwrapped from a nice, warm sleeping bag on a typical, cold summer night in the Cascades.

"I'm coming," he muttered, groping again for the flashlight with one hand and his pants with the other.

"Hurry!" Lily hissed.

"OK, OK," Dean said, handing me the flashlight. "Hold this damn thing, will you Jimmy, so I can get these infernal pants on." He grumbled as he pushed first one long leg, then the other into the stiff, unyielding jeans. All the time muttering, "Porcupines . . . what next." He went slowly over to where Lily had been sleeping under a big shelter we had erected over the tables, and shined the flashlight on the porcupine. "It's not very big," he assured Lily.

"I don't care how big it is," she sputtered. "Just get him off of me!"

"OK, OK," Dean sighed again, and went stumbling around the camp, the flashlight jabbing here and there, as he looked for something to move the porcupine.

"I've got a shovel," he said, walking back to where Lily and porcupine were resting. "Hold still and cover your face." He scooped the shovel beneath the porcupine.

That was something the porky didn't really enjoy, and with a great deal of indignant grunting, he reluctantly stumbled and was pushed off Lily's sleeping bag. He went grunting and grumbling off in the direction of Todd Lake. Dean kept it in the beam of his flashlight long enough to see him slowly turn around, give us what I thought was a dirty look, and shuffle off into the night.

Just as Dean was sliding back into his bag Lily asked, "Did you kill him?"

"No, woman. I did not kill him!" Dean answered with a sigh.

"Why not?" Lily asked.

"Because I want to get some sleep," Dean muttered, adding, "If you want him killed, you get up and do it yourself. Good night honey . . ." he mumbled, and was gone with a growing crescendo of snores.

The next morning I thought we had been robbed in the night as I woke up to Dean's cussing, throwing things around and kicking the hay bales. I jumped to my feet, got into my britches as quickly as I could, and ran over to where Dean was rampaging among all the horse trappings. He was standing there holding the bridle that he used on his big gelding, Mac.

"If I ever get my hands on that *&##@@! porcupine, I'll strangle him bare handed, quills or no quills!" I looked at the bridle in Dean's hands and could see the chewed straps, bit hanging loose, and the reins almost ready to fall off.

"I told you that you should have killed him!" Lily said, almost smirking.

That memory made me aware of the fact that Dean wouldn't tolerate that little skunk or anything else but chickens in the hen house. So I volunteered to collect eggs, which just improved my relationship with the little skunk. Then I got THE GREAT IDEA!

It was February at the time, and my birthday is March 27. "Wouldn't it be fun," I said to myself, "if, for my birthday present, I could pet a live, wild skunk?" The more I thought of the whole idea, the more I wanted to do it. In no time I had myself talked into it and got started.

That evening as I walked into the hen house, I broke the news to the skunk. "Hi, skunk!" I said, letting the door bang shut behind me. "Guess what?" I added, picking up the eggs from the box next to the one he was in. "You're going to get petted on March 27." He stopped eating just long enough to raise his tail as I got closer, which made me retreat quickly. "OK, OK," I said. "Don't get excited."

The next day I went into the hen house much earlier and picked up all the eggs. Then I broke two of them into a dish by the door and put a tiny bit of cat food in with it. I had my camp chair with me, and placed it

Spotted Skunk (It's the other end you have to watch out for!)

between the door and the dish, then sat down with the evening paper to wait. In just a few moments, Skunk came padding over, hind feet slapping the floor as he went to the box where the eggs used to be. He climbed up into the box, shoved straw this way and that, and gave me a dirty look, as much to say, "What did you do with my supper?"

After about five minutes of fruitless searching, the skunk dropped back to the floor and stomped his way around the room, visibly upset over the disappearance of the eggs, and perhaps my brazen presence. Just as he was ready to leave by his exit hole, he suddenly raised his pointed snout to the air and sniffed. He froze in that spot for a moment, sniffing the air and turning his head this way and that. I had a hunch he

had picked up the scent of the cat food/egg mush. Sure enough, once he got the right direction, he padded right to the dish. It was a little closer to me then he liked, so there were a few moments of indecision for both of us—whether he wanted to eat or whether I wanted to run—but we both managed to overcome our survival instincts, and in a moment he was at the edge of the dish, eating his supper, like any good "pet" skunk should do.

Well, that was the beginning of what could have been a wonderful relationship. Each evening I'd sit and read him the paper aloud, as he silently lapped up eggs, dog food, cat food, occasional meal worms, a mouse when it wasn't needed for the owls I was raising, and even some banana once in a while. Each day I moved the dish closer to my chair. Each day I read a little louder. Each day I rattled the paper a little more, and moved my hands closer to his furry, little back. By March 15, I was right next to the little guy, with my hand about an inch above his back, and nothing had happened to cause either of us great concern.

March 27 dawned a bright, beautiful day; I knew it was going to be a Great Day! Why not! That afternoon I even dressed in my new shirt and jeans, confident that this was no longer an experiment; this was a sure thing. I was going to pull it off. Little Skunk and I were going to become real pals. I was going to show him how friendly I was and, mutual trust now established, pet him like I would my dog. Noooo problem!

The day seemed to go slower than usual as I waited for the sun to slide over behind the big, old Ponderosa Pines that towered over the old Timberland Ranch. Then, not able to wait any longer, at about 4 pm I took the birthday treat to the barn. I had purchased the best cat food I could buy, mixed into a delicious-smelling pudding of fresh eggs, tuna, and a little smoked salmon. A dish fit to relax a king . . . and I wanted that little skunk to feel relaxed this day—for sure!

I walked into the hen house, all decked out in my new outfit, and wearing a big smile for Skunk. I had no sooner set the dish down when he came loping along. He didn't even hesitate, just walked up to his dish and started lapping it up. "Hi, Skunk!" I said, dropping into the chair beside him. "Lap, lap," was all I got in return. After I was sure he was into that birthday pudding I moved my hand. Millimeter by millimeter I lowered my hand until I knew I was just above his back. "It's now or never," I muttered, half to Skunk and half to me.

Closing my eyes, I eased my hand to where I could feel his silky hair and moved from his head to his back. Wham! He jumped back with a jerk, leaping up onto his front feet, pounding the floor as he hopped up and down. "Aghhh!" I almost gagged, as I waited for the burst. I squinched my eyes and nose shut as tight as they would go. If I could have rolled my ears shut, I would have done that too! I knew what it was going to be like; I knew what was coming . . . I'd been there before!

But nothing happened . . .

Slowly I opened one eye and glanced down to see what Skunk was doing. He was eating again, calmly lapping away at his mush. So I did it again, only this time even more gently.

Wham! Up he came again, but this time we were both prepared. He didn't stay on his front legs long, just a moment, and then he dropped back to eating. "Whew!" I sighed aloud. "That was a close call!"

Each time I petted him, he'd hop up on his front legs, but each time it was obvious he didn't have his heart in it. It was only a few moments before he was tolerant of my touching him, and stopped being so jumpy. I actually was able to lay my hand against his back, pushing the fur against his skin as I petted him from head-to-toe. I don't think skunks can purr like a cat, at least I didn't hear him doing it, but I did note that each time I petted him, he'd raise up his back just enough so that I sensed the movement. I have a feeling that he really enjoyed that as much as I did.

This would be a good place for me to end this tale—but I'm ashamed to say, I can't.

March ran or rather blew into April, and at the end of April, Skunk vanished. As I did chores around the ranch I also noticed that all the mice on the ranch had vanished as well. I knew it wasn't the barn cats, they were too lazy, living like kings on the expensive food Lily doled out to them twice a day. The only answer that made sense was the little skunk had gobbled them all up. I assumed that he had eaten himself out of

Contrary to popular belief, porcupines are friendly and easy-going; humans are their only problem.

mice and moved on. Then I remembered that great horned owls often prey on spotted skunks, and wondered if that's what might have happened to him.

I must admit, gathering eggs was no longer fun. I really missed that little guy; we had really become pals. I respected his rights to live on the ranch, and in his way, he respected my rights to gather up eggs—all except two that I left in his dish. He also helped to eliminate mice in the feed rooms. He trusted me as much as I trusted him.

It was almost May when I blustered into the hen house one evening, and got the surprise of my life! There, waiting at the door was my pal, Skunk, along with three, absolutely beautiful little skunk babies skittering around behind him. Only "him" was a "her!" I was so excited I could hardly contain myself. "Well, what do you know!" I shouted, dropping down to pet her like a long-lost friend. She backed up quickly, and the little ones actually tried to hop on their front legs. "Oh, oh!" I said, backing up and out the door. I ran to the house for the dish and after filling it with a feast fit for a Momma Skunk and her kids, I trotted back to the hen house again. There she was, patiently waiting for her dinner.

"Come and get it, momma," I laughed aloud, setting the dish down. She went to it immediately, but her little ones were a little slower. It didn't take more than three days to settle the small family in, and each evening I went into the hen house, there they were patiently waiting for their dinner. I loved it.

I told all my logger friends about it. Marion Grover, my favorite librarian down at the library, thought it was wonderful. Phil Brogan, down at the Bulletin said it was impossible. My caving pal, Phil Coyner thought I was nuts, and so did Doyle Shoults, a logger pal who I hunted with. But, I was happy with my achievement—and should have let it go at that.

One day someone—I can't remember who—remarked to me after I had told my skunk tale, "Say, you know what you should do? Trap them little guys, de-scent them, and then sell 'em."

Dollar signs went off in my eyes. "How much do you think I can get for them?" I asked without even thinking of the consequences.

"Oh, shucks," my companion answered. "I've heard of people getting forty to fifty bucks a piece."

"Fifty bucks a piece!" I thought. "I'd be rich!" And right then and there I set out to trap not only the little guys, but momma as well. I was going to de-scent the whole family and make a bunch of money! Anyway, I needed a new set of tires for my little Jeep, why not get the skunks to pay for them.

It was easy to live-trap them all, one at a time. They didn't even act scared as I carried them—carefully—out of the hen house and to the cage I had built to hold them. Once I had them all, it was easy to coax each one in the trap again, place an old towel over it and administer the chloroform I had got from the vet (who wouldn't do the operation himself, but said he'd show me how . . . so I was on my own). It took only a moment for the little guys to go under. I took a tiny clamp and carefully squeezed the end of the scent gland shut, gently pulled it from the anus and skillfully used a sharp scapel to remove it from the muscle that set it off. In no time I had all four of them de-scented, without so much as a whisper of a smell. I was really proud of my talents. Little did I know what was coming.

The word spread quickly that Jim Anderson, "Naturalist," had three "pet," de-scented, baby skunks for sale. The telephone jangled night and day. I was not only going to be rich, but famous too. It was pretty obvious that I had cornered the market on "pet" skunks, so I jacked up the price, seventy-five bucks each, take it or leave it. That's what I sold those little skunks for—and I got my new tires. However, I kept the little momma around.

Way in the back of my demented head a small bell was going off from time to time; a bell heralding the coming of a guilty conscience.

Momma Skunk didn't appear to hold a grudge against me for what I had done to her and her kids. Shucks, all I did was sell her babies and make her incapable of defending herself, that's all. She let me pet her and I cared for her like one of my own. She had the run of the house like a pet cat. I even got her a litter box. Then one day she found a small hole and vanished back to the wild.

That's when part of the awful truth of what I had done struck me. "She can't defend herself!" was the first thought that jolted me awake that night. I jumped out of bed, grabbed up the live-trap, and headed for the hen house. I knew that's where I could find her. I set the trap, then returned to the house for a restless night's sleep.

Next morning I rushed down and flew through the door. There she was! I had caught her again. "Oh, boy!" I said, scooping up the trap, "Am I happy to see you!" I tucked the trap under my arm and started to trot back to the place where her cage was standing in the shade of the big pine, next to the old shop Dean had hauled in from a construction site.

I hadn't got more than ten feet from the hen house when suddenly the world exploded in a pall of blinding, horrifying, yellowish, stinking mist that I will never forget. I couldn't believe my nose as I gagged for breath, looking through my tears at the cage under my arm. Staggering with dizziness and gasping for breath, I exclaimed, "This can't be!" I knew I'd removed scent glands. Then the awful truth struck me: I must have caught the male!

It was impossible for me to speak aloud now. I staggered along, finally reached the cage and shoved the trap in. I couldn't find anywhere to get fresh air; no matter where I went, the vile mist stayed with me, clutching at my throat. I was sure I was going to die of asphyxiation. I couldn't go into the house. I didn't dare jump into the horse trough— Dean or Lily would kill me, if the horses didn't kick me into the next county.

In the dim recesses of my mind, I heard the message telling me to get out of my clothes. "Got to get out of these clothes," I gagged aloud and right there I stripped down to my birthday suit, staggering around, trying to get enough breath to keep me alive—or so it seemed. This was an emergency, and I didn't care what neighbors,

Spotted skunk peeks out from under lava rock.

visitors, friends, or strangers thought or saw. (My grandfather used to say, "If they haven't seen it, they won't know what it is—and if they have—it doesn't matter.") I had to get away from that awful, gagging fog. As the last of my clothing fell away, I found relief from the awful stench and could breath a little easier.

I looked around and there, leaning against the side of the shop was the extra water trough left behind after the horses from the movie, *The Indian Fighter*, had been at the ranch. I rolled it near the hose and turned on the water. It took a long time to get enough water in the trough to submerge myself in, and that was almost enough to kill me too: that water was coming right from Broken Top's Bend Glacier, and just as cold!. Shaking with the cold, I washed and washed, first with dish soap, then with bath soap, then with dish soap again, then with shampoo, then with bath soap—nothing would carry away that awful stink. I would have used a Brillo pad if one had been handy. I was sure that stench would be with me the rest of my life.

After about an hour of that ice water and washing, I dressed, jumped into my Jeep, and headed for the Elkhorn Cafe, on south Highway 97 for a hot breakfast. Dorothy and Wade Collins ran the place and were good friends.

The minute I walked through the door every head in the place turned in my direction. I stopped in my tracks and stared back, from one face to the other. Dorothy was standing behind the counter as I began walking toward her.

"Stop, Jimmy!" she shouted, holding up the towel to her nose that she'd been wiping the counter with. "You smell terrible! Did you get sprayed by a skunk?"

"Pheeeewhehw!" the waitress exclaimed, making a wide detour around me as she headed for the kitchen.

"Oh, my gosh, Jimmy!" Wade laughed as he came out of the kitchen holding his nose. "You need a bath!"

"You better ged oud of here, quick!" a customer muttered, holding his nose. "I'm losing my abitite!"

I turned quickly and left the cafe, driving off to work without any breakfast. My boss took one whiff and left me alone, muttering, "You'd better go out to the pit and drill holes. No one around here can stand you!" Thankfully, I was out in the field by myself for most of the day, drilling holes, which we loaded with explosives to blast the over-burden off pumice. It was my partner, Daryl Stevenson, who gave me the last reminder of how badly I offended everyone with my skunky smell.

"Boy, oh boy, Jimmy," he said, laughing. "You got a smell that would gag a maggot!"

That evening, as I was lying in my bed, musing about my poignant encounter with the male skunk, I suddenly had the full vision again of that poor little momma skunk, out there in the wide world thinking she had the tools to protect herself—and didn't. I felt badly, but then I had another thought that made me feel much worse. Not only had I done her a terrible, personal injustice, but I had done something even worse than that. I had violated a trust, a trust that I had made with one of nature's lovely little creations. No! Not one, but a whole family. I trapped them, put them through a terrible physical ordeal, then sold them for tires for my Jeep. Even though my punishment fit the crime, I felt a lot like Judas then, and I still do today. It's important that one never violates a trust, especially with Mother Nature.

3 | LIFE IN THE "SWAMP"

The Harder You Work, The Luckier You Get

Years ago, when I first went to work for The Oregon Museum of Science & Industry (OMSI), in Portland, Oregon, I had the pleasure of being the part-time cook at one of the science camps down on the Oregon Coast. The regular cook, Eleanor Barrett (wife of the Education Director at OMSI, Ray Barrett), had cut her hand terribly on a big fruit can, and needed the help. I had just joined the museum as staff naturalist, but cooking was something I enjoyed too, so I pitched in to help.

You know, that's a trait that I believe everyone should have: to be prepared to pitch in where help is needed and not be afraid of work. Unfortunately this is something that seems to be fading in America. My old pal, Clyde Miller, can tell you a lot about the fun of working hard and enjoying it; he's been doing it for years. He and I have had a lot of fun together with kids and nature: like banding bats, crawling through lava tubes, and the time we went to Fossil Lake.

Each spring vacation of the public schools, I would take a busload of high school kids from the museum to dig fish at Fossil Lake, in Oregon's northern Lake County. This particular year we had a paleoichthyologist from Michigan State University with us. It was spring on the Oregon desert, but the day was warm and sunny anyway, a peculiar circumstance; the wind is usually blowing like a demon, and sand gets into your teeth, up your nose and into your very bones. The sun felt good on my back, the kids were great, and the "fishing" was wonderful. Clyde was digging alongside of me as a stranger walked over one of the rolling sand dunes and, apparently curious about what we were doing, stopped to watch. When he asked what was going on I told him. "You

mean you get paid to come out here and do this?" he said, shaking his head.

"Yep, sure do." I replied, carefully brushing some dust and sand from the skeleton of a big Dolly Varden about a million years old.

"Boy! You sure are lucky!" he exclaimed, stooping over for a closer look at my fish.

Clyde piped up, "Yeah, the harder you work, the luckier you get," and went on digging.

That's true. The harder you work, the luckier you do get. That's the opportunity that was facing me that morning at Camp Arago when Eleanor had cut her hand. There was a chance to do more than I was expected to. There was a job to do, and it had to be done. That was that.

Prior to that assistant cook assignment, however, I was one of the camp counselors. It was on my second day at camp that Ray Barrett, the Education Department Director, walked up to me with a worried look on his face.

"Jim," he, said with in an exasperated voice, "I can't find those three older guys anywhere." He was referring to three high school seniors who had come to the Camp Arago session with other things on their minds than learning about marine biology and geology. They hadn't been too cooperative about staying with our program, and now, with dinner-time at hand, they were nowhere to be found.

"I'll give a quick look, Ray," I answered, heading out the dining room hall door. I asked several people who were waiting to go in and eat if they'd seen them, but didn't get much help 'til I got in the lab.

"Oh, yeah," one of the counselors said. "I saw those three down by the boat dock about a half hour ago."

I trotted off in that direction, grumbling to

myself about kids that don't play the game right, and all that other grump, grump. Arriving at the boat dock I searched here and there, looked in several of the boats, into the office, and around the whole area, but still no sign of the wayward trio. Then I just happened to glance out over the small bay beyond the boat dock. There they were, the three of them sitting on their fat duffs in a small row boat about 100 yards off shore. "What the devil is goin' on," I mumbled to myself, heading back to find my binoculars. In a few moments I had them in focus and watched as they laughed together and sat there drinking something out of cans. As I watched, one of them light up a cigarette, the glow of the butt obvious through the binocs.

"Dad blast it!" I exclaimed under my breath, and headed for the dining hall. Ray was waiting just inside as I came through the door. "I found them, Ray," I announced, grumbling and holding the door open so he could see the direction I was pointing.

"Where?" he asked, looking out toward the bay.

"Right out there," I answered, pointing my finger toward them.

"What're they doing?" he asked.

"Drinkin' and smokin'."

"What?" he exclaimed in surprise.

"Yeah," I said. "I spotted them with the binocs. They've probably got a six-pack out there, and think they're safe from being discovered." Then I got a great idea. "Don't fret, Ray," I said, giving him an evil grin. "I'll go get 'em."

Without waiting to hear what he was saying I headed off to my room and jumped into my swimming suit. By using some overturned boats and buildings along the beach, I was able to ease into the warm water of the bay without being observed. Swimming slowly, I used quiet breast strokes to get closer and closer to them, concealing myself behind a couple of small boats riding at anchor. I could hear them laughing and making jokes as they drank their beer and did the "Big Guy" thing. In a few moments, I was just about as far as I thought I could go undetected, then I eased around the last boat, took a few big breaths, submerged myself quietly, and started for the boys underwater. As it is when you've got a real objective in mind, you can run faster, jump higher, learn faster, fly higher, and swim farther underwater to accomplish the purpose. That day I was able to go farther than I have ever gone underwater. Just about the time I arrived at the boat I felt a great bunch of goopy algae sliding past me, and another idea hit me. Holding what little air I had left, I pulled great handfuls of the submerged vegetation out of the muddy bottom and plastered it all over my head, shoulders and face. Then I reached up out of the water, grasped the gunwales of the small rowboat, placed my feet against the muddy bottom, and launched myself into the air, roaring like a mad sea lion as I came bursting out of the water like a breaching whale.

The effect was stupendous! In fact, it was more than I had hoped for. As I leaped out of the water, the kids was so startled that they jumped from their seats, arms flailing the air and shrieking their heads off. All this commotion went a long way to what took place next. With my weight on the gunwales, it was too much for the little craft to maintain stability, and it began to roll in my direction, the boys leaning over right along with it. Before they knew what was happening, all three were shouting, and pitched head-first into the water—complete with beer cans, cigarettes, good clothes, wallets, and all. They went right over me, and into the bay. Ker-splash!

I didn't wait to see how they were doing; the water was shallow enough to almost stand in, and they had the boat to hang onto anyway, so I vanished underwater, heading for shore. It took me perhaps half the time to escape as it did to start this mad scheme, but all the time I was heading for the beach, I was amazed at how much those kids had learned about the English language and how they had corrupted it!

I changed my clothes then quietly eased the door closed behind me heading for the beach and the group that had gathered to watch the boys drag their sodden craft to shore. I was suddenly surprised by a little laugh coming from alongside the side of the door as I passed.

"You found them, I hear," Ray chuckled,

patting me on the back as we headed for the beach.

Yep, you've got to always be prepared to help where help is needed.

While I was working in the kitchen I chanced to meet one of the people who helped me along the naturalist trail more than I can ever thank him for: Dr. Arnold Rustin, a urologist (that's a doctor who works on everything between your belly-button and knees). He also saved me from having a fatal reaction to penicillin, which we discovered I'm very allergic to—but that's another tale.

Dr. Rustin was at the camp with a bunch of other people from the Portland area who were studying under the Master Photographer, Minor White. Things were at their usual helter-skelter best as we were rushing to meet the scheduled time for dinner. I was bustling around, helping to get things in order, when Ray stopped me.

"Jim," he said. "I'd like you to meet Dr. Arnold Rustin." At that time, Dr. Rustin was on the OMSI Board.

I stopped for a moment and realized this was an important person to meet (everyone on our Board was important to meet), so I set my hot pan down, took a deep breath, and offered my hand. "How do you do, Dr. Rustin."

He looked at me for a moment shaking my hand, but without saying anything. Then Ray quickly added, "Jim is our newest employee, Dr, Rustin."

I stood there a moment longer and then repeated myself. "How do you do, Dr. Rustin," and then added, "I'm Jim Anderson."

"Yes, yes," he said, shaking my hand and giving me what I thought was a critical look. "I know that—but who are you?"

That took a moment to sink in. I didn't quite catch the thrust of the question at first, then I noticed something about Dr. Rustin I had missed when I first looked at him. There was a twinkle in his eye that suggested he was enjoying himself. He was looking for something, so I tried to give it to him. "Ummm . . . , I'm an omnoligist," I replied, grinning at him.

"Oh!" He said, turning away chuckling. "One of those damn, know-it-alls."

Over the years that followed, Dr. Rustin and I got to be good friends. One day he called me and told me to come by his house. Dr. Rustin never asked me to do anything, he just told me. I learned to live with that part of his nature because of the way he was, and it didn't offend me. There was something about him that I liked, and when he told me to do something, I enjoyed doing it. Father image? I just don't know, but he's only one of a very few people in my life who could tell me to do something and I'd do it without protest.

Anyway, I went up to his house one evening and we immediately retired to his library. Another trait Dr. Rustin had was getting right down to the nitty-gritty without any fanfare.

"Jim," he said, pushing a catalog over to me. "If you had a choice of photographic equipment, what would you like?"

I glanced down at the document in front of me and saw that it was from Asahi Pentax. I thumbed through the pages, lusting for each beautiful camera and lens I saw. What a wish book, I thought as I turned one page after another. All the time I was doing this he sat there watching me.

"Well?" He asked. "What did you see that you'd like to have?"

I was a little off balance with so many choices thrust in front of me, but I sat down next to him and pointed out a camera body with a normal lens, then a 135 mm lens, and a 28 mm wide-angle. "Is that all you want?" he asked, giving me a quizzical look, and then adding, "Wouldn't you like to have a telephoto lens?"

I turned back to the catalog, and just for kicks, I jokingly picked out the huge Super Takamur 500 mm, rack-and-pinion-focus, telephoto lens. "That one would do," I said, pointing to the lens.

"OK," he said, and then we sat there discussing various photographic details of his newest batch of black and white prints, which, by the way, were very, very good. Dr. Rustin has a great deal of talent, both in his profession, as well as in his photographic work.

It was about two months later that I got another call from him. "Hi, Jim," he said.

"Come on over and pick up your photographic equipment."

"What do you mean, my photographic equipment?" I asked.

"Well, the gear you ordered when you were over here a while back." he responded.

I stammered a little longer, then quickly drove over to see if he was serious. He was. I even unpacked all the boxes, fresh from Japan. It was all there, every piece of equipment I had picked from the wish book, including the huge, 500 mm rack-and-pinion-focus Super Takamur, Telephoto Lens! And, as it turned out, I had perhaps the first 28 mm wide-angle Takamar lens to be delivered in the US.

That was the beginning of my serious pursuit of nature photography. I worked hard with that gear, using the beautiful equipment to make several slide programs for the education department of the museum, as well as programs for fund-raising, scientific presentations, and for schools. I still have a bunch of Pentax gear of my own that I use today, including the first motor-drive that Pentax made, back in the '60s.

I only tell this tale because it opens the door to something my father, grandfather, and Uncle Harry gave me, along with Dr. Rustin's wonderful gift: the Work Ethic, which I've applied to my life-long love affair with Nature. They all go together.

As a kid on the farm I can recall watching hawks soaring overhead, never beating a wing as they used the lift that Mother Nature provides to those who know (learn) how to use it. It would be over thirty years later that I would put these same forces of Nature to work as a glider instructor and teach my students how to use various kinds of lift to go from point A to point B, the same way eagles do. My early reading of *The Birds of America*, which contains those unparalleled Finley & Bohlman photos taken way back in the early 1900s, captured my love for hawks, eagles, and owls for evermore. I couldn't believe the way those two men carried their equipment into the trees, cliffs, up and down and over rocks to capture the images of the birds, especially the condors, eagles, and hawks. That, at best,

was hard work—very hard work—but it was fun too.

In the '50s and '60s, I questioned the use of 1080, (a poison with no known antidote) used by government trappers to kill coyotes. I have always thought this stuff was a possible cause of death in raptors, especially eagles. Even though the government told me over and over that there was not enough poison in the horse meat bait to kill eagles, I found in the scientific literature that the stuff is accumulative, and if an eagle returned to the bait several times—as they would in winter when food was scarce—they could ingest enough to kill them. That opened another door, or perhaps better stated, an unoccupied niche.

Nature abhors a vacuum. If there is an area or an organism that's not filled or utilized by one or another of Nature's forces, it won't be for long. Something will move in to fill the void; that's the way it is. That's why the coyote is so successful. A predatory vacuum was created in many parts of North America when the wolf was removed from the top of the food chain; the coyote quickly filled that niche. He's a great opportunist. I'm the same way.

I found that no one was looking after the welfare of hawks and eagles in Central Oregon back in the '50s. No one seemed to care. I kept asking the Oregon Game Commission about poison and eagles until they were tired of hearing it. I haunted the government trappers until the head rat-choker threatened me with a law suit if I didn't let go of it.

I found eagles and hawks electrocuted wherever there were electrical lines and transformers that allowed the birds to come into contact with them. Along with other biologists concerned with the welfare of raptors, I hounded the power companies in an effort to implement safer conditions for hawks, eagles, and owls.

I also found misinformed farmers killing hawks and thanks to the cooperation of the Granges, I gave talks to farmers and ranchers about the economic value of hawks and owls in their business.

Then I found the plinkers—people with guns that just have to kill something—

killing eagles, hawks, owls, and anything else that provided a target. All these factors joined up to become a driving force and set me to interacting with raptors.

One of the Great People I've enjoyed over the years was Avon Mayfield. He and his lovely wife, Peggy, and I became good friends. Avon was an Oregon State Police Game Officer stationed in Bend. In the purest form, I can say that he was a True Gentleman. He and I fished, and spent a lot of time sharing ideals together. Most importantly, he enjoyed hawks, eagles, and owls as much as I did. Each time I heard of anyone who had shot (killed) a hawk, eagle, or owl, I'd call Avon and ask for his help. His reply was always the same: "Wait 'til I get my uniform on." Thanks to him, and officers like Kenny Roach, Gary Hayden, and Luke Scarlet, I have a hunch that many other members of this elite group became more interested in protecting nongame wildlife at a time when this philosophy wasn't popular. It would be over twenty years before the Oregon Department of Fish and Wildlife made it official. Avon went out among the stars after a bad heart attack that was probably helped along by his dedication and going the extra mile in his calling. I had the pleasure, and pain, of singing "Nearer My God To Thee" when Avon's body was committed to the Good Earth that he loved. A great many people still miss him, but will never forget him.

I asked for Avon's help one time when I watched a man shoot a beautiful Northern Harrier, known in those days as the Marsh Hawk. My old pal, Dean Hollinshead and I had gone sage grouse hunting one September weekend in the big sagebrush lands and hay fields on the east side of Fort Rock that belonged to Reub Long, and we were sitting in my little Jeep. We had each shot a grouse earlier in the day, and were just sitting there quietly drinking hot coffee in the late afternoon when we saw a man park his rig out on the county road east of the field and begin to stalk the grouse that he thought might be hiding in the alfalfa.

"Look at that guy," Dean exclaimed, pointing to the fellow as he pushed through the knee-high, last cutting, of alfalfa. "Reub

Avon Mayfield, state game officer and a true gentleman, "never turned Jim down."

'aint going to like him mashin' all his hay down."

"You're sure right, Dean." I agreed, picking up my binoculars from the seat to take a better look. As I swung the glasses toward the man, a sudden dark movement across the lens caught my eye and I quickly swung back.

"Hey!" I exclaimed to Dean. "Here comes a little male marsh hawk."

The hawk was hunting the way all marsh hawks do, slowly sailing along with lazy flaps of his wings, about fifteen feet above the fields, head down, searching for any tell-tale movements that would reveal a small rodent or bird, which is their favorite prey. Each time the hawk swung over the field it got closer and closer to the man also stalking through the alfalfa. As the hawk came within his range the man suddenly changed his stance and looked up. I knew what was going to happen next.

The old Gooch barn at Christmas Valley was a camping sight for the OMSI science students who took part in the annual Spring Safari. If the wind blew too hard, and the snows came, the barn was a refuge—of sorts. There is no place to escape the blowing sand of the spring winds.
(Photo courtesy of Larry Langley)

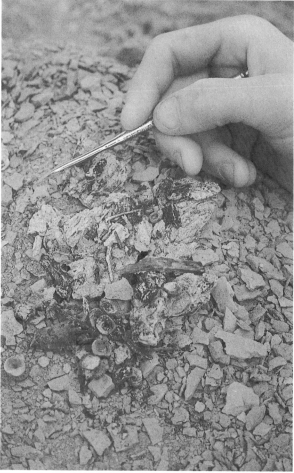

Typical deposit of fish fossils in the old lake basin of Fossil Lake in northern Lake County. Many of the fish fossils collected by the OMSI students from the ancient lake bed have been placed in a collection at the University of Michigan, and are still being studied today.
(Photo courtesy of Larry Langley)

Bruce Welton demonstrates the method of fossil searching at Fossil Lake: on his hands and knees.

"Blast it, Dean!" I exclaimed. "That guy's going to shoot that marsh hawk!"

Before either of us could say—or do—anything, the man raised his gun and we saw the puff of smoke before the sound of the shot echoed off the steep cliff of Fort Rock behind us, and we watched the little hawk fall to the earth.

"Blast!" I said again. Then I started up the Jeep and went roaring down toward the edge of the field. I pulled up in a cloud of dust and bailed out, jumped the fence, and ran toward the man, who, as I sprinted up, was grinding the hawk's head into the sand and alfalfa with the heel of his boot.

"Did you kill that hawk?" I shouted.

He looked up at me with what I interpreted as disdain and answered, "Sure I did," and then added, "hawks are no damn good!"

When I'm really mad, I have a very difficult time keeping my cool. I get the

"How long does it take for a mosquito to drink her fill?" asked a student while on an OMSI field day on the Oregon Coast. Dorothy Harvy holds the vial with a mosquito in it on Bruce Hendrick's arm, while Morgan Allara *(left)* and Paul Nemser clock the mosquito.

shakes, and I was shaking mad as I stood there watching that guy grinding that little hawk's head into the ground. Without thinking, I reached out and snatched the shotgun right out of his hands. He stood there staring at me as I jacked the unused rounds out of the chamber and then threw the gun into the sand and began to grind it into the ground with my boots.

"Hey!" he shouted, trying to push me off his weapon. "You can't do that! You'll ruin my gun!"

I ignored his shouts and just kept right on grinding away, stomping my feet up and down, mashing the grit into the weapon as hard as I could. Finally he managed to push me aside, reached down and lifted his gun from the ground, rubbing the dirt away.

"You stupid, jerk!" I shouted at him. "You killed that little hawk just for the fun of it, and I'm going to place you under citizen's arrest—right now!" I stood there glaring at him, panting from the work I had been doing trying to kill his shotgun.

"Look at my shotgun!" he exclaimed, thrusting it toward me.

I must admit, it was a pretty expensive looking weapon. There was a lot of fancy carving on the stock, and even the side of

the chamber. The barrel had some elaborate scroll work too, which was badly scratched up by that good old gritty, volcanic sand of the Oregon desert.

"I don't give a tinker's damn about your shotgun!" I exploded. "You killed a hawk that's protected by Oregon law, and by my soul, you're goin' to pay for it!" With that I spun about, and stomped off toward the rig.

As I climbed into the Jeep, old Dean was sitting there, smoking a cigarette and drinking his coffee. "You sure raised a lot of hell with that feller's shotgun, Jimmy," he said, giving me a funny look.

"What'd you expect me to do!" I retorted, and starting the Jeep, roared out of the field in a cloud of dust down toward the main road.

"Where're we goin'?" Dean asked, trying to keep his coffee from spilling all over his lap.

"To get that guy's license plate number, and then to find a phone!" I answered in a clipped tone.

"Now, cool down, old scout," Dean said, patting me on the shoulder, "You don't have to get huffy with me just because that feller shot one of your hawks."

I tried to give him a grin, but at that

Jim holds an adult Bald Eagle that was used in publicity photos when Georgia-Pacific presented him with a grant for eagle research on the lower Columbia River.

moment my heart wasn't in it. I just wanted to get to a phone, turn that guy in and then go back to Bend.

Things didn't work out that way at all. The first phone I found was in Fred Wright's trailer house, an old friend of Dean's who had lived near Fort Rock. Dean often called him "Fritz." As I talked with the State Police office in Bend on the phone, the first thing I learned was that the officer who would investigate what I called, "Illegal killing of game" would have to come out of the Gilchrist office, located in Klamath County, over thirty miles south of Bend. That meant Avon wouldn't be the one to investigate the incident. Which also meant that I had to stay in Fort Rock and wait for the other officer to get to the place where I was calling from. This meant Dean and I would be late getting back to Bend. That made me madder.

"Well, if we're going to have to wait 'til your State Policeman shows up, we might as well play some pinochle," Fritz said, reaching in the drawer for the cards.

We drank a lot of coffee, and played a lot of pinochle well into the evening. It was about 10 pm when the trailer house lit up with headlights of a rig pulling up out front. I got up and opened the door just as the policeman was walking up on the front step.

"Hi," he said, giving me a questioning look, "You Jim Anderson?" I told him that I was, and he came into the house, shook hands with Dean and Fritz, then took the cup of coffee Fritz offered him and sitting down said, "Now tell me about this illegal killing of game."

"Well," I began, "It wasn't exactly game, it was a hawk."

He raised his eyebrows as he sipped his coffee, lowered the cup, and said, "A hawk, you say. That's different."

"What do you mean, *different*," I asked, starting to get angry.

"Hawks aren't 'game'," he said flatly.

"Oh," was all I could say and waited.

"What kind of a hawk was it?" he asked.

"A marsh hawk," I replied.

"They're protected." he responded.

"Yep, I thought they were," I said. "Now what do we do?"

"Tell me about it, what happened, I mean." he said, pulling his big notebook from the pocket in his jacket.

So I told him about it, all about it. As I related the details he would touch his tongue to the end of his short pencil, write a note or two, watch me, then scribble a few more notes. That's the way it went until I got to the part about jumping up and down on the shotgun. As I launched into that part of the tale he lowered his notebook, and just sat there staring at me.

"You did that?" he asked, closing his notebook.

"I sure did!" I replied emphatically. Then the room got very quiet.

The officer looked at Dean, sighed, and asked, "He really did jump up and down on that guy's gun?"

"He sure did," Dean said, giving me a big grin, "It was a mess on the outside, and probably raised hell with the guts too." He added, grinning at me again.

More silence. Then the officer stood up, walked over and placed his hand on my shoulder. "Now here's what we've got to do," he said as I sat staring up at him. "We've got to go see this man, arrest him, and then we've got to go to Lakeview to talk to the judge . . ."

"Lakeview!" I blurted out. "Why can't we take him to Barney Martin in LaPine? He'd give him what he deserves . . ."

"Now, take it easy . . ." the officer interrupted, squeezing my shoulder. "We're in Lake County, we can't take him to LaPine, that's in Deschutes County." He waited for that to sink in, then added. "But there's another problem with taking him to Lakeview," he said, giving me a very serious look. "The judge in Lakeview is a good man, he'll do what the law says he must do, but he's also a sportsman who really appreciates a fine piece of workmanship in shotguns, and I fear that when he hears what you did to that man's weapon he may get a little upset."

Before I could interrupt again, he added, "Now we know who did the hawk in, and we know it was against the law." Then he gave me the first smile I'd seen from him since he came into the room. "Let's leave it this way. He can't drive through this neck of the woods again without making some kind of a mistake." With that, he closed his book, stuck it into his pocket, opened the door, and stepped out into the night adding, "and thanks for the coffee."

Not too long after that, I took to the air for the first time and began doing an aerial census of the hawks and eagles throughout Central Oregon, something that I still do today. During a recent summer, I flew into the Sunriver Airport with Dick Davis, a very talented aviator who flew me over the Deschutes National Forest in his Citabria (I'm between airplanes just now) doing an Osprey census for the Oregon Department of Fish and Wildlife. As we climbed out of the aircraft talking about the nests and Osprey, a man closeby overheard our conversation and followed us into the airport office.

After a few moments he said, "Do you get paid to go out and fly over the trees looking into Osprey nests?" I replied that I did. "Boy you sure are lucky!" he exclaimed.

Dick looked at me and grinned, "Yep", he said, "The harder you work, the luckier you get!"

Batchin' With a Bandit

One of the most cuddly critters that exists is a baby raccoon—ask anyone who has seen one and they'll agree. Kids from all walks of life have them as pet stuffed animals. Maybe that's how it all begins—stuffed animals. Perhaps the strong attraction for baby wildlife gets started in people's lives as they are given stuffed baby bears, tigers, monkeys, a wide variety of birds, frogs, and even snakes and dinosaurs. Yes, I'm sure of it, we're taught to love wildlife, especially baby wildlife, from the cradle up.

When the movement began to obtain stuffed teddy bears to assist in handling trauma in children's accidents, my son Reuben donated his to a police department in California. Since then, many other emergency units have discovered the value of stuffed animals to help small children over rough places. Pets in general are necessary in our lives, and have helped thousands of people heal hurts, loneliness, and other types of trauma.

I can remember being at the Oregon Coast at Sunset Beach one afternoon and spotting a woman trying to carry a baby sea lion up from the beach. I asked her where in the name of Heaven she was going with that creature.

"Oh," she said, looking at me with tears in her eyes, "Its mother has gone off and left it. I'm going to take the poor thing home." When I asked her how, and what, she was going to feed it, or where she was going to keep it, she looked at me with a blank face and couldn't answer. I helped her take it back exactly where she found it . . . where I'm sure the real mom would find it.

The raccoon is different. A baby raccoon has the look of an impish dwarf. The mask over the eyes suggests a cute little helpless waif. The appealing eyes and human-like qualities reach out and entangle even the most hard-hearted person, and the baby raccoon finds itself the occupant of a new home. They immediately take advantage of this situation, often more aggressively than their human parents would like. Then when they grow into adult raccoons, the fun really starts.

Sure, there have been cases where the parent raccoon has been killed, run over by a car, mangled by dogs (which is a very difficult thing for any dog to do), or sometimes the baby loses the parents in a sudden flight to avoid danger or escape capture. But in most cases, a baby raccoon is scooped up by a well-meaning person because that person thinks the baby is lost or abandoned. In reality the parent is closeby and will take her offspring away as soon as danger passes. It is (almost) always best to leave baby wildlife in the forest, stream, ocean, or wherever they were found.

In the Portland, Oregon area, and especially in the suburbs, raccoons are fed as wildlife pets by a great many people. In the Lake Oswego neck-of-the-woods, it's not uncommon to find two dishes on the back porch of many homes: one for the pet dog and the other for the "pet" raccoon. Sometimes there's a problem of overlap if the raccoon arrives at the time Rover is finishing his supper; a raccoon, bent upon having his own way, whether Rover is a German Shepherd, Pit Bull, or Bulldog, will usually get his own way.

A raccoon's skin fits over his muscular frame in such a way that when he's grabbed by a dog, it's possible for the raccoon to roll over and grab back. This has surprised a great many domestic dogs who then find they have a real problem. Male raccoons can run up to thirty or forty pounds. They have long, sharp claws on all four feet, and strong jaws armed with formidable teeth. I've seen

a male raccoon leap upon the back porch of a house near Portland, calmly walk over to the dog's dish of food and eat it all, while Rover, a ninety-five pound Irish Wolf Hound stands there, shaking in his boots. In fact, I've seen a male raccoon teach a German Shepherd to climb trees.

As you might gather from this preamble, I have a keen respect for the awesome offensive, defensive, and survival abilities of our water-loving carnivore, known to the scientific guys as *Procyon lotor*, which roughly translated means "first-bear-dog." So you can understand why I was so upset when Loren McKinley, the director of the Oregon Museum of Science and Industry, in Portland, called me into his office and showed me a young raccoon—not a baby raccoon—but a juvenile raccoon lurking in a cage in his office. It seems the folks who had picked it up as a baby had suddenly realized that babies grow, and this one was getting to be a handful. Juvenile raccoons are a big handful, especially when they begin to realize that they're a raccoon, which will happen in spite of all the human imprinting that's been attempted.

"You're our naturalist," Loren began, pointing to the large, wooden cage on the floor. "And as such we thought you'd like a new animal for your wildlife shows," he said, grinning at me. I had no choice; Loren was not only my boss, but it was next to impossible for me to say no to that red-headed character—besides—I loved him too much. I looked into the cage and sized up my new wildlife show partner. He sat there, eyeing me back with the confidence born of an animal who knows his potential.

"OK," I sighed, but I couldn't bring myself to say thank you as I picked up the cage and headed out the door.

In those days I was a bachelor, living in a small house out near Beaverton, west of Portland. It was an old two room house used in the past by the hired man. The bathroom was at one end and the bedroom/kitchen at the other. There wasn't too much room for a raccoon, and I already had a partner living with me: a little screech owl that had flown down a chimney in southeast Portland and needed a quiet place to get over it.

A fully grown male raccoon can teach a German Shepherd to climb trees.

"Oh, no . . ."I groaned, heading for the bathroom. As I opened the door my face fell: the place was a wreck. The teen-age raccoon was pleased to see me though, so he climbed out of the toilet bowl and right up my pants leg, wet "hands" grasping tightly and dragging that big, bushy trail along making sure I was good and wet. I tried to fend him off, but his long, sharp claws clung to me and he let me know he was used to being held. He clung to me like a leach.

As I eased back into the bedroom/kitchen, the raccoon spotted the little screech owl immediately, who at the moment was perched on the back of a chair. He didn't even hesitate, just launched himself directly for that little owl. I tried to grab his tail as he catapulted out my arms, but it was no use. He was gone like a furred rocket. Thank goodness the owl had seen us coming out of the bathroom, and had his eye on the lively menace. The raccoon hit the chair with a crash, but the owl was long gone, headed for the curtain rod above the big picture window that allowed the moonlight to come in on the few nights when it wasn't raining. The chair went crashing to the floor, followed by the raccoon who then jumped to the second one, leaped on the table, and made another jump for the curtain rod. He was good, but not that good; he just managed to land with a crash onto the bed, and then pull the covers off as he spotted his favorite object, the refrigerator. He knew what was in there, and would often swing on the door handle of his other "parents" cold storage, waiting for them to get out his meals.

Well, it only took an hour to clean up what he'd done in a minute, which wasn't too bad when you consider what he might have done had he been an adult. That's the way it went for about a week. I tried to give him away to several friends—thanks, but no thanks. I tried to give him to Dr. Maberry at the zoo, but they were already long on raccoons and had no room. (I think he lied to me!)

So I cleaned the bathroom of all playthings and put up with him for another week as I began building a cage outside for him.

While this domestic crisis was going on in

As I rolled home that evening I wondered how I was going to handle this new wildlife addition, but couldn't think of anything intelligent to do with him. I locked him in the bathroom for the night: that was my first mistake. A half-grown raccoon left on his own to find a way to entertain himself is a disaster looking for a place to happen. They're great climbers to begin with and this guy was no exception. The first thing I heard was everything in the medicine cabinet falling into the toilet bowl, bath tub, and floor.

Screech Owl

my home I met a very lovely school teacher who taught biology at Grant High School in east Portland. I was trying to impress her to the extent where she might consider me as husband material. This was met with considerable frustration within my home as it meant moving the raccoon out every time I wanted to take a bath, which, considering my matrimonial goals, had to be daily.

In the meantime, the raccoon continued to grow, the owl had to be cared for, and I fell heir to a big, aggressive Yellow Rat Snake. Snakes are a tasty dish for raccoons, so it was even more difficult to maintain equilibrium as I tried to assemble this menagerie in their separate locations as I ate breakfast, took a daily bath, and carried out my duties at OMSI. It all came to a head one evening as I was preparing to go out with the biology teacher.

I had arrived home at about four in the afternoon, giving myself plenty of time to feed the crew, and then bathe and dress for what I hoped was going to be a great evening. Coon was removed from the bathroom and placed back in his cage. This is easy to say, but he was about five pounds heavier than when we first met, and he knew the game. He didn't like going into that cage, so we had quite a tussle. After the shift of residence I cleaned the bathtub of what can be best described as a stinky mess, and ran the water for my bath.

While the bath water was running, it was time to clean the snake cage, put in a lab rat and fresh water for him, and then feed the little screech owl. I had placed a bunch of newspaper on the floor under the spot owl liked, high up on the curtain rod above the window. This made it much easier to clean up behind him, something I wish had been as easy for the raccoon.

Little owl was a lot of fun to work with, and he was quiet enough to sit on my finger, but did not like being stared at. If I stared at him for too long a time he would raise himself up into a thin column of feathers, squint his eyes shut and begin to hoot at me loudly. He would also do this when annoyed by the raccoon, who would always leap from side to side in his cage, trying to break his way out. It was sort of a rodeo at times.

Little owl was just calming down, and I was offering him his evening mouse, when I suddenly remembered the tub. I jumped down from the chair I had to stand on to reach the owl, and ran into the bathroom in time to shut off the water before it overflowed.

"Too much water—got to remember to let some out before I get in," I mumbled to myself as I went back into the kitchen to finish my chores. I should have been more alert to the fact that the raccoon was no longer rocking his cage.

"OK, little owl," I said as I climbed back on the chair to present his mouse. Just as I reached the owl I heard a "thump" on the floor behind me, and turned to see raccoon galloping toward the bathroom. "Oh, no!" I shouted, leaping from the chair and trying to cut him off at the pass. Too late. I don't know, to this day, how he did it, but he went sliding into the bathroom, hit the back of the door, which closed with a bang, and then to my unbelieving ears I heard the latch click into the locked position on the other side. "I don't believe this!" I groaned as I tried to open the door. Sure enough that blasted raccoon had not only made it back into the bathroom, but he had locked me out! Then, to add insult to injury he immediately jumped into the bathtub, which was filled almost to the top, and began to splash around, all the time giving forth with that delightful, but to my shortened patience, hideous, trilling sound that raccoons sing when they're especially pleased—or angry.

I banged on the door, "Raccoon! Let me in!" I shouted, like a fool. I began a frantic search for a way in. The hinges were on the inside, so I couldn't knock out the pins. Unlike today's bathroom doors that have a small hole on the knob where a nail or punch can be pushed in to unlock the door, this was an old timer with a small lever under the knob that could only be unlocked from the inside. I looked all around the door jam, but this was framed in by an expert many years ago. I would have had to almost destroy the wall to get the door off from the outside. The solution to getting at that blasted raccoon was only too obvious: the only way was by forced entry from outside. The hour was getting late, I was sure my date would be wondering where I was, and to make things worse, I didn't have a phone. I ran outside, grabbed the raccoon cage to stand on and looked into the bathroom window.

There he was, swimming around in the bathtub, water splashing all over the bathroom—my bath water splashing all over the place—and I could do nothing but watch. Then I gave the window a closer inspection. I ran back to my little Hillman Husky, opened the hatch in the back and grabbed a hammer, screw driver, nail bar, and wood chisel, ran back and attacked the window with a vengeance. It didn't take more than ten minutes to get the frame off the window, the window out of the sash, and then climb into the soggy bathroom. My patience was pretty thin at that moment, and the raccoon could read body language better than a student of Freud. He tried everything in the book to keep away from me as we splashed around in the bath water. It was hard work, but I eventually got hold of the back of that thrashing, soggy raccoon's neck and hauled him out of the bathtub.

Standing by the window I knew that his time with me had come to an end. I chucked him right out the window where he went sailing into the big, blackberry bush behind

the house. I poked my head out to see how he was doing just in time to see him crawl out from under the bushes, give me a very dirty look and lope off toward the forest at the edge of a big wheat field.

"Good-bye, and good riddance!" I shouted as he humped his back and galloped off across the wheat field. With a great sigh of relief I thought that was the end of it, but I was sadly mistaken.

It was probably three days later—rather three nights later—that we renewed our acquaintance. I had come home from a wonderful evening after giving talks to two different PTAs in southwest Portland and having a great time with my biology teacher pal. I was humming to myself as I crawled into my nice, warm bed. The evening was damp, with the usual rain falling. (The name that Ed Park, a fellow naturalist from the Bend area, and I have for west of the Cascades is: "The Swamp.")

I was looking forward to a good night's sleep and was just going under when I heard the faint click of the front door knob. It took me a moment to assemble the message that the door had opened, and just as I was about to unglue my sleepy eyes to see what was going on, I felt two, cold, clammy paws slide down my back. I let out a howl that probably was heard in downtown Portland, and grabbed for the thing that had assaulted me. It was that dadblasted raccoon! He let out a squealing chatter, and we got into it right there. I was trying to scrape him off my back, but he was trying to get reacquainted, probably because he was hungry, and I was the only friend he had. That didn't make much difference as I saw the mud all over the bed, smeared on the bed sheets, on my tee-shirt, and felt the cold goop running down my back.

"Sorry, old buddy," I rasped through clenched teeth as I finally got a firm grip on his nape, and for the second time in his life he had another flying lesson, landing again in the middle of the blackberry bush. We stood looking at each other as he clambered down to the base of the bush, unhurt, but mad as a hornet at me. My T-shirt was torn, and there were mud and deep scratches all over my back. The bed, floor, and front door were all gooped up with that good old Willamette Valley glue.

After I slammed the door shut, I changed the sheets and started the water running for my bath. Just as I was stepping into the tub I suddenly remembered one more thing that had to be done—lock the front door.

In spite of the raccoon problems, I had a lot of fun with the little screech owl I batched with. I mentioned once that he didn't like to be stared at. Well, I found that out quite by accident one evening. I had given him a mouse to eat, which he grasped in his talons while he was standing on a towel placed on the back of a chair. I was sitting on the other chair reading, but placed my book down and sat there watching to see what he was going to do with the dead mouse. The more I watched the owl, the more he watched me, unblinking. Soon we were both staring at each other.

Slowly, the owl began to pull all his feathers close to his body and as he did, his face lost the roundness and began to take on a long, thin, oriental look. He squinched his eyes down to mere slits, and then began to stretch himself into a taller shape. It was almost comical to see this tiny, round owl slowly become a skinny, squinty-eyed owl. As if the transformation wasn't enough to make me stop staring at him, he began to give forth a series of high-pitched, trilling hoots.

I had sense enough to stop staring, and raised my book and began to read, but I couldn't resist the temptation to slowly lower the book and stare at him over the edge of the pages. Once I did it when he was in the act of swallowing his mouse. That was unkind of me, for he immediately tried to make himself taller, but had difficulty doing so because of the fat mouse halfway down. I quickly raised my book and waited politely until he was finished before I peered at him again.

We played that silly game for about an hour. I would read a little, ignoring his stares, then lower the book and stare at him, staring back at me. Finally he got tired of me and with a little hoot, took off from the chair. He went round the room about three times then picked out his place to land—

which was a mistake. He swooped down and landed on the long faucet that was attached to the kitchen sink.

This was one of the chrome-plated jobs, with a surface slick as glass. As the owl dropped onto it he had trouble holding himself upright. I guess he was still a little weak, from what reasons I had no idea, and probably found it difficult to perch on the slick faucet. He rocked first one way, falling forward, but flapped his wings and recovered, then over-corrected and began to tip over backward. This caused him to madly flap, but he over-corrected and began to fall forward again. I set the book down and headed for the sink to help him, but I didn't get there in time. He over-corrected again, but this time he fell over backwards and clung to the faucet, upside down.

"Oh, nuts," I exclaimed, reaching out to take him from the faucet, but just as I did he let go.

"Ker-splash!" he went, head-first into a pan of water I had soaking in the sink. He panicked, flapped his wings, and thrashed around in the water to get upright again. Before I could get my hands on the poor little guy, he had got himself out, hopped up on the edge of the pan, gripped the rim as best he could, and rocked back and forth. I must admit, I had to laugh at the sight. He was soaked, feathers wet and soggy, and he had a very angry look on his face—if a screech owl can look angry.

I tried to get him to come and perch on my finger, but it was to no avail. He just ignored me, and looked above his head at that chrome faucet, perhaps trying to figure out why he hadn't been able to stay where he had landed. I left him there, and in a few minutes he made it to the drain board, then to the edge of the counter where he stood preening his feather, avoiding any eye contact with me. It was about 2 am when I woke up and glanced up to see where the owl was. I couldn't help but laugh when I finally found him. He was perched on the back of the chair, about a foot away, staring at me. I couldn't stare back, but I just went back to sleep with a smile on my face, thinking once again, "Nature sure is fun . . ."

Grab It Quick!

We were caught in the struggling traffic, trying to cross the Burnside Bridge in Portland, Oregon. It was rush hour, and I wanted to get to Sandy Boulevard where I had a reservation for dinner at "The Broiler" with the young lady who was with me in my little Hillman Husky. We only had an hour or so to eat, then I had to travel across town to do a nature program for a PTA at an elementary school in Oregon City. But things just weren't going well at all . . .

About two weeks before, while traveling to a school with "Owl" perched on the back of the seat and, "Snake," a gentle, four-foot rat snake, safely tucked away in the overnight case I carried him in, I was driving a little too fast when the traffic light ahead of me suddenly turned red. I jammed on the brakes to avoid a costly collision with the automobile ahead of me. Owl was capable of handling surprises like that; he just sunk his talons into the back of the seat and gave me a dirty look. Poor old Snake, on the other hand, had a tough time of it. The overnight case went crashing to the floor where it hit with a bang. I glanced down at it, thinking to myself that was a pretty nasty bump the snake received; but the case was padded inside with foam rubber, so I was pretty sure he was safe from harm.

Imagine my surprise when I arrived at the school and found the case had popped open when it hit the floor, and Snake was nowhere to be found. I would have tried calling him, but snakes can't hear. Then I thought of using some kind of bait, but he had already gobbled up his weekly meal of three big lab rats just two days before, so that was out. I made a quick search of the floorboards, the bottom of the seat and other more obvious places, but still no snake. In as much as I was usually operating on naturalist's time—that is, late for everything—I didn't have time to look any longer. I just cranked all the windows up tight, put Owl on my shoulder and dashed off to the school program.

My pal, the owl, was in such a fine state of mind that day that he positively wowed the kids with his performance. He flew around the cafetorium, landed on the microphone, and hooted up a storm. Then when I called him back after he had gone to perch on the basketball back board, he glided down and landed on the microphone again for his lunch, two young lab rats.

At this point in the program, I used the rats to demonstrate the flexibility of an owl's neck. I'd slowly rotate the rat in front of the owl's face and slowly move it all the way around him. Usually the owl would also slowly rotate his head to about the 270 degree point—as far as an owl can move his head without moving his body. If I continued to move toward a point behind him, he'd swing his head back the other way, so quickly at times you would miss it, and pick up the movement from the other direction. This would often put the kids into an uproar.

Then I'd ask them how an owl could do that when we couldn't. That opened the door to a comparison between our neck vertebrae as compared to an owl's, and the fun started: owls have twice as many vertebrae as we do, they can't move their eyes, etc, etc.

(Sam Moorehouse, an old buckaroo from the Fort Rock country told me of an experience he had with a Burrowing Owl once: "I was ridin' along on my pony when up ahead I seen one of them little 'Coo-coo' owls a-standin' on an old fence post. Well, I rode my horse right up to him and that little owl just set there starin' at me. I rode all the way around him and he just kept turnin' his head clear 'round. So I rode around him again, and he turned his head clear 'round again'. Well, you know, I done that three more times. You know what happened then?" he asked. I said, "Sure. The owl's head fell off!" He grinned at me and said, "Nope! My horse got dizzy and fell down!")

I played the game of "Hold-Back-The-Rat"

until I could see that Owl was rapidly running out of patience, and past time for his reward. As I took my attention off of him, he would snatch the rat out of my hand, hold it for a moment, then swallow it in one gulp. The kids would usually clap, sometimes they'd even cheer. I could never figure out why that was something worth cheering about. Teenagers eat the same way—gulp it down whole, and away they go.

Well anyway, back to the missing snake. I spent the next few days after the school assembly trying to find that blamed snake, searching the car high and low, but failed to find a trace of him. Then, as I opened the door one morning to go to work I found a "trace" of him. He'd left a nasty pile of undigested rat right in the middle of my seat. Luckily, I saw it before I sat down. The mornings turned cold for a couple of days, and I turned the hot water from the engine into the interior car heater, but I was afraid to turn the fan motor on for fear old Snake was coiled around it and might get chopped into snakeburger.

I continued my search for over two weeks, but I couldn't find him. I became a little worried about his starving so I turned a couple of small lab rats loose in the car one evening, and never saw them again, so I was reasonably certain the snake was alive and well—somewhere in the Hillman.

The traffic wasn't moving on Burnside, so I smiled and chatted with my companion about schools, weather, kids, and music. I wasn't really thinking about snakes or owls. She smiled back and made a comment about how heavy the traffic was for this time of the afternoon, which I agreed with, listening to beeping horns, and looking ahead at the snarled traffic. Then, all of a sudden she let out a terrified screech and almost jumped clear out of her seat.

"What's that!" she screamed, pointing to the dashboard.

It was Snake! Well, there he was, sticking his head out from under the dashboard.

"Grab him! Quick!" I shouted, pulling up the hand brake. I won't tell you what she said . . . it was quite a shock for me, too. However, it could be summed up this way: "If you want him—you grab him!"

It began to get kind of busy in the little station wagon at that moment. My lovely, composed, date was coming unglued. She was panting, pushing her skirt down—which was trying to do other things—as she made some brave attempts to leap into the back end of the tiny station wagon—without opening the door. I was trying to get a hand on Snake by slumping down in the seat, reaching around the gear shift lever, and trying to get a look up under the dashboard—but from the outside of the car it probably didn't look that way at all. In fact, it probably looked very interesting to the car directly behind us who was blowing his horn often and loudly.

"You're blocking traffic," my date whined.

"Help me," I pleaded with her, as I tried to get a better grip on the struggling snake.

"I hate snakes!" she uttered painfully, all the while trying to slide higher up the back of the seat. Her head was touching the ceiling, but I don't think she noticed.

I glanced in her direction to see if I might be able to get some assistance in my struggle, but it only took a second to see that she was ready to either tear the seat out of the car and beat me to death with it, or open the window and jump out. Something had to give—and it did. I had just got another good grip on old Snake, who had a half-hitch on everything under that dashboard, when a voice thundered from outside the car.

"What's going on in there?"

I tried to twist my head around to see to whom the voice belonged, but the steering wheel, gear-shift lever, and my companion's thrashing feet made that almost impossible. So I just kept pulling gently on my snake.

"What's going on down there?" came the question again, only this time it was more agitated and with considerable authority.

I had a hunch now who was talking and thought it imperative that I do something to acknowledge that I had heard him.

"I'm trying to get my snake!" I grunted, giving the infernal creature another gentle pull.

"You're trying to get your what?" the agitated voice inquired.

"I'm trying to get . . . my . . . snake," I repeated, grunting, shaking my head to get my dinner companion's foot off my ear, all the while pulling on the snake with both hands.

"All right! Out of the car!" the voice ordered.

I almost had the snake moving in the right direction. I could feel him relaxing as I slowly unravelled him from the wires, cables, braces and whatever else those clever Englishmen had put under the dashboard. I didn't want to let him go now.

"Out of the car!!" the voice commanded again, as the door swung open.

Well, someone had to surrender. The horns behind me were blowing pretty loudly. The young lady with me was almost a basket case. I had lost the initiative with the snake who was gaining a new grip on things, and now I thought I was about to be dragged out into the street. So I let go of the snake, and began to unravel myself from the gearshift lever, steering wheel, and thrashing feet. I must admit, it was a relief to stand up straight as I stepped out, but the very angry policeman glaring at me ruined that feeling.

"I'm sorry, officer . . ." I began to mutter, reaching in my back pocket for my wallet to show him my license. Then I noticed he was not looking at me any longer, but at my companion who was still struggling to get out of and over her seat.

"What's going on in there?" he asked again.

"Well, you see. I lost my snake in the car about three weeks ago, and we just found him under the dashboard. I . . ." I wanted to explain this silly situation, but he wasn't listening to all of it. So I thrust my license at him and said, "Here's my license, you want to see it?"

The officer gave me a wicked look and replied "No, I want to see the snake!" With that, he bent down and tried to get a look under the dashboard.

Everything looked like it was very quickly going to hell in a hand basket, especially when the officer's partner unsnapped his gun, looked me right in the eye and asked, "You having a problem, Fred?"

Now anyone who can remember the old Hillman Husky knows it was a very small station wagon. The doors were adequate for entering and escaping—even though my companion apparently hadn't thought of trying it yet. The car was built close to the ground by American standards, and to look inside, a person had to stoop over in a very awkward position. I was standing next to the door, not daring to move, keeping my hands in full view while the policeman was headed for the dashboard.

Please remember the snake. That animal had been handled by at least ten thousand children. He was a gentle soul, had never offered to bite anyone, even when squeezed almost breathless by kindergartners. He had shed into a new skin only two weeks before, was in the pink of health and had a good disposition. I have a feeling he was also very curious—probably why we got along so well together. As the policeman was heading down to see the snake, the snake must have been curious about where I suddenly disappeared to and was on his way out. They met under the dashboard.

"Yeeeeooooooowwwww!" the policeman screamed, yanking his head back and trying to escape the interior of the Hillman. Unfortunately, that was impossible the way he was about it. He bounced off the steering wheel, then slammed his head against the top of the door opening. It only took a second for him to make the trip, but I was watching his partner who was ready to go into action—I thought it was taking an hour. As the policeman stood erect, holding his head, he turned to me and declared, "That is a snake!"

"I told you it was," I replied, trying to smile, but too scared to say much of anything else—an unusual situation for me. I kept my eye on his partner all through this, and was relieved to see his shoulders come down and his hand moving away from his right thigh.

"Do you want to see my license?" I asked above the din of horns.

The look that policeman gave me would have frozen hot water! He stood there, slowly rubbing his head and then said, "Get your car off the road, and get that ---- snake, now!"

I jumped into the car, started the engine, quickly drove across the bridge and onto a side street with the flashing lights directly behind me. As I came to a stop I let out a great sigh, and sort of sagged into the seat. I noticed my companion was also back into her seat, but her feet were jammed against the right side of the interior, and she was staring at the dashboard. I looked at her and grinned—I thought it might help. Then I thought of the snake and opened the door so I could get on its trail again.

This time it only took a few minutes to unravel old Snake from his hold. I think he too was a little relieved to be back in familiar hands. I thought he certainly recognized my chemistry, my odors, my warmth. As I gently lifted him out from the dash I glanced at my companion, fearing she was going to spook like a young colt. I had to admire her

courage for she remained as still as could be, and even managed a brittle smile as I walked to the rear of the station wagon to put the snake in his padded shelter.

It was at that moment that I noticed that the flashing lights were gone, the policemen along with them. I couldn't believe my good fortune. They apparently weren't even angry, or unhappy about the traffic jam I had created. I was slowly shaking my head in wonder, walking back to the car when I looked up just in time to see my lovely dinner companion flagging down a taxi. As she climbed in she shouted, "Thanks for the floor show! Don't call me! I'll call you!"

A Bird in the Hand Should Have Been Left in the Bush

"You'd better do something about that turkey vulture," my wife Harriet said, as she looked out the window at the bird wandering across the tiny lawn of our house on the west side of Portland, Oregon.

I was working as a naturalist for the Oregon Museum of Science & Industry (OMSI), an up-and-coming science education institution, back in the mid-60s, during the glory days of Science Fairs and Sputnik. My position required me to be on the road a great deal: fund raising, conducting field trips, helping to staff science camps, and looking into new outdoor natural history programs to offer the community.

The turkey vulture came into my possession very much like the golden eagles, raccoons, opossums, and barn owls I had to take care of. Usually it was someone who had assumed it was easy to keep wild animals soon tired of the incessant struggle for an adequate and proper diet, and handed them off to me.

In the case of the vulture it was a young man who wanted to use it on a science project he had in mind. He had been a member of a group of about twenty high school kids who were with me on the OMSI bus headed for a marine science camp on the Oregon Coast, near North Bend. South of Cottage Grove, we were about five miles

west of Drain, a lovely little town between Eugene and the Coast, when suddenly one of the boys in the back of the bus shouted, "Hey, Jim! I just saw a big, dark bird walking down the road!"

I glanced in the rear view mirror, and sure enough, just as we were rounding a curve, I had a glimpse of a large bird. I found a place to turn the bus around and headed back the way we had come, and as I approached the place where the bird had been sighted, all the kids stared out of the windows.

"There it is," a girl in the front of the bus shouted, pointing toward a spot near a curve sign.

I slowed the bus down looking at the bird as we rolled by. "My gosh!" she blurted out, "That sure is an ugly thing!"

"It's a young turkey vulture," I announced, slowing up abreast of the vulture who looked up at the bus and stopped. There was no traffic behind me, so I just stopped the bus and hailed the bird.

"Hi there, vulture!" I shouted. "Want a ride to the coast?" The bird just stood there, staring at us.

Before I could drive on, one of the boys leaped out the doorway of the bus, snatched the bird up, and leaped back in. The vulture and I were both surprised.

"Let's take him to camp with us," the boy

said, holding the turkey vulture around the wings and body in a tight grip. At that moment I spotted a logging truck coming around the bend behind us and got the bus rolling down the road quickly, closing the door. The die was cast; we had a vulture to take care of.

All the way to the camp we talked about vultures, their role as nature's cleanup crew, and how important it is for young birds to have not only the proper food, but also plenty of it. A juvenile bird must have all the food and nutrients it requires to build bones, flesh, and feathers. If it is starved for longer than twenty-four hours, a "hunger streak" will appear in the feathers which will weaken them and cause them to break, creating a severe handicap for any young bird fresh out of the nest.

Everyone on the bus promised they would be responsible for the bird and insure its health, which they did faithfully—all the time we were at camp. The vulture gulped down meat scraps from the table, fish parts from the docks, and road-killed rabbits which were barely enough to curb the bird's voracious appetite. It wasn't more than a week before it was in the pink of health, flight feathers growing strongly, and becoming used to being fed by the young people.

It became the pet of the camp. Each new session the young people assumed the responsibility for caring for it. This arrangement worked out beautifully until the last session of camp.

As I was driving back toward Portland with the last busload of kids, I took the vulture along with every thought in mind of releasing it with other vultures, near the place where we found it. However, as we drove back toward Drain, a long discussion began over whether the bird was capable of taking care of itself or not. The majority of the people on the bus voted that it was unable to do so and should be kept in captivity. Even though the vulture was almost capable of flight, it had no idea how to forage for its food, and we had no one on board with the talent to teach it.

However, one boy, a senior from Beaverton, was really impressed with the bird, and said he would like to use it for a science project. He had read that vultures had the ability to find food by using a sense of smell, and wanted to satisfy himself that they really could. We decided the vulture would go off and live in Beaverton. I should have talked to his parents first . . .

As we rolled up to the museum, most of the parents were standing around, waiting for their offspring. I parked the bus and began to climb the ladder to the top where the camping and personal gear was stored in a rack. As I was climbing I heard a loud hissing coming from somewhere inside. Glancing in the windows I spotted the young man from Beaverton chasing the vulture down the aisle, grabbing at it as it wiggled, flapped, and ran under the seats.

This isn't going to work . . . I told myself, but started to unload the bus. As the last pieces of gear were handed down and the crowd of parents and young people began to thin out, I spotted the young man standing in front of two adults showing them the bird.

"Honest, Mom," he was pleading. "I'll take good care of him! I really need it for a science project!" It didn't look like he was very convincing, but he kept at it anyway. "Ask Mr. Anderson. He'll tell you I can take care of it."

I didn't want to get in on this, but suddenly I was, so I walked over and made myself known to the parents. After some lengthy discussion of what the bird would eat, where it would be kept, and how much trouble this was going to be, I could tell the parents were going to go along with the whole idea—but very reluctantly.

"You say that we can bring the—" the women said, glaring at the poor vulture through her bifocals "—bird, over to you if this doesn't work out for Jeffy?"

I assured her she could, but didn't mention that I was hoping the vulture would escape and fly away to Drain before that happened.

The vulture project had lasted almost two weeks—longer than I thought it would— when I was paged from the OMSI admission desk. Someone was at the front door of the museum who wanted to deliver something to me. Walking up to the entrance, I saw the boy's parents standing in front of a well-taped up, big box. I was sure it was the traveling turkey vulture.

"I'm sorry, Mr. Anderson," the man said, apologetically, pushing the box toward me, "but this is just too much for our family to care for, and the odors . . ." He gave me a sheepish grin and added, "I'm sure you understand . . ."

I did, and thanked him for trying and went home with the box full of bird. I didn't need a turkey vulture, but I was the one who was driving the bus. I was the one who went along with the camp pet business. I was the one who agreed that the science project was a good idea, and I did say I would care for the bird. I was stuck with it.

I tried to send it off to the Portland Zoo, across the parking lot from OMSI, but they were long on vultures at that time of the year, having received several in the same way I had. There was no other way, it had to come to SW 75th with me and my family.

"You'd better do something with that vulture," Harriet reminded me again.

I looked out the window at the bird, sitting on an old hawk perch I had, and agreed. But what? I was up to my ears in teacher workshops, classes for young science students, and the Science Fair was coming down the road. I was also about to take on an extra job teaching an eighth grade ecology class at a local private school, Catlin-Gable.

Time was at a premium, and during each week that went by, the vulture was flying more and more. I had rigged it up with jesses, the leather straps falconers use to confine birds, and had it tethered to the comfortable perch. Unfortunately, it was somewhat domesticated, which is saying a great deal for a turkey vulture, and it accepted the food I presented: dead rats, meat scraps, and when I could get it, meat from road-killed deer and rabbits.

"I'll take it to Drain this weekend," I said.

It was about noon when I received a frantic call from my wife, exclaiming, "I can't find the vulture! It's not around the house!"

"Is the leash there?" I asked.

"Yes," she replied. "It must have broken the snap and swivel and flew off."

Thank goodness! I thought to myself, it's not hung up on a wire somewhere, and hopefully it's on its way back to Drain.

That evening when I arrived home I spent several hours searching for the bird, hoping not to find it. I looked under the hedges, around the garage, especially on the roof of the garage, just in case it had tried to cuddle up with the owl I used in my school assemblies, and had got eaten. (My neighbor had been by about two weeks earlier and asked if I had seen his cat. I knew where it was all right. A week before, I had been walking by Owl who was peering down at me from his perch on the roof of the garage.

I looked up and could see he was about to cast up a pellet. So I held out my hand and caught it. I had never caught an owl pellet before and thought that was a neat experience, but as I looked at it I suddenly became alarmed. It was not made up of lab rat fur, the diet he was on. It was an angora color. It could only have been one thing, so I climbed up on the roof of the garage and looked around. Sure enough, stuffed away in a dark corner were the remains of my neighbor's cat. I told my neighbor that the last time I saw his cat it was over here for dinner. He didn't pursue it, and I wasn't about to . . .)

Several days went by and the vulture vanished from my thoughts. I was pretty certain it had flown away to Drain, taking the leather jesses with it, which would rot off by the end of winter. In my mind's eye I could see the bird soaring away to the south, joining its relatives for the long flight down to Sacramento or the Imperial Valley of California where many of the vultures from the Northwest spend the winter. The OMSI switchboard operator ruined that image when I answered the phone and heard my wife's alarmed plea, "There's a very angry State Police Officer here who wants to see you—right now!"

It just didn't seem like a good idea to keep an angry policeman waiting, so I dropped what I was doing and dashed over to my house, located only about five minutes from OMSI. As I came through the front door, I was greeted by a police officer who was indeed, very upset.

"Mr. Anderson," he asked, with a grave look, "do you have a turkey vulture?"

Oh! oh! I thought, that poor bird has come back to haunt me. "No, I don't have a vulture," I answered, hoping for the best.

"Let me rephrase that question," he said, holding up bandaged hands. "Did you have a turkey vulture?"

Now we're getting technical, I thought, but truth is truth. "Yes, I did," I replied, trying to avoid looking at his hands. "Umm . . . do you have a turkey vulture?" I asked.

He glared at me for a few moments, then raising his hands so that I couldn't miss the bandages, he said, "No, I don't have it any more. It's over at the zoo now. I received a complaint from a woman that lives about two blocks from you who heard something knocking at her door. Guess what was standing on her doorstep?"

"The vulture," I replied.

"Yes, the vulture," he replied. "It about scared her half to death, and she called the office. When I got there the bird wasn't around, but after a search I found it in her garage, eating dog food. When I tried to pick it up, it tore my hands up like this." he said, waving his bandaged hands. Then he asked the million dollar question, "Mr. Anderson, do you have a permit to keep a turkey vulture?"

I got that sinking feeling most people probably get when they know they are about to find themselves on the wrong side of the law. "I don't think I do . . ." I replied, adding quickly, "But I do have one for the owl." I never cease to be amazed at the patience police officers demonstrate in situations like this.

"I'm sorry, Mr. Anderson," he apologized, taking his ticket book from under his arm. "I'm going to cite you for having a turkey vulture without a permit."

He almost reminded me of one of the Keystone Cops as he fumbled with the ticket book, trying to write with his bandaged fingers. I also realized it was sheer madness on my part to even smile, and I really did feel sorry for him—but I must admit, I would have laughed—if he had laughed. I had been beaten by vultures, eagles, hawks, owls, and kicked by cows. I knew the pain he was in. "I hope you're taking good care of those hands," I offered. "Those birds carry some pretty bad germs in their beaks and feet."

"Thank you," he said, without a hint of a smile, handing me the citation. "I'm undergoing treatment from the doctor once a day. He said the same thing." Then he pointed to the ticket and added, "I tried to set your appearance at a convenient time for you, in the Beaverton court house."

The following Wednesday I appeared before the circuit court judge with my turkey vulture citation in hand. As I walked up to the front of the bench I introduced myself, and I'll never forget the judge's remark.

"Oh, yes," he replied. "You're the one who keeps vultures . . . I keep chickens myself." I thought that was a good beginning for what could have been an unhappy ending. The judge was very understanding when I explained how I had come by the vulture, and what I had done with it in Drain that weekend.

"I understand, Mr. Anderson," he replied. "Perhaps you should get the proper permits very soon." Then he laughed. "You never know, you may end up with a bear." He let me off without a fine.

I thought I was through with turkey vultures for a while, but Mother Nature, and Reub Long had other ideas. Reub was from the Fort Rock country, located out on the high desert of Oregon. He was writing a book about the Oregon desert, in cooperation with Mr. E.R. Jackman, a retired professor from OSU who gave me a call and asked if I had some photos that might be suitable for their book. I thought that would be a lot of fun, so I packed up all the stuff I had on the high desert and gave it to Reub and Jack to pick from. About two days later I got a call from Mr. Jackman, asking if I would come down to their hotel in Portland and talk about the photos. We sat in the room while I told them about the various animals, flowers, and other subjects they wanted to use in the book. Then we got to the turkey vulture photos.

"I just don't know, Jimmy," Mr. Jackman began, shaking his head, "I want to use a photo of a buzzard in the book, but I can't find anything I think is appropriate."

Turkey vulture on Reub Long's horse skull.

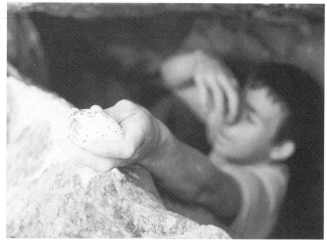

Roger Watkins gags from the nest odor as he shows a turkey vulture egg near Powell Buttes.

Juvenile turkey vulture tries out his wings while perched on old fence post.

"Holy cats, Jack," I stammered. "I've given you at least thirty pictures of buzzards, look at them all." I picked up the sleeves holding the transparencies, raising it to the light. "Here's one of a vulture sunning itself on a fencepost; here's another flying; here's a bunch of them on the tower at French Glen . . . how about this one?" I said, picking a photo of a juvenile vulture standing on a fence post.

"No . . . .," he said, slowly. "I don't think that one will do . . . I really don't know what I'm looking for. Do you have any ideas?"

I didn't know what to say, I was so frustrated. Then I muttered, "I suppose you want a picture of a buzzard standing on a bleached out old skull of one of Reub's damned horses!"

"That's it!" Jack exclaimed.

"I know where there's an old skull, Jimmy," Reub piped up, giving me a lop-sided grin.

"Me and my big mouth," I complained, laughing. "OK, I'll go out on the Silver Lake road, set out a road-killed deer and when a vulture is packed full, I catch it and shoot a picture of it standing on your horse skull. Will that make you happy?"

"That will do it, I'm sure," Mr. Jackman said. "But you'd better hurry. I think the publisher is getting nervous with us. They may think we were only fooling about doing a book."

All you can see are George Gates' feet as he crawls into the turkey vulture cave nest.

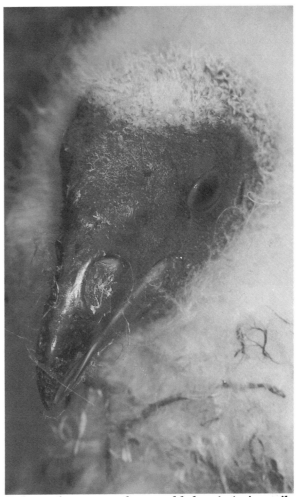

Only a face a mother could love! A juvenile turkey vulture.

George and Jim band turkey vultures.

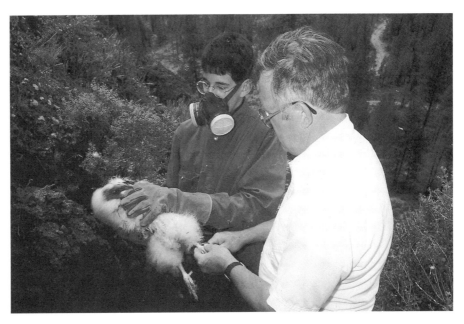

For the next four days I tried every way possible to catch a turkey vulture. I set out road-killed deer along the side of the road, where deer were being run over frequently. I parked my Hillman a long way away, and I watched with my binoculars as magpies, ravens, hawks, eagles, and turkey vultures free-loaded. I even placed the bleached out horse skull nearby, hoping a vulture would perch on it and I'd get the photo with my trusty 500 mm Pentax lens. But I got impatient.

Each time the vultures got filled up I would dash down the road with the car, leap out and try to catch one with a big salmon net. The magpies would see me coming and spook everything else as they started squawking and flying off. I gave it the best I had, slipping and sliding in the offal the vultures upchucked as they hopped and flapped along the road, trying to rid themselves of the food so they could fly. After several days of this nonsense I decided the birds had got the best of me, and I headed back toward Bend, defeated.

I had lived in Bend for several years, before moving to Portland to join OMSI, and as I was approaching the city I suddenly remembered seeing young vultures on the west side of town, just outside the city limits where I had worked for a pumice mining outfit. I could picture the little draw they were in perfectly, and headed out that way.

As I slowly drove west on the old Skyliner's Road, I spotted the draw I had seen the vultures in years before. I got out of the car, reached in for the old, bleached-out, horse skull, grabbed up my camera, and walked up the draw. I know this sounds unbelievable, but it's true. There was a young turkey vulture standing on a rock, about twenty feet away! I placed the skull on a rock in the sunlight, grasped the bird firmly around the wings and body, set it on the skull and shot three pictures before it had enough of me and flew off.

As soon as the photos were developed, I took them to Corvallis, where Mr. Jackman lived, and showed them to him. "That's perfect, Jimmy!" he exclaimed happily, holding the transparencies up to the light. "I'll use this one, right here."

Young turkey vulture peers curiously at Jim after being banded at The Rock in the Deschutes National Forest.

The photo he picked is in Reub and Jack's book, *The Oregon Desert*, published by Caxton Printers of Caldwell, Idaho.

Throughout the years the turkey vulture has sparked interest among avian biologists, and naturalists like myself. I've always been curious about the longevity of the vultures that nest in the Central Oregon area. Where do they winter? Do the same vultures who nest near Bend come back and nest here again the following year? What is the biggest threat facing vultures? Are they electrocuted the way eagles and hawks are? Do people shoot vultures? All of these answers, and more data could be collected from a banding project.

In other areas of the country various bird banders have placed a US Fish & Wildlife band on the birds, but over the years biologists found serious problems with the bands. Turkey vultures feed on carrion; that's the primary advantage of their "bald" heads. There are no feathers that will be fouled as they stick their heads into the body cavity of a cow that's been lying in the summer sun for two weeks. It was that business of walking around in rotting flesh that put a stop to banding vultures. The offal would get stuck beneath the band and cause serious infections to the bird, sometimes causing death. Because of this, a moratorium has been placed on banding turkey vultures. Prior to the moratorium I was banding all the vultures I could in an attempt to answer the many questions I had about their natural history. I thought it would be wise to have a file started on the vultures of this area in the event a land manipulation project came along that had the potential of impacting the welfare of the birds.

There used to be a large turkey vulture colony that nested on the lava flow cliffs in the Cove, along the Deschutes River, near Madras, but when Lake Billy Chinook was formed behind a dam, the ancestral nesting area was flooded. I had to beat the brush, literally, to find vultures to band.

Apparently a turkey vulture is somewhat like a killdeer when it comes to nest site selection. Just about the time the female is about to lay an egg she starts looking for a place to put it. If there's a hollow log nearby and she can fit into it, that's the nest. If the hollow is too small, then she'll nest behind it, or under some brush next to it. If a cliff is handy that's OK too. One of the places I found that was ideal for a turkey vulture to nest in was a pile of lava rock on the Deschutes National Forest known as The Rock.

I was doing my annual, aerial Osprey survey on the Bend District of the Deschutes which took me right over The Rock. I had a homebuilt aircraft that was ideal for the job, a Stits Flut-r-bug that I had converted to a tail-dragger. It had a sixty-five horsepower Continental engine with a metal prop, would

The lookout tower at the Malheur National Wildlife Refuge is a favorite roosting spot of turkey vultures.

fly low and slow, and had a big closed cockpit that afforded a great view as I circled over the nests. Osprey usually build their huge stick nests right in the very top of a tree, which gave me a good opportunity to count eggs and young. As I flew over The Rock I spotted a turkey vulture which appeared suddenly from the lava, and I knew it had a nest there.

George Gates and I were conducting an Osprey/cormorant study at the time on Crane Prairie Reservoir, about ten miles away from The Rock. After a day of climbing trees, banding Osprey and collecting cormorant food remains, we stopped by The Rock to see if we could find the vultures' nest. It only took a few moments to find the small lava cave the birds were using. We smelled it long before we saw it.

According to the literature, vultures apparently locate food by scent long before they see it. That small lava tube had a smell that would gag a maggot. The first turkey vultures I banded were a long time ago, and I did them myself. A nestling vulture is something to respect. They can bite, tear with their sharp talons, and be downright unpleasant. As my sons got older they took over the responsibility of banding, while I did the bookkeeping. That day my two boys were off doing their own thing and George was it. I had brought along a breathing mask for him to put on as he scrambled into the tube to bring the nestlings out. I also equipped him with goggles to keep the dry vulture poop out of his eyes. He dressed in a set of stout coveralls, put on welder's gloves, tied his pants legs and sleeves tight to keep out the dirt, and started crawling into the cave.

I had to give those birds credit, they had picked a cave that was almost inaccessible. George went in as far as he could squeeze and had to stop about a finger's length away from reaching the three young birds hunched in the very back of the tube. "I can't reach them . . ." he grunted. I got down and looked into the cave but all I could see was the bottoms of his size eleven boots. I let him slither back out while I went back to our pickup and returned with a length of baling wire from my tool box which I bent into a "chicken snatcher" and he crawled back in. That did the trick, he was able to snag each bird around the leg, and haul them out.

We banded all three and let each one run back into its lair. George was pretty upset by the awful pile of rotting offal that the adults had taken back into the cave for the young to feed on. Even with the breathing mask I guess it was pretty hard to take.

"George," I said. "I've never asked anyone to do something that I hadn't all ready done."

"That's easy for you to say," George laughed as he removed the mask, took a breath of fresh air, and watched the fuzzy little turkey vulture scramble back into its smelly cave.

Miss that Snake!

The "Sputnik Years" were exciting for our nation. Science was in, and the Oregon Museum of Science & Industry (OMSI) was determined to serve the Portland area community in every way possible. Science fairs ran amok among the schools. The final competition found the museum swamped with exhibits from every sphere of science, and still the education staff felt there was more to do—and we did.

I was the staff naturalist during those golden years, which meant that I conducted all the outdoor science activities. One of the many services we offered the schools was a guided tour from Portland up the Columbia Gorge to the Maryhill Museum, across the river from Biggs Junction, then back down the Washington side to Cascade Locks, west of Hood River and then back to Portland via Highway 30.

I was often asked to give nature talks and fund-raising pitches for many organizations, schools, and service clubs throughout the community. On a typical day I would take my traveling nature show and do school assemblies in the morning, and a service club luncheon at lunchtime. Then in the afternoon I'd do another school assembly, and rush back to the museum for a teacher in-service work shop. In the evening I would give a talk to a PTA, and on more than one occasion, do two PTA talks in one evening, rushing between schools.

OMSI was on a roll in those days. Science education had a high profile, and was a large part of the overall school curriculum as teachers and students met President Kennedy's challenge to outrun Russia in space. It was necessary for everyone at the museum to go the extra mile in order to fulfill the programs we offered to the community. Loren McKinley was the director in those days, and Ray Barrett was the education director, and a better team never existed.

Ray could come up with more programs for students and teachers in five minutes than most other educators could in a week. He also had the capacity to listen and the imagination to see how a program would meet the educational goals of the community. There was rarely a time when he didn't listen to one of my ideas for an outdoor natural history educational project and give it his OK. We always made certain we gave Dorothy Mason, our secretary and helper, the opportunity to polish the rough spots and make the program run smoothly.

The dynamo head man, Loren McKinley was a genius at shaking the money trees of the Portland area to get enough money for us to give the science students what they needed—and wanted. That's the way we obtained a contract from a school district in eastern Portland for a series of field trips up the Columbia Gorge for eighth graders. Instead of using the OMSI bus, the school system decided to use their bus and driver, saving insurance and costs, and giving me more freedom to talk about the geology, history, and natural wonders of the Gorge.

It was important to establish clear behavior patterns and educational standards on the first trip, so when I got to the bus for the first trip I was a taskmaster, setting some tough goals for the kids, as well as for myself. I explained the route to the bus driver, a short, tough-talking woman who had apparently been driving buses for years.

A trip up the Columbia River Gorge from Portland is exciting and filled with interests from all aspects of nature. The geology of the gorge is spectacular, and waterfalls and scenic wonders abound. I used a trip-guide, written by Dr. John Allen, head of the geology department of Portland State University to interpret the geology and selected historical features of the gorge. I knew a great deal about the natural history and was able to pass along many of these subjects to the eighth graders.

The main theme of the program revolved about the conservation ethic. While I always used the "holy-cow, gee-whiz" approach to teaching, I hit the conservation issues with more emphasis. I was hoping to bring the kids back with a new sense of appreciation for the variety of resources that could be found in the Columbia Gorge, and the world about them.

When we reached Biggs Junction, about 100 miles from Portland, we'd cross the Columbia on the Sam Hill Bridge and travel up to the Maryhill Museum, located on the Washington side of the gorge. There's a beautiful replica of Stonehenge close to Maryhill Museum, which was also on the itinerary. (As far as I know it is the only replica of Stonehenge in the country.) In those days the road from the Sam Hill Bridge went through the tiny railroad community of Maryhill, and then up a steep grade to a road on the flood plain high above the Columbia. (The old road was subsequently destroyed by a huge flood in the winter of '62.)

Maryhill Museum is a wonderful institution. It seems strange to find an art and history museum of its stature so far from any central city, out in the middle of nowhere, so-to-speak. The old, early 1900s building itself stands alone against the stark, wind-blown grassland of the Columbia steppes. The museum exhibits range from pieces by Rodin to beautiful tools and clothing of the Klickitat Nation, Native American people who once roamed the grasslands of central Oregon and Washington. This segment of our tour always excited the kids and provided many of them with their first visit to a museum of this stature and varied interests. I can still recall the giggles of the girls and the gawking of the boys as we walked into the foyer of the museum where we were greeted by a beautiful marble statue of Diana, the Huntress—without any clothes on.

After leaving Maryhill, we'd slowly return to Portland down the Washington side to the Bridge of the Gods at Cascade Locks, where we'd park the bus and I would tell the Indian legend of Mount Hood and Mount Adams.

One of the places I always stopped was at a small roadside lake not too many miles out of Portland where the hatchery at Bonneville

Locks held about 100,000 salmon for release. This was the site of an environmental disaster that took place in the early '60s when a crew from the Oregon Highway Department came by spraying weeds and killed almost all the fish in the lake. I never failed to tell that story, and used the incident to expand on the dangers from chemicals used throughout our environment, and especially in foods.

I was pretty pleased when I returned from that first trip. The principal of the school was on hand as we rolled into the school yard, and as the kids got off the bus, he grilled them at random, asking questions about the geology, history, arts, and the natural history of the gorge. I must admit, those eighth graders got more than I thought they were hearing. That evening I reported to Ray and Loren, and bragged about how the kids had picked up so much. I thought we had a good thing going.

The trips were scheduled every other day, which meant Wednesday was my next trip. I got to the bus a little early that morning, and discussed a few small changes in the itinerary with the driver. We chatted about the new stops, among them a chance to spend more time talking about the geology of a small island where rock had been removed for the big jetty at Astoria, and another small island in the middle of the Columbia where many of our Native Americans were buried. All went along smoothly until we crossed the river at Biggs Junction.

I was standing in the front of the bus, where the PA speaker was available, and I could point out the various features of the gorge as we traveled along the route. It was a splendid day in April, perfect for enjoying the beautiful balsam root and lupines that were coloring the slopes with golden-yellow and blue. The tiny town of Maryhill looked almost idyllic in the late morning sun. Just as we were rolling into town, I noticed an unbelievably long gopher snake lying across the rode just ahead of us and called it to the driver's attention. "Do you see that snake ahead?" I asked quietly.

"I see it," she answered.

The distance closed quickly as the big,

yellow bus rolled along on a direct course, heading right for the snake. Suddenly it occurred to me she wasn't going to turn aside, or even make an attempt to avoid the snake. "MISS THAT SNAKE!!" I shouted.

"I hate snakes . . ." the driver grunted through clenched teeth, and drove the bus right across the middle of that beautiful gopher snake!

I couldn't believe it . . . I stared at her in disbelief. As she turned to me I could see a grin on her face. She had done something she was really proud of—and every kid on the bus knew it. "Stop the bus!" I shouted.

"Why?" she asked.

"Stop the bus!" I shouted again, throwing the lever over that opened the folding door. That got her attention. She stomped down on the brake pedal and the bus skidded to a halt as I leaped out the door. Running back I could see the snake thrashing on the road, mortally wounded by the three, big tires that had rolled over it. I stood there looking down at that beautiful animal, and I'm not ashamed to tell you today that tears streamed from my eyes. What a tragic waste, I said to myself. This beautiful animal had been lying on the warm road trying to digest the two gophers that were now lying alongside the remains of its insides, when—Wham! Life ended.

I picked up the writhing snake as carefully as I could and slowly walked back toward the bus. As I came alongside I was conscious of every kid on the bus looking at me. The closer I got to the front door the more angry I became, and as I started up the steps I looked at the driver and let fly. I rarely used profanity when I was around kids—and don't use it today—but that day I had been betrayed, and I was holding the harmless victim of that betrayal.

"You haven't been listening to one damn word I've said about respect for Nature—have you?" I thundered at the driver. She sat there, stunned, not having the slightest idea that she had done something wrong. She must have been driving over snakes all her life. "Look at this animal!" I shouted, "Look at it!!" I shoved the snake close to her face.

"Get that away from me!" she screamed, trying to leap out of her seat.

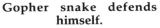
Gopher snake defends himself.

"Don't worry," I said, backing away and turning to the kids. "You see this snake?" I asked, holding up the now lifeless body. "This is a gopher snake, a harmless animal that does more good for man than probably any other snake in this area. It not only eats gophers and other rodents, but it is also known to eat rattlesnakes." I turned so the driver could hear the word, "rattlesnake" very plainly. "This snake was lying on the road," I continued, "digesting two gophers it had eaten sometime last night. It could never do any harm to anyone, and yet, this . . ." and I turned to face the driver, ". . . this . . . this . . . misguided woman drove right over it without even giving it a thought! She hasn't paid one bit of attention to anything I've said about conservation and the importance of ecological thinking when dealing with all aspects of our world." Then I walked back and glared at her, saying, "She just hates snakes . . ."

The driver knew she was in trouble. She could see the kids' faces reflecting back in the big mirror over her head. Not a one of them was friendly. "I . . . I . . . I'm sorry," she muttered.

"So am I," I grumbled, and stepped off the bus to place the snake's body in a patch of balsam root flowers alongside the road. As I turned to get back on the bus I was suddenly overwhelmed again with image of that beautiful reptile writhing on the road. I knew I couldn't go another mile on that bus. I stepped in, picked up my daypack, books, and binoculars, and stepped out to the road.

"Where are you going?" the driver asked.

"I'm going to walk home," I said. "I'm not going to ride another foot with you. There is no way I'll go with anyone who is so blindly stupid about the need to understand and protect all forms of life, whether you like them or not . . ."

"You have to go the rest of the way with us," she wailed.

"The hell I do, lady!" I shouted. "You take this bus back to the school, and you tell the principal why I'm not on it. I won't go another mile with you!"

"You can't leave!" she shouted again, stepping over to the door.

"I have," I said over my shoulder and started walking back toward the Columbia and the Sam Hill Bridge.

"You come back here!" she commanded once more, but I was long gone by then, knowing I had made my point with every one of those kids on the bus.

As I walked up to the toll booth I wondered how much money I had in my pocket, and how I was going to get back to Portland, over 100 miles away. It cost fifty cents to walk across the bridge in those days. It was a great hike watching gulls soaring overhead and mergansers in the Columbia as I slowly walked over the bridge back into Oregon. When I got about half way I turned and looked up on the flood plain far above and watched the yellow bus slowly heading west, toward the Maryhill Museum. I still felt vindicated as I stepped back into Oregon at Biggs Junction. Now what, I said to myself.

The Columbia River Highway, US Route 30, is a major artery where trucks coming from north and south meet trucks going east and west at Biggs Junction. I walked west, along the route to Portland, stuck out my thumb, and smiled as trucks and cars whizzed by without even slowing down.

Suddenly I began to hear Loren McKinley's voice in my mind . . ."You got off the bus because the driver did what . . .?" Then I could see Ray's face, pouting a little as he tried to understand my outlandish behavior. Then I saw the face of the school principal beginning to focus when suddenly I heard the hiss of airbrakes and a familiar voice shouted, "Hey! That you Jim Anderson?"

I looked up and could see a Bend-Portland Transfer rig stopped on the highway shoulder ahead and an old friend and horseman from Bend was standing on the running board. "Want a lift?" he asked.

"I sure appreciate this," I said, as he went up the gears putting the big rig in motion toward Portland. We talked about Bend and the old friends we knew, then he got around to asking me what I was doing thumbing a ride to Portland. I must admit, even with the memory of that beautiful, snake still vivid in my mind, my explanation of why I was afoot didn't sound too convincing to me. He was quiet as I tried to explain what had taken place, stumbling along. At last, I finished my tale and sat back, relieved.

He glanced over at me and grinned, "I'll be damned. Wait 'til I tell Old Dean about that . . ." Then he started to laugh. Each time he looked over at me, he laughed all the harder. "You left the bus . . . because . . ." he laughed, and then tried to watch where he was going. "Oh, Jimmy," he said. "You're really something . . ."

As it was, I arrived back in Portland long before the bus did. I took a cab up to the school parking lot where I quietly drove my car back to the museum. I knew I was going to have to tell someone about what happened, and it would be best to do it before the news arrived secondhand. With that thought in my mind, I walked into Loren's office and sat down.

"Loren," I said, "I've got a story to tell you . . ."

Loren sat there, quietly listening to every word, every once in a while nodding his head. As with my friend in the truck, I had a tough time sounding convincing, but I did my best, and ended my story with a positive thought about how much the kids learned by my leaving the bus.

"No doubt," he said, "those kids will never forget this day!" Then he looked at me and grinned for the first time. "I don't think anyone will!" He picked up the phone, called Ray Barrett and asked him to come into the office. "Now you tell him what you told me," Loren laughed.

The next day we received a phone call from the school principal with an apology for the behavior of their driver. There was no mention about cancelling the trips or shortening the program. Apparently we were going to do business as usual. When I arrived on Friday, I walked onto the bus to find the new batch of kids already on board and a new driver. As I was placing my daypack on the front seat, the new driver said in a clear voice, "I like snakes!" All the kids cheered. It was going to be good day.

Who's Flyin' That Thing?

"Jim, you'd better get down here and get this golden eagle out of my office before Jack trades it off for a monkey!" the zoo veterinarian, Dr. Matt Maberry, exclaimed over the telephone.

"OK, I'll be right down, Matt," I answered, pushing the receiver button down and dialing the switchboard operator. "Barbara, this is Jim—is Ray there? I just received a call from Dr. Maberry down at the zoo. He's got a golden eagle that should be released back to the wild and wants me to come down and get it immediately. I'd like to see if Ray will let me get away for the rest of the day." I waited while she connected me up with Ray Barrett, the Director of Education for the Oregon Museum of Science and Industry (OMSI), a museum in Portland, Oregon where I was employed as the staff naturalist.

"Hi, Jim," Ray's voice came over the phone. "What's up?"

I told him about Dr. Maberry's phone call and what might happen to the eagle if it weren't released as soon as possible. "You say you're going to use your Piper Cub to take it back over to Central Oregon and release it?" Ray asked. "Isn't that dangerous? That's over 120 miles from here, and if my math is correct, it's going to take you two hours to just fly that little airplane over the Cascades—one way—you're sure you can keep that bird quiet on such a long trip?" He hesitated. "What happens if it gets loose in the plane?" I assured him I knew how to handle the situation. "OK, Jim," Ray replied, "but you be careful!"

I thanked him and was just gathering up my jacket and hat when the phone rang again. "Jim! This is Matt. You'd better get right down here; Jack was just in here giving that eagle the eye and he's gone back to call his animal dealer over in Vancouver. You know what that could mean."

"I'm on my way!" I said, dropping the receiver onto the phone and heading for the door.

Dr. Maberry's office was located right next door to Jack Marks' office, the director of the zoo, and as I ran through the door Matt put his finger to his lips in a sign to be quiet. As he softly closed the door he turned, and pointing to a large box by the door, he said, "This bird was picked up across from the Warm Springs Indian Reservation along the Deschutes River. It had apparently hit something, the right wing was damaged, but not too badly. We've been caring for it for a month now, and from what I can see in the x-rays and the way it can move that wing, I think it will be OK." He walked over to the large cardboard box and slowly opened the lid, "What do you think. Is it a female?"

Taking a quick look, I could see a huge, golden eagle staring at us with those piercing eyes, its head feathers erect, a sign of alarm and anger. "It sure is a big one, Matt," I responded. "Yeah, I think it's a female, for sure." I was just about to take a closer look when the bird suddenly tried to leap out of the box. "Look out!" I shouted, as Matt slammed the lids closed, forcing her back into the box. "That was close!" I exclaimed, helping him to fold the lids back into place. "Did you see the large white patch at the base of her tail?" I asked.

"Yes, I noticed that when we were working on her," Matt replied. "She's a juvenile isn't she?"

"I'd say so," I replied, "probably last year's bird. You know . . . that's what my banding returns have shown. A young eagle less than three years of age is more likely to get into trouble than an older, experienced one."

Dr. Maberry snorted, "Yeah, sort of like people aren't they? A kid just learning to drive and might be going too fast is more apt to get into a wreck than someone who is older, and with a great deal more experience."

"Yeah, Matt," I said. "Speed can kill . . . whether you're an eagle or a human."

We would probably have gotten into another of our philosophical discussions I enjoyed so much if there hadn't come a loud knock on the door. "Doc, you in there?"

"It's Jack . . ." Matt said. "Give me a hand with this tape and we'll seal the box right now and you can get it out of here. Just a minute, Jack!" he shouted.

"Holy cats, Matt!" I rasped, "I can't take that eagle across the mountains in a cardboard box. She'll tear it to pieces before I can get there!"

"Sorry, Jim," Matt replied, handing me the tape. "It's now or never—" then grinning, he said, "—what you see is what you get!"

"What the hell are you doing?" Jack angrily shouted from out in the hall. "Oh, forget it, I'll be back when you're not so busy!" he grumbled and we heard him go stomping back down the hall to his office.

"That's it, Jim," Matt said, sticking the last bit of shipping tape to the side of the box, "You want me to cut some air holes in the box?"

"Yeah, but make 'em small. And only on the top!" I replied, looking at the box with apprehension.

In a few moments, we were out the door and the box was in the back of my little Hillman Husky station wagon. I closed the back door and was just getting in when Matt came over to the passenger's side and opened the door. Poking his head in, he gave me one of his big grins that I miss so much today, and saluting me he said, "Happy Landings!"

I kept my little, yellow Piper Cub at a small airport located in those days in downtown Beaverton, where it was close to the museum and close to home. The trip from the zoo to the airfield only took about fifteen minutes. On the way I stopped at several stores looking for a better box, but couldn't find anything stronger then I already had. As I drove into the airport and parked my car I glanced over to the east, and could see big, white, puffy clouds building up. I had been flying around Oregon for several years, and clouds like those, early in the morning at that time of the year, usually meant thunderstorms by late afternoon. I wanted to be back home long before things got wild and wooly. I didn't want to use anymore time looking for something better to put the

eagle in, so looking the box over once more I talked myself into the idea that all was well—no problem . . .

When I called the Flight Service Station to check weather, the briefer verified what I had expected: thunderstorms forecasted for late afternoon. I filed a flight plan from Beaverton to Lake Billy Chinook, where the State of Oregon has a 5,000 feet, dirt strip. I looked the box over once more, loaded the eagle, and took off for the dry side of the Oregon Country.

It was an absolutely beautiful ride up the Clakamas River drainage, over the clear cuts of the Willamette National Forest (I find clear-cuts offensive to this day—even though the haul roads would make a good place to land in the case of an engine failure . . .), and past the north flanks of one of my favorite volcanoes, 11,000 feet Mount Jefferson.

I was just beginning to make out the outline of the Deschutes River canyons west of Madras when I turned around the hundredth time to see if all was well in the back end of the Cub. It wasn't!

"Oh, no!" I groaned aloud. The eagle had been picking away at the wall of the box and had managed to get a hole started. Over the next half hour things went from bad to worse as I watched the hole get bigger. Instinctively, I looked for some place to land, but no clear cuts or roads were in sight. Nothing but beautiful Douglas fir with scattered western red cedar, hemlock, lodgepole pine, and small, hidden lakes.

"Blast!" I shouted. Each time I turned to look at the box my skin would crawl . . . "I'm not going to make it! Eagle!—" I shouted, "—stay in that box! Please!!" That's when I transferred some of my altitude into airspeed. Gently pushing the stick forward, I opened the throttle all the way, and hightailed it for the Lake Billy Chinook strip.

The Piper Cub is, in my opinion, one of the most wonderful airplanes ever built. I leaned to fly in one, and have flown that aircraft with a variety of engines. I used to fly a surplus WWII military version to haul freight, which had a ninety horsepower engine and metal prop. That little machine could get in and out of short strips and rough roads with a wide margin of safety. I even hauled a calf in the back of it—once. However, the one I owned at that moment was a stock 1947 Cub with a tired sixty-five horsepower engine and wooden prop. Downhill and wide open, the best I could get was ninety miles per hour, which was really pushing it more than was good for her. I kept the petal to the metal and pointed her nose straight for Lake Billy Chinook.

Each time I looked in the back I could see more eagle. First it had been just the beak and the eye; now I could see the entire head as she thrust it out of the hole, chirping and looking wildly for some place to escape. "Three more minutes!" I shouted above the din, diving for the field. I looked all around to make sure no one else was heading for the same place . . . "Murphy's Law" can get a person in situations like this, one problem developing into another one. I looked everywhere to make sure no one else was making the crazy approach I was to get on the ground in a hurry. "Hang on, eagle!" I shouted, as we lined up with the runway, still going like a bat out of hell. As an old logger pal used to say, "I was as nervous as a pregnant fox in a forest fire!"

When I knew we had the strip made, I began to throttle back, trying to slow down. As things got a little quieter I could hear the unmistakable sound of cardboard being torn to shreds. I turned for one last look and about swallowed my Adam's apple; the eagle was almost out of the box!

"Blast!" I shouted again, and with one hand on the stick I opened the double doors on the right side of the cockpit, first the upper one that latched into a catch on the lower part of the wing, then the lower one that dropped against the side of the fuselage. If the bird got completely out, I hoped it would just leap out of the side door and be gone.

The aroma of sagebrush and juniper filled the cockpit as the doors opened, a smell that always fills me with a sense of well-being. I knew we were going to make it in safely. We were still going pretty fast, so I put the little Cub into a hard side-slip to lose more airspeed. At the last moment I straightened the plane up and we dropped onto the dirt strip, but we didn't stay down long. I was still too hot and the little Cub just floated back up again, wanting to fly on ground-effect. I kicked the rudder hard, left and right, using it as an air brake, and we dropped down again to the dirt, and stayed there rolling along. At that moment the eagle slapped the back of my head with her powerful wing, then I caught the awful stench of an eagle's breath.

"She's out!" I shouted, and switched off the engine and fuel.

The poor eagle had no idea I was even in the cockpit. All she could see was blue sky, juniper, and sagebrush. She was home and she knew it. With no regard for where she was, she began battling her way toward the side door. That was enough for me! The airplane had almost stopped so I bailed out first. I hit the ground and rolled to avoid the horizontal stabilizer, then jumped up, watching my little Cub slowly rolling down the runway.

A second later the eagle came flapping out the door. She also did a full flip as she hit the runway and rolled over. Scrambling to her feet, she looked at me and decided that wasn't the way to go. She turned and started running, then hopping, and finally flapping down the runway. Unfortunately, her muscles weren't toned up due to her long time recovering from her injury, so she couldn't get up enough steam to fly, but she made a brave attempt at it. The last time I saw the eagle, she was going for all she was worth down the long, dirt runway, her head thrust way out ahead of her as she made a supreme effort to get airborne. At the end of the runway, she turned off into some junipers and vanished from sight.

The Cub slowly rolled to a stop, her tail swinging around, as if to look back at me, wondering what was going on. I was very thankful that there were no holes in me, no bent pieces on my Cub, and the eagle was out of the plane safely. As I was slowly walking up to the airplane, a voice behind me asked, "Say. Who was flyin' that thing?"

I turned around to see an older man standing there, grinning from ear to ear, "We both were," I answered. Then I introduced myself and explained what the airshow had been all about.

"Hi, Jim," he said, as we shook hands laughing. "I'm John Hinchey. I run the store over there," he continued, pointing to some buildings near the wind sock. We spent a few moments discussing birds, flying, and the beautiful land he had built his home and business in. Then, looking at the ominous clouds all about us, I asked him if he would keep an eye out for the eagle, leaving instructions that if it got into any trouble, please to call me or Dr. Maberry.

I beat the thunderstorms back to Beaverton that evening, arriving home just in time for dinner. As I walked in the house, the phone was ringing.

"How was the trip?" a familiar voice asked.

"Just fine, doc," I replied, "but wait 'til I tell you about your eagle packaging skills." I laughed and explained what had happened.

As I finished my story I could hear him chuckling. "That's OK, wait 'till we go over to Pendleton next week in my Mooney. You'll have a chance to get even; we're going to haul some peacocks back . . ."

Two weeks later I received a phone call from John Hinchey who was all excited about a big golden eagle he had been seeing for the past week, soaring along the rim of the canyons adjacent to the store. "Do you think that's your eagle?" he asked.

"Might be, John," I replied. "But I think that eagle belongs to nature now, and let's hope it stays that way." We passed some more time, and I promised to come and see him again. As I hung up the phone, I said a silent prayer of thanks for the eagle, Dr. Maberry . . . and the old Piper Cub.

More About Owls

Owls and I just seem to have a good time together. In spite of the fact that my earliest introduction to them was having to eat one for shooting it (or perhaps because of that experience), I really find myself attracted to owls. As it is with your human family, you're not supposed to have favorites, but in spite of that well-known error in judgement, we always seem to be attracted to one of the kids just a little more than the others. Oh, we love them all! But one is sort of . . . well . . . "Special." I guess the Great Horned is the one that qualifies for me.

"Owl," the Great Horned wh-o-o-o-o shared school programs with me, spent most of his time sleeping on a perch I had on my office desk at OMSI, or on a perch next to my home garage near Portland. He was a constant source of wonder to visitors and staff alike. One day a salesman was walking past my office and glanced in.

"That's a terrible job of stuffing an owl," he said as he stepped back to take a second look. The owl never opened his eyes.

"Oh? What should it look like?" I asked.

Jim and "Owl" give a lecture to high school science students.

Nature" for the series. In as much as birds were my strong suit at the time, I decided to begin the series with that subject. The studio lights came up, and the theme faded, and the camera focused on a little chick calmly seated in the palm of my hand. Watching the monitor, I welcomed the TV audience to the show, and explained that today we were going to talk about birds.

I was pretty pleased with myself; the opening looked good and had lots of pizzazz. As I turned my head to give a cue to the cameraman, a silent breeze swept by me.

"Oh no!" I exclaimed, jerking my head back to look at my hand—just in time to see the chick swept away by Owl.

"Holy cats!" the cameraman shouted. "The 'blinky-blank' owl just ate the chicken!"

Sure enough, Owl came to rest on the top of the second camera, clutching the lifeless little chick in his talons and crunching the skull with his powerful beak. The second cameraman swung his camera around and

Rich Steeves holds a baby great horned owl on a banding trip in Wasco County, Oregon.
Courtesy of Greg D. Paul

"Well, owls have beautiful eyes," he said. "And they have big wings. That one should have been mounted with his eyes and wings open."

"Oh, like this?" I asked, interrupting him and giving the owl a little push on his chest.

Owl snapped his eyes open, gave a big flap with his wings to catch his balance, then gave me a little hoot of surprise at being suddenly awakened from his nap so thoughtlessly.

The salesman jumped back and, with his eyes bulging, asked, "Is that owl stuffed?"

"You bet he's stuffed," I laughed. "And you'd better be careful what you say about him, because the guy that stuffed him is pretty Big Medicine!"

When I went over as the head honcho of the Children's Zoo in Portland, I was invited to present a series of TV programs for KOAP, the Public Television station for Oregon. We settled on the name "Curious

"Owl" and Dean Anderson guard the homefront.

"Owl" returns home with a fat rat, caught near Jim's backyard, west of Portland.

Great horned owls usurp the goose-nesting platforms of Malheur National Wildlife Refuge. These owls are feeding on muskrats that swam by.

recorded the whole scene for posterity. I couldn't help but laugh—oh, I felt badly about the chicken, to be sure—but if it had grown up, my family and I would have eaten it sometime or another anyway. It was just the way an owl takes advantage of a prey item, that got me. Owl didn't wait for the lab rats I had for him; he just got to do his thing before the cue.

Then there was the herp show when Al St. John dropped the rattlesnake on the studio floor as he was trying to get it back into the snake sack. One of the cameramen leaped on top of his camera . . . but that's another tale. It was a good thing we were taping the series . . .

I had a fellow call me one morning at the museum and ask me if I wanted a dead owl. I asked him what kind it was, and he said he was positive it was a great horned. Then I asked him what shape it was in.

"Oh, really good," was his enthusiastic reply. "There's not a mark on him," he continued. "The only thing is, his eyes are closed."

I assured him that was perfectly normal, asked him where he lived, and since it was close to a school I was headed for that afternoon, told him I'd be by to pick it up.

"What'll I do with it in the meantime?" he asked.

"Oh, just put it in a plastic bag and lay it in your freezer," I told him.

That afternoon, about one o'clock, I pulled up at the man's house, rang the bell and was invited in.

"It's right in our big storage freezer out here," he said, pointing to an older model upright freezer in the garage. I followed him in, and stood closeby as he unlocked and opened the door. As he swung the door open he suddenly exclaimed, "What the h---!"

I looked past his shoulder and couldn't believe my eyes. A large, adult great horned owl was standing there amongst pieces of plastic bag, blinking at us. Before I could stop the man he slammed the door shut, turned to me and said, "It's impossible! That thing's dead!" Then he turned back, opened the door a tiny bit and peered inside, then muttered, "Uh . . . was dead."

The gingerbread in the gable of an old ranch house is a favorite perch of this adult great horned owl.

In the corner of the roof, the owls have moved into a raven's nest to raise their young.

A female great horned owl attacks George Long while he attempts to band her young.

It's time to duck! A female great horned owl attacks the camera.

In the crotch of a limb filled with pine needles, the adaptable owl lays her eggs.

Young long-eared owls don't fit into the nest any longer.

Inside the magpie nest, mother long-eared owl peers out with a baleful eye.

Apparently the owl had only been stunned by a passing vehicle and was still in some kind of shock when the man brought it home. When it came out of shock, it just tore the plastic bag to shreds and got to its feet. I don't know how long an owl could live in a freezer if all it had to combat was cold. Obviously, if deprived of oxygen it wouldn't be very long, but otherwise with the wonderful insulating quality of the owl's feathers, it would die from starvation before it froze to death. In any event, we chuckled

about that incident for quite some time. As it turned out, the owl did have some type of brain damage, but if I remember correctly, the last I saw of that owl was at the zoo where he was on display.

During the brittle cold winters in central Oregon, food is always a problem for the raptors, owls not withstanding. They have to scratch to find enough to eat, as well as compete with eagles, coyotes, badgers, and wintering hawks. If a jackrabbit is foolish enough to wander into the cold night and try to hide himself from an owl, he's usually dead meat pretty quick.

One very, very cold winter morning, when the thermometer had sunk to ten below zero, I happened upon an adult great horned owl, just east of Bend. He was standing on the icy snow holding a jackrabbit. The only camera I had with me was my old, 4 x 5 Graflex, so I slipped out of the car with that beautiful old blunderbuss and grabbed a shot. As I was pushing the dark slide back into the film holder, the owl looked up and gave me a piercing look, but didn't offer to fly. I cranked the shutter up again, turned the film holder over, pulled the dark slide, walked a little closer and took another photo. Still the owl stayed put, so I put another film holder on and eased up a little closer.

By the time I had shot five pieces of 4 x 5 film, he was still hunkered down in the snow with no indication of leaving. So I walked right up to him and filled the frame with owl, snow, and rabbit. Then I took my time, held my breath, and the camera steady, and knocked off the last piece of film I had with me. That photo is really unique, one of my favorite owl pictures, and because it's on a large piece of film, it can be blown up to almost to the size of a billboard. I made an 8 x 10 print of the owl's eye once, and in the reflection, I can see myself standing there, head down, looking into the top of the Graflex, shooting the owl's photo!

The criteria for nest-site selection in owls is probably like that of the Killdeer. They just keep flying around until they're about to lay an egg—and that's the place. Killdeer seem to stop running long enough to lay their eggs, no matter where they happen to be: parking lots, along road shoulders, in the middle of a gravel road, corrals, sandy beaches—you name it. I once found a great horned owl nest—if you could call it that— in the crotch of a pine tree limb where a handful of needles had settled, that was all. When the owls hatched, they were branchers almost immediately.

Sometimes an owl will use a golden eagle's nest, and that could be the end of the world for the owl. Eagles usually use the same nest year after year. Owls usually do not, and because owls nest long before eagles do, they will sometimes use the eagle's nest. When the eagle comes back and finds it occupied, she'll sometimes eat mom, dad, and all the kids. I've found adult, and juvenile owl feathers in pellets of an eagle nest that was once occupied by the (unfortunate) great horned owl.

Young long-eared owls line up in a Finley & Bohleman pose.

"Will they bite?" asks Dean Anderson.

Short-eared owl does a fly-by.

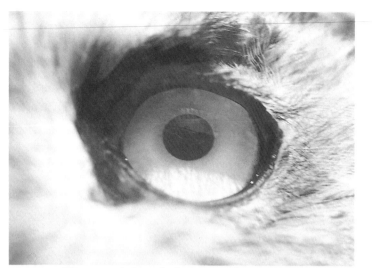

The eyesight of the great horned owl, day or night, is twenty times better than that of a human, while the volume of the owl's retina is greater than his brain.

After a false alarm on the way to the hospital to have a baby, Jim and his wife decided to go bird-watching. They discovered this short-eared owl perched (not nailed!) on a fence post near the Portland airport.

Nothing great horned owls do surprises me anymore—well—almost nothing. The biologists at the Malheur National Wildlife Refuge have gone to great lengths to place Canada Goose nest platforms in places that (more-or-less) insure the safety of their eggs.

by using an automobile tire with a screen in the bottom, mounting it on a steel pipe, and placing it in open water. I wasn't a bit surprised to drive by one day and see a great horned in one, with three happy, stuffed babies. Between the ducklings and muskrats, the owl was living high on the hog. Come to think of it, I wouldn't be a bit surprised if they nested on the roof of a pig-pen and took a pass at a piglet now and then.

I had an opportunity to see what I interpret as an example of significant friction between great horned owls and golden eagles, back in the middle '50s when I was living at Timberlane, the Hollinshead's place in Bend. I was using the library resources a great deal in those days, and got to know the librarians pretty well. One of them asked if she could visit a great horned owl nest some time. Well, I knew of one just east of the ranch, high up in an old red-tailed hawk nest, located in the top of a Ponderosa Pine. Had I know what was going to take place I would never have invited her to go along.

One late afternoon after work, we hiked from the ranch out to the big pine. As we approached the nest, both owls began their hooting, leaving no question of how much they were annoyed at our presence. Wanting to impress the lady with my professional abilities as a naturalist, I invited her to climb to the nest with me for a first-hand look at the baby owls. This was long before the days of women's lib, but my librarian friend exhibited all the spunk that has helped to keep this movement alive and well.

"I'm capable of climbing the tree myself," she stated, and began looking for a way up. I had to give her a little help to the first limb, but after that she was on her way and doing great. So I just found a comfortable place nearby which allowed me a good view of her progress, and sat down to watch the fun. Both owls hooted at her, but neither of them made any effort to attack—something that surprised me—but made me feel a great deal better.

Just as she reached the uppermost branches the owls suddenly stopped hooting, and the male took off like a shot for some junipers about fifty feet away. I thought that was strange, and was just standing up for a better look when suddenly, the sky was filled with the sound of thrashing wings, and a golden eagle almost crashed into her! I really can't recall exactly what happened next, it all happened so swiftly, except that the woman let out a scream, grabbed the limbs in a death grip, as the female owl left the tree with a slapping of wings, and crashing of branches, with that eagle right behind her. The owl was going headlong toward a willow thicket along the irrigation ditch about 100 yards away, and was only a split hair ahead of the eagle as they both crashed into a big bushy willow. It was something to behold!

The eagle dislodged itself then hopped around the willow, trying to reach into the interior again and again with its' powerful feet. Five minutes probably went by as the eagle kept looking for ways to dislodge the owl from the willow. I started to walk toward the willow when suddenly the eagle spotted me, jumped into the air with a chirping sound, and swept over the junipers and out of sight.

Then I remembered the librarian in the tree and headed back in a hurry, thinking well, I sure blew that one . . . There she was, still clinging to the upper branches, not making a sound. I shouted some ridiculous encouragement, but I should have saved my breath. I even offered to come up and give her a hand, but she was one of the best, and descended without a word. "Did you see that?" I exclaimed, as she reached terra firma again.

"How could I miss it!" she answered, her eyes still as big as golf balls. "Did the eagle get the owl?"

I told her that I didn't think it had, and we both retired to about 100 feet away to watch what would happen next.

It took about thirty minutes before the owl began to untangle herself from the willow thicket. As we watched quietly, she crept toward the edge of the willow, all the while sweeping the sky with those huge, bright, yellow eyes. Confident that the eagle was gone, she hopped out onto the bank of the ditch, shook her feathers into place, and

Great horned owls are fastidious. Here "Owl" takes his weekly bath.

"Owl" dries off after his bath.

on silent wings flew back to her nest. As she was settling into place again, a timid hoot could be heard coming from the junipers closeby, which she answered. The male appeared then and he too flew back to the nest. For some reason I don't understand, I never had the opportunity to invite that librarian out to watch wildlife again.

I once visited a great horned owl nest to band the babies, and almost upset the apple cart very seriously. It was an old red-tailed hawk's nest in a tall juniper, about ten miles east of Bend in the BLM Badlands, now a

Owls rehabilitated in captivity often have to be coaxed to fly. Ross Anderson uses road kill to encourage this youngster.

Wilderness Study Area. I walked to the nest from where I'd parked my pickup, and both the female and male came out to meet me, hooting mad, and clacking their beaks. I slowed down some, assuming the owlets might be too young to band, which is usually the case when the parents are so protective. I climbed a small juniper so I could see into the nest with my binocs, and, sure enough, the little guys were quite tiny.

I had just returned to the ground and was turning back toward my pickup when I heard that familiar squawk of a raven. Turning around, I saw it making a run for the baby owls. Both momma owl and I rushed toward the nest—both with the same thought of protecting the youngsters. The raven shied away just as the owl landed back in the nest, where she quickly covered her babies. At that moment, another raven appeared, and did a remarkable thing. BOTH ravens landed in the nest with the owl and began to make some of the darndest sounds I've ever heard come from a raven. If I could have interpreted them it would have probably been some of the most awful insults that any raven ever heaped on an owl. Time and time again, they hopped around on the nest: chirping, cawing, croaking, squawking, trying everything they could to drive the adult owl from the nest. All she did was hunker down deeper into the cavity of the nest and close her eyes.

I tried to drive the ravens away, but each time I started toward the nest, the female owl would get fidgety. I guess the ravens were one thing, but a man was something entirely different.

I had caused this mess, and I felt it was my responsibility to solve it, but I didn't have any idea how to do it. I felt miserable, but could only think of one thing to do, and that was slowly back away. As I did so, the ravens became even more incorrigible, and one of them actually hopped on the owl's back and pecked at her head.

I was just about to rush back when suddenly, way back in the trees I caught the flash of movement. It was the male owl. He was skimming over the top of the sagebrush like an F-16! I didn't believe an owl could go that fast! He flapped his wings only once or twice and sped on, straight for the nest, skimming the sandy surface between sagebrush bushes. Too late, one of the ravens let out a terrified squawk and both jumped into the air. The faster of the two was already out of reach as the owl zoomed up and slammed

Female owls are bigger and more alert than male owls.

"Move, mamma!" shouts Dan Green. "We want to band your babies!"

Jane Stevens, a wildlife rehabilitator from Bend, coos to a baby long-eared owl.

into the other raven. It was like a falcon striking a crow. Raven feathers exploded as the owl struck, and both went tumbling end over end, crashing into the sagebrush.

The silence was overwhelming. Not a bird made was making a sound; the silence was deafening. The owl on the nest never moved a muscle, and the other raven had vanished. After what seemed like ten minutes, the male owl raised himself where I could see him behind some brush, and then he appeared, dragging the body of the raven. As I left, the owl was plucking his victim, probably preparing it for transfer to the nest to feed his mate. I drove away from the site realizing I may have witnessed an incident not commonly seen in nature.

We even found a great horned nesting in an old raven's nest that had been constructed under the eaves of a deserted, pioneer ranch house located out among the wheat fields. That male owl owned the house. He perched in the gingerbread along the eaves and dared anyone to try and move him.

Juvenile great horned owl postures in a typical defense pose, making himself look twice as large.

"What are you doing up here, Reuben Anderson?"

The toughest owls I ever met were a pair about two miles away in another old raven's nest. George Long had climbed it, and the owl parents gave him such a shellacking I thought he was going to have to go to the hospital. More than once they bounced off his leather jacket, knocked his hard hat off his head, and really gave him a beating. I can recall George's groans as he finally clambered to the ground, sore all over, long tears in his leather jacket, and nasty gashes on his back. "I sure hope you appreciate

what I do for you, Jim," he grimaced—followed with his usual grin. I did.

We learned that one of the young from that nest wandered clear over two counties to the east, and lived to the ripe old age of fifteen years!

Long-eared owls are always great to be around. They sometimes hiss like snakes or bark like a dog, depending on their frame of mind at the moment. I can remember being out with Rich Steeves banding owls, hawks and eagles in Wasco County, the land of the rolling wheat fields and rows upon rows of orchards.

We were working in a big tree plantation that had been planted when the homesteaders were "proving up." It was surrounded by wheat fields when we were there. The magpies had built their huge, fortress-like nests in the high branches of the nut trees. These big bunches of sticks were often used by great horned owls. They'd jump up and down on them to form a cup in the top, lay their eggs inside, and call it home.

As we approached the grove of trees I saw a long-eared owl slip away quietly, trying to hide from us. I knew there was a nest somewhere, and like all the owls, they do not build one of their own. The first, big, magpie nest had to be it, so I gave it the once over with the binoculars, but couldn't see an owl in the top. As I began to climb the tree next to the nest, the male owl came back and started to protest my getting so close, so I knew I was on the right track. However, I didn't really expect what I saw as I was passing the bulky magpie nest. A big, yellow and black eye was staring at me from inside the nest. How that owl managed to cram herself into the nest, then have room for her eggs was beyond me.

When we came back about three weeks later to band her young there were five of them on top of the nest; there was simply no room for them inside. I can also remember my son, Dean, who always asked if owls would bite, sticking his finger in one of the baby's beaks. Oh, my, yes! It did bite!

Short-eared owls are diurnal: they hunt during the day. They're also ground nesters. The wheat fields of Oregon and Washington

Anderson Family Portrait, 1981. Left to right: Owl, Reuben, Jim, Ross, Owl, Dean, Owl.

are favorite places for them to nest, and at times, that gets them into deep trouble. The wheat farmers I've met have the right idea about owls. They understand that owls eat rodents, and the short-eared is an expert— finding gophers to its liking—and when owls eat rodents, they save the farmer money. As the farmers leave their wheat fields to fallow (a resting time for a year), I will often see a small area of wheat stubble still standing, not turned under with the rest. That's usually the site of a short-eared owl's nest that was left unmolested by a thoughtful farmer.

However, if the farmer waits too late into the spring to start plowing the stubble under, he can sometimes interrupt a nesting pair at the moment when they are the most protective. That's what happened when a farmer was out plowing. The female actually struck the tractor again and again, and the farmer couldn't stop her. She eventually killed herself with the repeated attacks on the tractor. The farmer felt pretty badly about it, so he picked up her eggs, which were at the hatching stage, called the Oregon Department of Fish and Wildlife, who in turn called me.

My wife and I jumped into our Citrabria, the tow plane we were using for our glider

A bird in the hand can often be a wonderful experience for a child. This little black-capped chickadee landed on Caleb Anderson's hand for a sunflower seed handout at Ed Park's place.

operation, and flew up to the farmer's strip to pick up the eggs. They hatched the next day. Unfortunately, the eggs chilled just enough so that most of the little owls died from "stretch," a terrible malady that strikes birds making them unable to assimilate anything from their food. The good news is that we saved one of the owls by placing copious amounts of vitamin C in with his food—dead mice. That was the beginning of my belief that vitamin C can fix anything.

We named the survivor "Shorty." He became a part of the family, travelling with us everywhere, and became quite an entertainer at local nature shows and school rooms. He eventually found a more 'proper' home at the Sunriver Nature Center where my wife worked. One of his favorite tricks was untying children's shoelaces as they came in to visit, much to their delight. Unfortunately, Shorty met his demise one night when a wild great horned owl undergoing rehabilitation escaped from his cage and ate Shorty, who liked to sleep in the bookcase. Sometimes the best intentions just don't work out the way you planned them. All is not always "nice" in the World of Nature . . .

Respect is the key. Respect for the rules that nature dictates to her plants and animals. As I've said before, owls are opportunists. The easiest to catch is what they'll use as prey items. If it's barn cats, that's that. If it's mice, rats, or other animals that cause economic and health problems to people—all the better for us. If there's one comment that is the height of absurdity, it is "Oh, that owl is really mean." There is only one creature walking the face of this earth that has the capacity to be mean: that's you and me.

'Possums in the Glove Box

Our native Opossum (*Didelphis marasupialis*), the only marsupial in North America, enjoys a wide distribution all the way from South America to Vancouver Washington. It more than likely wandered north from its home range in South America into the United States on its own, crossing the isthmus of Panama into Mexico and Texas, then spreading throughout the Southeast.

I have a hunch Man got into the picture and helped spread our only marsupial even further. He may have helped move its range into the Northwest. Documented records show that the CCC boys back in the '30s brought it to the far west, where there are populations in southern California, western Oregon, and southern Washington today. Almost everywhere it has been introduced, the opossum has been successful, a tribute to its tenacity for survival. My interest in the opossum began while I was living near Portland, while I was employed with the Oregon Museum of Science and Industry as the staff Naturalist.

The Portland City Club asked me to be their speaker, which I accepted, choosing the opossum as my subject. Many of the members were Isaac Walton League members and had good feelings for the natural world. It was an opportunity for me to share information about the opossum in the Northwest, as well as gather new information for myself.

The talk was a lot of fun, as they usually are for me. I enjoy doing talks, especially when the subject is about one of my friends from the natural world. At the end of the talk, a man walked up to me and launched into an emotional outburst condemning the opossum and accused the animal of every crime against nature that he could think of, focusing most of his wrath on old 'possum's alleged role in pheasant nest predation.

It seems that when someone gets all worked up about a specific species of wildlife, anger bursts to the surface when the particular animal is getting something that man desires. In this case, it turned out I had a very irate sportsman who had been hunting pheasant in the Willamette Valley ever since he was a kid. He had watched the unfortunate decline in pheasant populations to the point where there were few places to hunt them anymore, especially near his old boyhood haunts.

On the other hand, the opossum population had been expanding ever since they had been introduced by the CCC boys back in the early '30s. As more and more road-killed opossums were observed more frequently each year on the roads all over the Portland-Astoria-Salem triangle, it was only natural that someone who had lost his pheasant populations would put the blame on this ever-increasing population of "exotic" animals.

To make his argument more believable he said, "You know, those damn opossums will eat anything!" He was correct with that statement. Although they prefer the quick protein of flesh and bones, they will eat anything they stumble upon. I wanted to bring out the point of land changes throughout Multnomah, Washington, and Clackamas counties; houses are now standing on what once were the beautiful, open fields of corn and grain, waving in the warm Willamette Valley summer sunshine.

I wanted to debate the scientific credibility of the man's opinion that the opossum was the culprit destroying his pheasant hunting, but I had nothing but an opinion on that myself. However, it did set me to thinking about what I could do to gather data on what the opossum was really doing to—or for—the various species of wildlife that had survived progress of land-use planning within the Portland-Beaverton-Hillsboro areas.

As I did with many of my proposed projects, I sat down and discussed it with my old pal from the Portland Zoo, Dr. Matt Maberry. He had his usual good advice, and offered to supply me with a variety of colored ear tags which I could use to identify specific individual opossum for longevity, reproduction, and distribution data. Armed with twelve "Havahart" live traps, several cans of expensive dog food, a few rotten bananas, some rotten liver, and a bunch of ear tags, I set out to begin the opossum project.

I needed a specific study area, and one of the people who helped me with this was a friend on the Beaverton Police force who was interested in all the subjects of nature. People often called the police station about opossum that were making a nuisance of themselves. The officers had to respond to these calls, which often made them late or unavailable for robberies and other serious crimes.

I was living in Beaverton, so I went to the police station and asked if they would call me with their opossum complaints. I received an enthusiastic welcome, and a promise that they would immediately call me on every opossum complaint. I set my study area within the boundaries of the Beaverton Police Department.

Night after night, I wandered afield, setting my live traps baited with dog food, rotten liver, old bananas and anything else that smelled. Night after night I caught cats. Cats, cats, and more cats. It became abundantly clear that the most prolific animal around the Beaverton area wasn't the opossum, but the feral house cat. Oh, sure, I caught opossums as well, but at a ratio of eight cats to one opossum.

Winter dropped on Beaverton with the usual downpour of rain and snow that soaked western Oregon. I was out nights, slugging around in the mud, catching cats, an occasional skunk, and a few opossums. Each morning I visited my trap line, freeing cats, ear-tagging the occasional opossum and then driving a route I had established to search for road-killed opossums. Winter was hard on the opossum, especially when the freezing east wind came blasting out of the Columbia River Gorge, carrying the Arctic Express. I began to find many of the opossums with smaller ears than normal, the ends frozen off by the cold temperatures. On a few occasions I caught an opossum with one of my ear-tags, and was excited to see how close they stayed to home. However, I did find an ear-tagged male, dead on a county road, over fifteen miles west of Beaverton.

My favorite stops on the opossum route were the firehouses. There was always a pot of hot coffee going, and guys sitting around, bored with television, and eager to discuss what they knew—and thought—about opossums. As my study progressed, I found that a great deal of the information shared by the firemen was very usable and accurate. I can recall one individual who had his own ideas about what was going on with the pheasant populations in his neck-of-the-woods.

"It's those damn cats!" he exploded. "I've lived here all my life, and like the guy you were telling us about in the City Club, I also enjoy hunting pheasant. But my dog flushes cats more often than pheasant these days." Then he walked over to a drawer and rummaged around for a moment, returning with an open cigar box. "Take a look at these," he said, placing some photographs in my hand. I thumbed through photos of his house, his hunting dog, himself holding some ducks, then I stared at a photo of a man holding a huge, dead cat, not the normal-sized, domestic house cat, but a monster of a cat! It was as big as a male raccoon and as muscular.

"What is it?" I asked, passing the photo to him.

"That is one of those cats I told you about," he said. "That's my dad holding it; he shot it one morning after it had just killed one of our domestic ducks and was hauling it off." Then he waved the photo at me and said, "I'll tell you, Jim, the feral house cat is the biggest threat there is to our native wildlife. You'll see!"

One evening I was forced awake by the incessant ringing of the telephone and as I picked it up, a male voice said, "Mr. Anderson, this is the duty officer from the Beaverton Police Department. Could you meet one of our officers over at . . ." and he gave me the address. "We have a woman there who thinks she has a rabid 'possum on her back porch." I agreed and immediately got my warm clothes on, ran out to the car and headed for the address he had given me.

As I drove into the yard, I could see the patrol car parked to the side and several flashlight beams swinging around in the general vicinity of the back porch. I ran around to the back, and swinging my powerful spotlight beam, I spotted the opossum's eyes reflected back at me.

"Mr. Anderson's here . . . give him room," I heard someone say, as I passed several people with flashlights, and walked slowly toward the opossum, crouched along a wall on the porch. As I got closer it began to hiss, growl, and open its mouth wide, saliva drooling down to the porch floor. Then I could see the foam around its jowls.

"See!" a woman cried out. "It's foaming at the mouth. It's rabid!"

There was a scurrying of feet as most of the group began to retreat toward the house. I glanced behind me and all I could see were two police officers left, still holding their lights dead center on the opossum's pointed nose.

"Be ready, Bill," one said. "If it goes for Mr. Anderson, shoot it!"

Adult 'possum poses on a fence near Portland.

I didn't think we'd get to that point, but it was encouraging to know there was fire-power available, should the opossum be rabid and lunge at me. I stepped to the side, just in case shooting was necessary, and approached the opossum closer. I had never seen a rabid animal in all the years I have studied wildlife, so for all I knew, this one might be rabid. Then, I had never read about a rabid opossum in the literature either, so I had an interesting mystery to cope with. Was it rabid or not? I asked myself.

"Keep an eye on it, will you?" I asked the officers, and went back to the car for my live trap and a big piece of burlap I used when transporting an animal.

It only took a moment to steer the opossum into the open live trap. There was a little thrashing around as the opossum tried to pry the doors open, but those Havahart traps are stout. The more the animal pushed, the tighter the doors closed. I threw the burlap over the cage and the animal stopped struggling almost immediately. Then I took the whole shebang out to the car, placed it in the trunk, and returned to the house.

As we sat inside the warm house discussing the evening's excitement I told them I was going to keep the opossum isolated and see if it developed additional indications of being rabid. I asked them to tell me about the incident at their house, from the beginning.

"Well," the woman began. "I was washing dishes at the sink when I heard a clatter on the porch, so I turned on the outside light to see what it was. Imagine my surprise when I saw this big, ugly grey animal out there! I thought it was a big rat, with the naked tail and all, so I called George," she said, pointing to her husband, "and he said it was an opossum."

"Yeah," George interrupted. "Then I saw the foam around its mouth and told the missus to call the police." Then he added, "That's not the first one we've seen like that, you know!" That perked up my interest immediately, and I asked the occupants of the house if they had many opossum around the place, which got a mixed response. The wife said no, while the husband said yes. I looked at them both, waiting for them to settle their dispute.

"You're damn right," the man ejaculated. "I think we've got a whole mess of those rabid 'possums around here!" He waved his hands toward the back yard. "I've seen at least four of them on warm, summer nights blundering around out there, foaming at the mouth."

The mystery was becoming more interesting. A group of rabid animals was extraordinary, but it would appear that the infection would spread to other mammals of the area which would result in a serious outbreak among house pets. I was beginning to be a little skeptical about what I was hearing, but George insisted that all the opossums he saw in his yard had been foaming at the mouth.

Then I had a thought. "Do you leave food out for animals?" I asked.

"Of course we do," was the immediate reply from the Mrs. "I see a raccoon once in a while, but I don't care what gets the food, as long as they're all healthy."

"What else do you have out on the porch?" I asked.

"Well . . . nothing that I can think of," George began. "Potted flowers . . ." Then he snapped his fingers and added, "Wait a minute . . . we do leave a pan of slug-bait out there too."

I glanced at the policemen standing nearby with a look of relief.

"May I see the slug bait?" I asked. As I read the instructions and the list of the ingredients, I thought I had the answer for the "rabid" opossums. Those poor creatures were eating the slug bait, which induced a foaming of the mouth and probably a very upset stomach, perhaps even death to some. We had a discussion about the effects of slug bait on wild animals, which was a surprise for the people who owned the place. They promised they would be more careful of how and when they put out the bait.

The "rabid" opossum was placed on a diet of meat and vegetables and watched closely. After six weeks, Dr. Maberry thought the animal had recovered, so I placed a tag in the animal's ear and released it to the wild. The mystery of the "rabid" opossum was solved.

Spring came early to Beaverton that year. The rhododendrons were budding out in early February, giving everyone an indication of how beautiful it would be in May and June. I was still catching cats and an occasional opossum, along with a stray, small dog once in a while, but I had yet to find an opossum with pheasant parts in their droppings or stomach. Each road-killed opossum was autopsied for stomach contents, and I tried to pick up as much possum poop as I could to determine their diet.

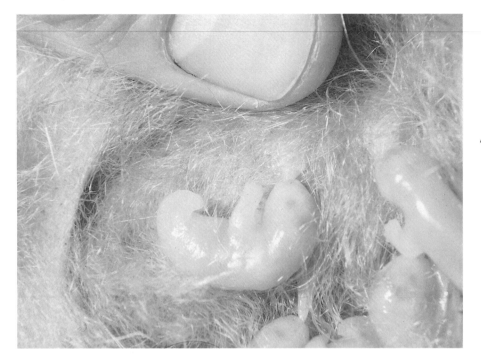

'Possum in a pouch

The bulk of the opossums appeared to be eating vegetation, dry dog food, table scraps—especially chicken and beef bones raided from the garbage cans—and other human-type food left out for wildlife by kindhearted residents of Beaverton. But no pheasant remains. I still had spring to go, perhaps I might find pheasant nests raided by opossums then, I thought.

It was a warm night about two weeks later that I was jarred awake by the phone. It was my friends from the Beaverton Police Department, but not with a call about a "rabid" opossum this time. Rather, a resident was very upset with strange noises coming from the interior walls of his home, and he was sure it was burglars.

I drove out to the address the officer had given me and was greeted by a very exciting scene: red lights flashing from three patrol cars parked in front of a small, older house, and flashlight beams slashing the night air. The house was on a big lot which had an old, dilapidated board fence on three sides. I walked into the house with my collecting equipment and other tools I thought I might need and found a great deal of commotion going on in the kitchen.

"I tell you!" a man was shouting at an officer, his nose almost touching the officer's, "I heard somebody trying to get into my house!" The man turned and pointed toward a wall. "There were all kinds of noises coming from over there by the door. I heard it!"

"I understand, sir," the policeman said. "But I don't think it was anyone trying to break in." He looked up and saw me coming and added, "Oh, here's Mr. Anderson. Perhaps he can help us to find what was making the noise." The officer in charge took my arm and led me around his car and whispered, "I don't think he's got human visitors, Mr. Anderson. I think he's got some critters in his house. Would you mind giving it a look?"

I walked over and introduced myself, asking if I could get the whole story, which the man enthusiastically gave me. He had been hearing strange noises in his house for about a week, and was sure there were thieves trying to get in and steal his valuable gun collection and other treasures. Then he swung around, looked at the policeman, and said, "I called you, because I heard them guys that were trying to get into my house—right there—under that wall." He finished, pointing at the interior wall of the kitchen.

Old car bodies make good 'possum houses.

We walked back into the kitchen and I took an old stethoscope that Dr. Maberry had given me out of my tool kit and placed it against the wall, listening for any strange noises. I almost jumped back as the cup of the stethoscope touched the wall. It sounded like a thunderstorm going on in there! I couldn't believe my ears! Loud grumbling, crunching, slithering noises came from within the interior of the wall. I slid my scope toward the floor, and the noise became louder and louder. Right at floor level it was the loudest. I stood up, and pointing to the spot said, "It sounds like your visitors are really working away right about there."

"See!" the man said. "What did I tell you!" Then he glanced over at me and said, "Mark the spot where you heard that sound the loudest . . . I'll be right back."

I did as instructed, marking a place on the wall with my pencil, and in a few moments the man returned with a hand-held sabre saw. "That the place?" he asked, plugging the saw into a nearby electrical outlet.

"Yep, that's the place," I replied.

With that he placed the saw against the wall and hit the switch. He didn't slow down as the sawdust flew. After he had cut a line about a foot long, he went around the bend at right angles and continued to cut another foot, ending up with a square hole in the kitchen wall. As the saw came to the place where it had started the panel suddenly popped off, right into the room, and as it did an avalanche of paper sacks, plastic bags, old rags, paper towels and leaves cascaded into the room.

"What the hell!" the owner exclaimed, jumping back.

At that moment a shout came from outside. "Hey! Come out here and see this! There's an army of . . . rats . . . no . . . 'possums running out from under the house!"

We all started for the back door, and as I reached the porch I saw at least ten opossums galloping out toward the back yard. "What the hell is going on?" the owner grumbled again, watching wide-eyed as the opossums ran out from under his home, spreading out into the yard.

"They're heading for those junk cars!" a policeman shouted, waving his flashlight in the direction of a running opossum.

Then I was the one who was shocked. The back yard was packed with every type of foreign car ever made. Piles of them. It looked like a football field made of junk cars. As my night vision began to adjust I could make out that the bulk of the cars were vintage Volvos, and English cars, and the opossums were vanishing within the folds, bends, doors, windows, fenders and bodies of the assorted automobiles.

"Well, now I've seen everything!" a policeman exclaimed, grinning at me. I had to nod my head in agreement. "Jack!" he shouted to an officer close to an old, beat up black Volvo, "See where that possum is headed for right behind you!"

The officer almost jumped in an attempt to get out of the way of the scurrying opossum. He swung his light on the animal as it dashed for cover within the body of the car. "It's gone in there somewhere," he shouted back, "but I'll be darned if I can see where."

"I'll get that son-of-a------," the owner shouted, running toward the car with a short two by four. We all watched as he jerked the driver's side door open and slammed the stick against the steering wheel and then the body, which made a sound like a steel bass drum. Again and again, he beat the seats, doors, panels, and interior of the car, but no opossum ran out. Then he leaned on the roof and peered inside, saying, "I don't know where that son-of-a------ went, but if I get my hands on him I'll kill him!"

I walked over to the old Volvo and looked into the empty engine compartment, then leaned over, listening for some clue to where the opossum was hiding. As I reached the firewall, where the glove box was located, I could hear faint hissing, and a shuffling noises. "I think it's here," I said, pointing my light at the spot.

The man rushed over with a screwdriver and proceeded to remove a panel on the firewall, adjacent to the glove box. As the panel dropped away another avalanche of plastic bags and newspapers spilled out, along with the snout and beady eyes of an opossum. "There it is!" the man shouted, grabbing his stick again. But before he could assail the animal it suddenly tumbled out on the ground. We put the beam of our flashlight on it. The mouth was slack, jaws open and saliva dribbling on the ground. "The

son-of-a------ is dead," the owner said, poking at the opossum with the end of his stick. There was no movement, for all practical purposes, it was dead. "I'll bet I scared the damn thing to death!" the man announced proudly, prodding at the opossum again. As the man turned his flashlight I saw a movement around the opossum's mouth as it slowly raised it's head, looked about and then scrambled under the car to safety. "I got one anyway," the man boasted, swinging his light back to the spot where his victim had been. "What the hell!" he blurted, bending down for a closer look, "It's gone!" I didn't have the heart to tell him about opossums playing 'possum . . .

After all the excitement died down we went back into the house for a discussion about all those used automobiles and opossum in the yard. The policemen decided that it was probably against city rules to operate a used auto parts storage, or business, in that location, and the situation looked more dismal for the owner as the officer discussed the possibility of additional health hazards from the animals using the cars for shelter. Then I was asked to try and do an inventory of the opossums using the autos—and the house—for a shelter.

The next day I returned to the house and asked the owner if I could go out into the back to try to count cars and opossums. He agreed, grumbling a lot, knowing that he was going to have to move them in a short time. I went out into the yard and began to tap bodies, fenders, trunks, glove compartments, seats and the upholstery. It seemed no matter where, or what, I touched, an opossum would hiss at me, growl, and then scuttle off deeper into the interior of the car. I found twenty-five opossums using the old car bodies as a shelter from the wet and cold winter weather. They had packed in every conceivable type of plastic, along with hamburger wrappers and paper sacks to line their shelters. It appeared they had hauled in tons of the stuff. I had to chuckle as I thought about the role the 'possum was playing as a street cleaner!

As I was about to leave, the owner called me over, "Hey, Jim! Come here and see this!" I walked to where he was standing and looked down at the ground, and could hardly believe my eyes. There was a deep trail in the grass which began at a crawl hole beneath his house and spread like the spokes of a wheel out into the cars in the back yard. "I've been a friend of them guys for a long time, ain't I?" the man asked, grinning at me. "Do you suppose I could make this a wildlife preserve and keep my cars . . .?"

A Rattle in the Trunk

If there is one animal on the face of this earth that is a whipping boy for man, it's the poor old rattlesnake. It's been accused of doing more injuries to people than the mosquito (which has done far more damage to the human race than all the snakes in the world combined). Even the American Red Cross First Aid instructors seem to get all lathered up when they get to the part on venomous animals. In reality, the automobile is the greatest cause of death in the US, but to hear some people talk, you'd think rattlesnakes are capable of exterminating man. That's a shame, as the rattlesnake is usually a retiring reptile who would rather be left alone. Oh, sure, there are always exceptions, sometimes surprising ones.

I can remember when my son, Dean, and I went out on a road near Douglas, Arizona and met a big Mojave Rattlesnake that would have made a grizzly bear back peddle. We had never seen a snake that big or that beautiful. I parked the car on the shoulder of the road and got out to see if we could photograph it. Shucks, we had no sooner set our feet on the pavement then that big guy coiled up, stuck his tongue out at us, and started buzzing. The closer we got the louder he buzzed. We could see that big tongue flicking in and out and could almost sense the vibrations coming from him. He was BIG!

I grabbed up my loyal old Pentax, with the 105 mm lens on it, and started to focus. Dean shouted, "Look out, Dad! He's headed your way!" Sure enough, I could see him sliding across the pavement toward me, still coiled up, inching along slowly. That big dude was downright aggressive! That's the exception, however, rather than the rule.

Speaking of Dean. He got his education on the speed and agility of the Twinspot Rattlesnake while we were living on the Ramsey Canyon Preserve, in southeast Arizona. I was employed by the Nature Conservancy, who operated the Preserve, as the Preserve Manager. Part of my responsibilities was to take people on guided walks through Ramsey Canyon. We had several species of rattlesnakes there: the big, bashful, and beautiful Blacktailed was a common resident throughout the Preserve, while the Twinspot, Green Rock, and Willard's Ridge-nosed rattlesnakes lived higher up in the Huachuca Mountains on Forest Service lands.

What a gentleman that Blacktailed is. We would collect them up each spring as they wandered around the preserve. Even though they were very shy, retiring beauties, the upper level management thought it best to try and remove them from immediate contact with the guests and visitors. So every spring Rick Hewett, who was the Mile-Hi manager, would join Dean and me and we'd set out to capture and transfer the Blacktails to locations outside of the Preserve. I can remember one that was waiting on the trail each morning just outside the office of the Mile-Hi cabins; we thought he wanted to be petted.

Throughout the summer, Rick, his lovely wife Connie, Dean, Sue, Carroll and Joan Peabody (the original owners of the Mile-Hi facility), and I would conduct guided walks for people visiting the Preserve. Dean was a young man at the time (he's now a First Lieutenant in the US Air Force and a hot-shot F-16 driver). He was, and still is, good at taking people on guided walks, and recognizes birds better than most people. He also knows a great deal of other wildlife, including the rattlesnakes, and is fearless when it comes to picking them up.

I can recall when he was about four and we were on a bird-banding trip through Wasco County, in Oregon. We came upon a very large Gopher Snake lying across the road, sunning himself. Dean had never displayed any fear of getting bit, and I was afraid he might try to pick up a rattlesnake someday. When I saw that big fellow lying across the road, I stopped on the shoulder and asked Dean if he wanted to catch it.

"Where, Dad?" He asked with excitement, leaping out of his homemade car seat.

"Right there, in front of us," I answered, pointing to the six foot beauty.

"Oh, boy, Dad!" he exclaimed, and hit the road running.

"You're not going to let him try and pick up that snake, are you?" my wife asked, giving me a 'mother whose kid is going to get hurt' look.

"Sure," I replied, then shouted to Dean, "Go get him, son!" Then added, "Besides, if we don't get him out of the road someone will surely run over him."

Well, that snake never had a chance. One minute he was at peace with the world, probably digesting a couple of ground rodents, and the next minute that kid had him by the tail, trying to drag him away. I guess the snake decided that he'd had enough, for in a flash he had a big mouthful of Dean's right hand.

We could hear Dean draw in a big breath as the snake nailed him, but that didn't relax his grip one little bit. Dean had the back end, but the snake had Dean's hand. With his other hand he started to gather up the rest of the snake and before I could get out of the van, he had it all scooped up and was carrying it back to show us. He struggled up to the car, trying to keep a firm grip on the writhing mass, and exclaimed proudly, "I've got him, Dad!" Then, with big tears running out of his eyes, he added, ". . . and he bites too!" I thought that might put a little respect into his life for snakes, and it did too—well—a little . . .

The behavior of getting a closer look at nature prevailed when he was a volunteer guide at Ramsey Canyon, and still prevails today. One day he took a small group up the canyon while I took another over to Carr Canyon looking for trogons. Dean is a hiker, so he elected to take his group above the preserve and onto the Forest Service land above, and was still out in the field when I returned with my group. I dropped everyone off at the Mile-Hi and was walking back up to my house when a man came running down the road, spotted me, then started shouting.

"Dean . . . g . . . bit . . . by . . . a . . . rat . . . nk!" He was too far away for me to hear what he was shouting, so I speeded up a bit and met him. As we pulled up to each other he took a couple of great gasps of air and blurted out. "Your son, Dean has been bitten by a rattlesnake!"

If I said I wasn't concerned, that would be a big lie. I was very concerned. "Where?" I asked.

"Up in the Box Canyon," my breathless messenger gasped.

"No, not where on the preserve," I asked, a bit exasperated. "What part of Dean did the rattlesnake get?"

"Oh!" he replied, thoughtfully, raising his eyebrows. "Ummm, on his hand . . . I think."

"What did he do about it?" I asked next.

The messenger held his breath a moment, and I could see he was trying to remember what he had seen before he bolted down the canyon to look for help. "Oh, ummmm, he was sitting on the bank of Ramsey Creek holding his hand in the water."

"Good!" I said, relieved to hear that the bite was on his hand and that Dean had placed his hand in the cold water of the creek. "Do you know what kind of a snake it was that got him?"

"Oh, yes!" he replied immediately. "He was showing it to us at the time, and was just about to release it when suddenly he let out a little yelp and said, 'Son-of-a-gun! That little guy got me!'"

"What kind of a 'little guy' was it?" I asked again.

"I think he said it was a Greenrock Rattlesnake," he replied, searching my face for a reaction.

"Ok, let's go up and see how he is," I said, trying to keep my anxiety to myself best I could as we turned up canyon.

When we arrived at the Box Canyon, the most beautiful place on the Preserve, there was Dean sitting along the creek holding his hand in the cold water, and all his party looking on anxiously. "Hi Dad," he said sheepishly.

"Hi, son. How do you feel?"

"Like a dunce," he replied, looking away.

I took his hand out of the water and looked at it. No swelling was evident, and no sign of where the snake got him. "Where'd he get you, son?" I asked, holding the hand for all to see.

"On the end of my finger," he replied, showing me the place. I got down to look more closely and finally could see a faint, white blush at the end of his middle finger.

"Well, it doesn't look like he got you very hard," I said, helping him to his feet. "Do you think you can walk out on your own?"

That's all a stout teenager has to hear. He looked at me, gave me his big grin and said, "I sure can, dad. Let's go."

For years, first aid for snake bite has been the cut-and-suck method. I've never believed in it myself. The human mouth is a cesspool when it comes to germs, and the idea of using a dirty (not always sharp) tool to inflict another wound where someone's already been hurt, and then sucking away on it with your mouth is like pouring rat poison on it.

The tourniquet was another tool that folks used. I think more people lost their appendages due to that method then all the snake bites in the world. The American Red Cross does not recommend a tourniquet for anything any more. For a while, ice was the prescribed first aid treatment for snake bite, but now that's also gone by the wayside.

I would suggest that the best advice today is to stay calm, and don't get yourself into a lather. If you get excited, you'll speed up your heart and that will pump the poison into your system quicker. As my seventh grader says, "Stay cool, man." Keep the poison below the level of your heart and maybe use a little cold pack to slow down the spread of the juice. But above all, stay calm and get to a hospital as quickly and safely as you possibly can.

That's what we did on our hike down the canyon. We watched Painted Redstarts flitting along the banks of the creek, and Dean called out the big, beautiful, Blue-throated Hummingbirds that went zipping by. When we reached the house, my wife had the pickup already pointed toward town, and we climbed in.

Our arrival at the hospital was greeted by a little panic, until the admitting people heard where Dean had been bitten, what first aid had been applied, and how he had responded. Unfortunately, the doctor on call was out having dinner with his wife and friends, and was less than happy to be called away to care for some dumb kid that got bitten while playing with rattlesnakes. At least that was his frame of mind when he came through the door. It didn't help much when he asked Dean where the snake was. "I let it go," was his response.

"You let it go!" the doctor responded, a bit put out. "How can I tell what kind of a snake it is now," he added, angrily. Then he gave Dean another grim look, and said, "We've got to know what kind of a snake it was in order to treat you correctly."

"It was a Greenrock Rattlesnake," Dean said, quietly.

"How do you know?" the doctor responded.

"Because I know," Dean answered.

Before this could turn into a quiz show, I stopped the doctor and explained how and why Dean knew it was a Greenrock, and what he had been doing with it when he got careless.

"Oh, that's different," the doctor said, and got down to inspecting Dean's index finger, muttering to himself, "Should have brought it in anyway . . ."

As it turned out, the injuries from the snake were nothing compared to the digging the doctor did trying to find the poison. He cut and cut to be sure there was no poison left. Some rattlesnakes have a strong enzyme in their poison that will digest flesh for a long time after the bite, so I was relieved to see how thoroughly the doctor cleaned Dean's finger to insure that no poison or other foreign body was in there, eliminating the chances of tissue digestion or infection.

For at least three weeks after that event

Mojave rattlesnake on Arizona roadway

A rare snake, the Greenrock rattlesnake is found in southeastern Arizona.

Dean would apologize for getting bit, which was very unnecessary. I'm happy I didn't have to apologize to him for all the times I let him down . . .

He was with me the day we were coming back from Tucson, and saw a guy in a car, parked in the middle of the road, leaning way outside the window, slowly inching up to a big Diamondback who was sunning himself on the road.

"What's that guy doing, dad?" Dean asked.

I couldn't figure it out either. He was hanging on the door, peering out at the left front wheel and inching forward. Suddenly it dawned on me.

"Oh, blast it, Dean!" I groaned. "That jerk is going to run over that big Diamondback!"

Sure enough, before we could stop him he rolled his front wheel right over that big, beautiful snake. Guts flew in all directions as the snake burst beneath the weight of the car. Dean and I both almost got sick watching that barbarian.

"What did he do that for, Dad?" Dean asked with a gulp, and looking a little pale.

"I don't know, son," I replied, "but I'm sure going to find out!"

I bailed out of the pickup and walked up as the guy was backing his car away from the flattened snake. "Hey!" I said, very unfriendly like. "Why did you do that?"

The guy glanced up at me with a look of surprise on his face. "Why the h--- not? Those blankity-blank snakes 'aint no damn good!" And then, as to get his point across, he slammed his door and added, "I'm glad I killed the blankity-blank thing!" And drove off in a smoke-screen of burning rubber.

I'm not ashamed to say that both Dean and I had tears in our eyes as we looked down at the poor, squashed snake. Then I got mad. I got steaming mad. I had noted the license plate of the car, and we headed for Sierra Vista where I got on the phone and called my friend Pat O'Brien, the Arizona Game and Fish Officer who worked our area.

"Pat!" I almost shouted over the phone. "Dean and I just witnessed a guy killing wildlife with his car—on purpose! It was an out-and-out act of senseless killing, done deliberately!"

"What kind of wildlife, Jim?" Pat asked.

"A Western Diamondback," I replied emphatically.

Pat was one of the best wildlife officers I ever worked with, and was a good snake man too. He and I teamed up and apprehended several snake crooks trying to get away with the rare and endangered Willard's Ridge-nose that lives in the country just above the Preserve. I knew he was the man to sic on that screwball.

"A Western Diamondback, you say," Pat replied.

"You bet," I said.

Silence. "You there, Pat?" I asked.

"Yeah, I'm here," he replied slowly. Then with a note of sadness in his voice he slowly added, "I'm sorry, Jim, but that species just isn't protected. There's nothing I can do."

And that was that.

Incidentally, July is the best time to see rattlesnakes on the road in the southwest. During the magnificent thunderstorms, the snakes spread out over the countryside and also spend time on the roads. We'd go out on those nights to photograph the fantastic lighting storms, and roadhunt afterwards. I was out one night with Ross, Dean's kid brother (who is also a First Lieutenant in the Air Force and an Instructor Pilot today), and we got some lightening photos of the Preserve getting smacked that were spectacular.

I got to feeling a little guilty, though. My wife was up on the preserve with our newborn son, Reuben, at the time, but when she saw the photos all was forgiven. Then there was the time the whole family was out roadhunting and found the Colorado Toad, the largest toad in North America. I tried to convince Dean that if he kissed it, it would turn into a princess—but that's another tale.

In the Northwest, we have only one species of rattlesnake, the Western Pacific (but according to my herpetologist pal, Al St. John, there are several subspecies). He's also a beauty, sometimes getting to about four to five feet out in the wilder areas where he can grow to an old age without being molested by people. Unfortunately, Oregon's rattlesnakes don't have much protection either. The folks who run the Hampton Store, half-way between Bend and Burns, instigated an annual rattlesnake hunt for a couple of years which I hope will die due to lack of interest. There's also a few people who think it's neat to have rattlesnake hatbands for their cowboy hats, while others like to use the hides for wallets, knife holders, and hang the rattles from the rearview mirrors in their pickups. Folks in the Fort Rock, Christmas Valley, and Silver Lake areas get a little jumpy at haying time if they pick up their hay bales by hand; rattlesnakes like to get out of the hot sun by hiding under the bales.

The Blacktail rattlesnake is commonly found in the Huachuca Mountains of southeastern Arizona.

Willard's ridge-nosed rattlesnake is often poached.

Al St. John, an old pal and fellow naturalist, is a herpetologist who's been studying snakes all his life. He knows where every rattlesnake den is in Oregon, but if you twisted his arm off, he still wouldn't tell you where they were.

I've got to tell you a tale about Al. I had heard of him years before I actually met him. As a kid he was always keeping snakes in his home near McMinnville, a great little town located between Portland, Salem, and the coast. When he was in high school, Al had a big Egyptian Cobra escape from him once, which about turned McMinnville inside out while everyone searched for it. After they found it (in Al's garage), the city passed an ordnance prohibiting anyone from keeping poisonous reptiles within the city limits—just for Al.

It was about 1968 or so, while working for OMSI, that I was driving down Highway 97 heading to Bend to visit with my mom and dad. Between Redmond and Bend I suddenly looked in my rear view mirror to see a State Police car bearing down on us, lights blazing away on top. To my surprise he pulled up behind me, and I pulled over quickly, wondering what I had done wrong this time.

I was just getting out of the car when the officer came up to me and asked, "Excuse me, sir, but are you Jim Anderson?" I couldn't believe it! I've done some speeding in my days and got my fair share of tickets, but I didn't think they knew me that well.

"Yes, I am," I replied, with a questioning look.

"You have an emergency phone call from Salem, Mr. Anderson," he said. Then pointing to his car, added. "If you'll follow me to a phone, I'll guide you." With that he went back to his car, pulled around me and headed for Bend.

As we rolled down the highway following the policeman, I explained to my wife and children why we were being escorted to a phone. "Who do we know in Salem?" she asked.

"I don't know," I replied in a worried tone, as we sped along.

The first phone we got to was on the north end of Bend. I called the Salem number the officer gave me, and the Salem hospital answered. I told the operator who I was, and she replied, "Oh, yes, Mr. Anderson. Just a moment and we'll connect you with Dr. McCallum." That rang a bell. Dr. McCallum's wife, Gail, was a nurse who had served several sessions with me when I was at OMSI's Camp Hancock, located near Fossil, Oregon. She helped me save a young camper's bacon when she got herself dehydrated—but that's another tale too.

"This is Doctor McCallum . . ." the voice said. "That you Jim?" I assured him it was, and asked what was up. "I remembered you just returned from a poisonous animal seminar that was held at the Southwest Research Station in Arizona. We've got a young man here who was bitten by a rattlesnake and we were wondering what you might have to offer as a treatment." After a lengthy discussion, we decided that it would probably be best to use the anti-toxin serum as part of treatment.

I asked him where the young man had been bitten. "On the end of his finger," He replied. Then I asked him how the kid managed to get bit there. "Oh," he replied, "He was reaching under a rock for the snake."

"Is that kid's name Al St. John?" I asked.

"It sure is, how did you know?" Dr. McCallum replied, then added, "Do you know him?"

"Yes, I know of him, but I've never met him." I chuckled. "But if I ever do, we'll have a lot to talk about." Then I laughed. "You tell him to lay there and suffer. Anyone who has the audacity to reach under a rock to catch a rattlesnake bare-handed deserves to suffer."

Al is one of the people I enjoy most out in the field today. We often go out together with our families to enjoy the beautiful world of nature in the Columbia River Gorge country. He taught my kids how to make nooses to catch lizards, and to expand their knowledge of the world around them. Yep, he's one of the best all-around Naturalists in the Northwest.

Before we leave Al, I should tell you about the time we were doing a TV taping for educational television in Portland and he almost got bitten (again), and . . . Oh, shucks, let's save that one for another day . . .

I've saved the "best" rattlesnake tale I've ever been involved with for last. This took place when I first went to work at the Oregon Museum of Science and Industry (OMSI) in Portland. As I may have mentioned before, the museum is located just above the Portland Zoological Gardens (called Washington Park Zoo now), a wonderful place to find a variety of wildlife.

One day I got a call from the zoo veterinarian, Dr. Maberry, who told me to hurry on down. In the past when he said to "hurry on down," he usually meant just that, so without haste I told Dorothy Mason, whom I worked with in the Education Department, where I was headed, and scooted on down. As I walked in the service door, Doc met me and held his finger to his lips in that universal sign to be quiet. Voices were coming from Jack Marx's office, the Director of the Portland Zoo.

"I tell you Jack, I got the best load of blankity-blank rattlesnakes you've ever seen in your blankity-blank life," the voice boomed out.

"Well, we'll just have to see them before we can make any kind of a deal," Jack replied.

"Come on!" the booming voice ordered. "And I'll just let you feast your eyes on them babies!"

Doc took my arm and pushed me back into his office as they swept out of Jack's office, down the hall, and out the door. I looked at Doc and asked him what was going on. "Oh, that guy has been coming here for years selling Jack snakes," Doc replied. "Come on, let's go out and see what he's got."

We walked out into the drizzle just in time to see the man unlocking the trunk of his car and saying to Jack, "Now wait 'til you see these babies, Jack. I got some in here from over near Rome that's big as your leg!"

"Yeah, I'll bet," Jack replied skeptically.

"OK, wise guy," the man said as he flipped the trunk open. Then he froze. "What the h---!" he shouted and slammed the lid down with a crash. "Every one of them things has got out of the sack, Jack!" he wailed, jumping back from the car.

I thought Jack was going to burst, holding back a loud laugh. "What are you talking about?" he guffawed, pointing to the car. "You mean they're all loose in the trunk?"

"Yeah," the man whispered almost to himself, and with eyes wide, he looked at Jack, then to Doc, "They're all loose in the trunk!" Then as though the whole picture suddenly bloomed in his mind, he jerked around and, staring at his car, asked, "How am I goin' to get home? I can't drive that car!"

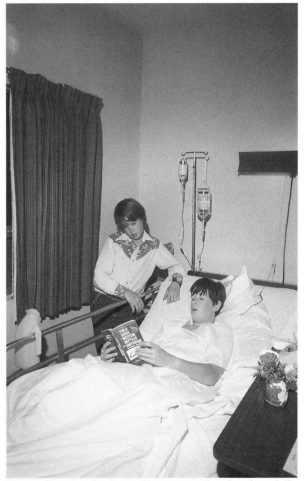

Dean lies in bed reading a snake book while Ross visits.

Doc was trying to be serious, but he couldn't keep the humor out of his eyes as he shrugged his shoulders and said, "Beats me."

"I've got an idea," Jack volunteered, laying his hand on the man's shoulder. "Why don't we call a wrecker and have your car hauled to my garage."

"What good'll that do?" the man interrupted, shaking his head.

"Now, wait a minute, will you," Jack glowered. "Let me finish. We'll have your car towed to my place and seal it in my garage, then call an exterminator who'll gas the snakes. After they're all dead, we'll take them out, and you can have your car back."

"Good plan," the man replied, and they walked off to make the call.

"What do you think?" I asked Doc. He just shrugged his shoulders and grinned.

About an hour later we heard a commotion out by the sidewalk and went out to see what was going on. As we emerged onto the sidewalk we saw a big wrecker pulling up to the front of the car full of snakes. The man got out and began hooking the chains to the front bumper, getting the car ready to hoist. "Who's got the keys," the man asked as he finished chaining the car to the hoist. Just as Doc was about to tell him, the owner came walking out of the office. "You got the keys?" The wrecker driver asked, starting to crank the front end of the car off the ground.

"Uh . . . you won't need 'em," he said, avoiding eye contact.

"Hey, mister," the driver said, as the front end of the car went higher off the ground. "I've got to have them keys to make sure your car is in neutral, and to make sure the brake ain't on."

"Just a minute," the man said, and came over to Doc. "How am I goin' to get the door open, Doc?" he asked quietly, trying not to move his lips. "Them snakes might be . . ."

"Snakes!" the wrecker driver shouted. "What about snakes?" He looked at Doc, then to me, and than back to the owner. "Is there snakes in that blankity-blank car?" he thundered, not waiting for an answer. Then, without any more comments he went over and hit the catch that was holding the car up in the air. Wham! The front end bounced back on the pavement. "I ain't takin' no snakes anywhere!" he shouted, unhooking

the chains from the bar that raised the car off the ground. "No sir," he repeated to himself, then he stopped and looked at the owner who at this point hadn't said another word. "That'll be fifty bucks, mister! Cash!"

After that no one said a thing about snakes as the next wrecker hooked on the car. Doc opened the door gingerly and knocked the car out of gear, then made sure the brake wasn't set. The last we saw of the load of rattlesnakes was the car bouncing along behind a wrecker, headed for Jack's garage.

I didn't get in on the end of this tale, but this is the way I was told it ended . . .

The plan went off just as Jack predicted. The exterminator came and shot his gas into the sealed garage. All the snakes in the car were killed, and everyone, except the poor rattlesnakes, was happy about it—that is, until the weather got warm. It turned out that the owner only found a few of the snakes he thought he had. The rest had crawled into hide-aways within the body and framework of the car where they died. As the weather got warmer and summer began to set in, the pungent smell in the car got higher and higher, until the owner couldn't stand it anymore. The last I heard, the car was towed to a junk yard and quickly sent to the recycling smasher—snakes and all. I wish Jack were still alive today to read this tale; I can see him guffawing, slapping his leg, and adding the details that I've forgotten. I'm glad I can't remember who the car belonged to . . .

An Elephant in the Trunk

"Say, Jim . . ." a familiar voice asked. "How would you like to gather up your cameras and come up to Seattle and photograph an autopsy on a young elephant that just died."

The familiar voice belonged to Dr. Matt Maberry, the veterinarian of the Portland Zoo back when I was working for OMSI in the '60s. He and I had gone out to photo-

graph whales together, conducted in-service teacher workshops, picked up dead snowy owls across Oregon, and shared many other adventures. He knew I wouldn't be able to pass up something as big as an elephant autopsy.

"That sounds like a great photo assignment, Doc," I answered. "But you'd better not plan on me 'til I call home."

"Oh, yeah," he replied. "You do have that brand new little baby boy at home, don't you?"

My wife was a biology teacher who shared most of my interest in wildlife, but I wasn't sure whether she'd want to get in on an elephant autopsy, especially with our three-month-old son, Dean, to watch over.

"What do you think, Hatt?" I asked, holding the phone away from my ear in the event this wasn't a good idea.

"That sounds exciting, Jim," she replied, "but what about Dean . . .?"

I had built a big plywood box that resembled a cradle, with removable rockers, and planned to place it in the back of the old station wagon we had in those days. It was only a three-hour drive to Seattle from Portland.

"That sounds good to me," she responded after I explained how I thought it would work. "I'll pack up some sandwiches and hot coffee for you and Matt. You know how he eats like a horse when he's working . . ."

"OK, Hatt," I said. "I'll be home in about an hour, and we'll gather up Dean and my cameras and head off for Seattle."

As always on excursions with Matt, I only knew half the story when we started out. It seemed that there were other disciplines involved in the elephant autopsy. A crew of biologists from the primate research center near Beaverton was also going to get in on the project. Ted Grand, who was a specialist on muscles and locomotion, was interested in the way elephants walk and rest. Another scientist was going along to study the nerves and muscles of the trunk, while another was interested in the load-carrying capacity of elephants. There was even a biologist who wanted to learn more about the digestion system of elephants and wanted to look at the viscera. It appeared the elephant wasn't going to go to waste.

It was about 7 pm when we rolled into the Seattle Zoo, and another hour before we got everything prepared for the autopsy and I was all set up to shoot 35 mm, 4 x 5, and movies of the project. As the group got busy, pieces of elephant began to fill the laboratory where we were working. Harriet stayed with the project, when baby Dean

would let her, making sure Matt and I were well fed and supplied with plenty of coffee. Matt always said, "I'll have coffee, before, during, and after my meals." There were more than wild animals to feed at the zoo.

Soon the elephant was straying into the next lab as skin, muscles, circulatory systems, viscera, and bones spread out.

"Oh! Wow! Look at this!" Ted would exclaim as he held up the muscles from the elephant's rear leg. Then he carefully placed the leg on the floor and slowly dissected each muscle from the bone. I kept hearing: "Jim! Photograph this!" That's the way it went up to about 1 am: scientists calling for photographs, their voices excited as they discovered new information, while the elephant slowly dissolved before us into a mass of flesh and bones.

"Hey, you guys!" Dr. Maberry suddenly shouted. "I can't hold another cup of coffee, and I can hardly keep my eyes open. I've got to operate on a tiger tomorrow afternoon, and if I don't get back to Portland, I won't wake up 'til next week. Come on, let's head for home!"

"OK, Matt," Ted responded. "Just give me another ten minutes on this foot. It's beautiful!"

"I'm ready to leave," Harriet said, packing up the remains of our picnic and carrying little Dean in his cradle to the old station wagon.

Slowly, each member of the group packed up his tools and notes and began to shuffle out to their vehicles.

"Are you sure you got enough photos of these legs?" Ted asked me, waving a tibia at me.

"Yeah, Ted. I'm sure I've got more than you'll use in a lifetime," I answered, packing my Bolex into its carrying case.

Ted walked out the lab door with a bunch of his notes and surgical kit and then came back in, grinning at Harriet and me.

"Hey," he said, "you've got a station wagon!"

"Forget it, Ted!" I said, giving him an evil eye.

"But, if I had those legs at the center I could put them in my carrion beetle tank. They would clean them up in about a month, and then I could study the bones in detail . . . come on, Jim . . . please . . ." Ted pleaded.

"Forget it, Ted!" I said again, going out with another armload of cameras. As I turned to open the door, he was turning the charm on Harriet. I feared I was about to lose the battle . . .

As I walked back in for the last load, I heard Harriet say, ". . . oh, I don't think those legs will take up much room if we pack them close to Dean's cradle."

"Ted Grand!" I said, "this is going to cost you dearly . . ."

"Oh! Thanks!" he exclaimed, picking up the elephant's legs and carrying them out to the station wagon.

Just as he walked back into the room, Matt gave me a wink and said, "Hey, Ted. You've got some room in the back of your Karmen Ghia. How about hauling the trunk back to the lab with you—in your trunk," he laughed.

"You bet he will!" I said before Ted could respond.

Then Matt laughed, "I'll take that bucket of guts too if you want me to."

"I'll find room for the skull," another man chipped in, and before long almost the entire elephant was loaded in a variety of vehicles, headed for the primate center.

On the way down the freeway, I had a big laugh at what someone might think if we were involved in a wreck: elephant bones and human beings all mixed up in the wreckage. "I don't think it's that funny," Harriet said, frowning at me.

We didn't have a wreck, or even have a close call. However, when we came to the toll station at the interstate bridge over the Columbia, between Portland and Vancouver, Washington, we caused a mild sensation. It was about four in the morning and the man on duty had probably been there all night, taking the toll fees from truckers and cars as they entered Oregon. I could see he was sleepy as anyone would be stuck in that booth all night long. I slowed to a stop adjacent to the tiny window he used to handle the cash toll, and as I was handing him the coins he suddenly jerked to his feet, and almost pushed his nose against the window. "What the hell is that!" he exclaimed, pointing to the back of the station wagon.

I turned around and could see just the top of Dean's cradle up against the back of my seat. "Oh," I responded, "that's my son."

"NO!" he shouted. "Not the cradle . . . all those bones, and other parts!"

"Oh, that . . ." Harriet said, leaning over me so she could see into the booth. "That's an elephant . . . we found it along the road back near Olympia and thought we'd bring some of it home for soup."

"What the ----," he exclaimed again.

Just then I saw Ted's Ghia slowing down in back of me, and I thought I'd get into the act. "Yeah, we've got the legs, but the guy right behind me has the trunk in his trunk, and there's a couple of cars behind him with the rest."

As I drove away, that poor man had his head stuck out of the toll booth, staring at Ted's little Ghia. I knew Ted wouldn't let such a good thing die—and he didn't.

The Show Goes On

Doing school assemblies with an owl, hawk, and a snake is a lot of fun, but also a great deal of hard work. Show animals are nervous, which in turn, places me under a strain as well. I was responsible for their welfare, and at times this created problems, especially in schools' schedules: like the times I had to cancel a school assembly—for a second time. "I'm sorry," my apology would go, "but my hawk isn't feeling too well today. I've got to cancel the program." I could get away with that once, maybe twice, but the third time would be pretty hard to explain to people who operate on schedules like Amtrak does.

Hawks are like that. Some days they're as

docile as a kitten, other days they'll about tear your arm off when you try to work with them.

I had a goshawk that a logger gave me a number of years back. The logger had felled a big fir tree on the rim outside Newberry Crater on the Deschutes National Forest. When he went out to limb it, he found the remains of a stick nest with a goshawk chick buried in the debris. I raised the bird and trained it for hunting sage grouse and jackrabbits.

The goshawk was a female, best for hunting because of their fearless nature and their large size. In the old world, the goshawk was known as the "pot hawk"—if anyone was going out to hunt for meat on the table, they took the goshawk because it rarely missed and a person came home with something for the pot.

Training it is sometimes like playing Russian roulette—I never knew what the bird's mood was going to be like, morning or afternoon. I could walk up to her on some mornings, and she would actually cluck at me like a chicken. Other times she would sit on her perch and glare at me, then suddenly bolt straight at my face.

Buteos, the soaring hawks such as the red-tail, were usually more relaxed. I used a trained red-tail that I named "Hawk" in my programs. It was a bit temperamental, but I could almost always tell when he was in a fit by his activity in the mornings. If he immediately bolted off the perch as I approached, snapping the leash tight, I had a hunch it wasn't going to be a good day for an assembly. However, he would usually calm down after getting a lab rat or two, and then we'd go out and do two assemblies in the morning and two in the afternoon.

On the other hand, my great horned owl, "Owl", was about as solid as a rock. The only thing I ever saw him get excited about was someone in a wheel chair . . . or a female owl. He bolted once when I was going up in an elevator in the Cosmopolitan Hotel in Portland, Oregon, where I was to speak to a garden club. The elevator stopped, and when the doors opened, there was a man in a wheel chair waiting directly in front of the doors. It was quite a shock for

Owl, he leaped off my shoulder and went sailing down the hallway. Unfortunately, the elevator operator was already spooky about the owl perched on my shoulder, and when it suddenly dashed out of the elevator, she panicked and hit the "up" button. The doors closed, leaving the poor man in the wheel chair and Owl on the floor below.

"Stop the elevator!" I shouted—which she did . . . on the next floor above. I ran out and down the hall, sailing through the exit door and down the stairs, three at a time. As I burst through the door on the floor where the owl had been left, I didn't know what I'd find. I looked down the hallway, but no owl, just a bewildered man in a wheel chair. I looked down the other hallway, no owl. I ran down another long hallway and looked first left—no owl—then right. Way down at the end, three ladies were standing like statues, staring at something at their feet.

I had a hunch I knew what or who it was, and headed down the hall at a trot calling, "Hey, Owl, here I come! Don't worry, I'm here." I felt a great sense of relief when I heard his familiar chittering call, his way of letting me know he had heard me. As I walked up to the three women, one of them turned her head and said, "Oh, my . . ." then she turned back to stare at the owl sitting on the floor by her feet.

"I'm terribly sorry," I apologized, bending down to pick my pal up off the floor.

Then the magic spell broke and the ladies got their wits about them and began chattering away, saying all the sweet things ladies always did when Owl turned on the charm. He was chittering softly as I placed him back on my right shoulder, where he snuggled up to my ear, carefully grasping my ear lobe and pinching it lightly in his beak. One of the ladies said, "Oh, look . . . the owl is biting his ear, isn't that cute . . ." We walked back to the elevator, made it to the Top of the Cosmo where Owl and I proceeded to give our talk to the ladies of the garden club. Owl was his usual big hit . . .

One of the things I enjoy about doing slide shows, assemblies, and talks is the way education works like a two-way street. I can recall vividly the time I took my big rat snake, a gopher snake, a rubber boa, and a tiny, ring-necked snake to do a talk on reptiles at a school in West Sylvan. I had just made the statement, "Snakes are cold-blooded reptiles and cannot control their body temperature, but are at the mercy of their environment." ZOOM! A hand shot up about halfway to the back of the room.

I knew I had just put my foot in my mouth, and was about to learn something. I took the microphone off the stand and walked to the edge of the stage (holding the gopher snake in the other hand) and called on the person with the hand waving like a Boy Scout semaphore flag. "I see a hand waving back there. Would you come up here and tell everyone what you want to say." All the people in the auditorium turned to look. I waited, but no one stood up. "Come on up here, please. I think what you have to say is valuable to us all. Please come on up here." It was wonderful to see that little fellow walking down the aisle toward the stage, each step a timid move toward something I'm sure he had never done in his whole life. As he approached the stage I hopped down with the microphone and squatted down alongside him.

I asked him his name and he responded in a whisper, "Tommy . . ."

"Well, Tommy. What do you have to share with us?" I asked, placing the microphone in front of his mouth.

He was silent for a moment, then he took a deep breath and with the voice of a zealot, little Tommy told the whole world, "I lived in India when I was a little boy, and when I was in the jungle with my Indian friend, he told me that the female reticulated python is capable of raising her body temperature five degrees when she is incubating eggs!"

I led the entire auditorium in a big hand of applause for Tommy. I had learned something—again.

I had to cancel out one assembly two times for a school near Longview, Washington because each time my red-tail had been acting silly. On the day we were scheduled to go, he was in a worse twit. He just wouldn't settle down, no matter what I offered him. He was then two years old, it was March, and the season for mating was

upon us. Perhaps that had something to do with his mood—in any event—he was a terror. It was just impossible for me to cancel again, so I gritted my teeth and put Hawk and Owl in the Ford "box" I was driving in those days and headed for Washington.

All the way up the freeway it was like an airshow in that van. Hawk just would not stay on his perch. We almost got into a wreck when he suddenly flew into the front and landed on the steering wheel, obstructing my view as well as making steering very difficult.

Owl, who was usually calm, cool, and collected, seemed to catch a bit of the agitation the hawk was stirring up, and he started acting nutty, hopping from one side of the van to the other, and pooping on everything. The hawk squirted across the van, hitting the windows, windshield, and even the seat I was on—it was not a good trip, and I was relieved to see it end.

I walked into the school with Owl on my shoulder, stopped by the office and announced my arrival, and immediately went to see the room we were going to use for the assembly. It looked good—a cafetorium—combination lunchroom, gymnasium, and auditorium. The windows were up high, and covered with a heavy, wire mesh. A small stage had been set up with a standing microphone for Owl to perch on and a towel was draped over a chair for Hawk. I set Owl on the microphone and walked outside to the van with a better feeling for the day, but was quickly reminded of what was probably coming.

Hawk was perched on the steering wheel—facing the windshield—and there were two, long streaks of white down the driver's seat. "Blast!" I grumbled angrily, and prodding the hawk on my glove, I headed for the cafetorium. I usually handled him bare-handed, but with the mood he was in, I decided it was wise to use a glove. He seemed to settle down somewhat when I coaxed him off onto the familiar foothold of the padded chair back.

The assembly got off to a rough start with Owl behaving nutty, probably because of all the antics of the hawk during the long drive

Jim and "Snake." This gopher snake has the distinction of being petted by 10,000 children.

from Portland. He didn't respond as he usually did; he only ate one rat—reluctantly—and flew around the room only once—reluctantly—and he hooted only once when he came back to perch on the microphone. To make matters worse, all during the owl's part of the show, the hawk was frittering away on his perch. He'd jump to the floor, trying to drag the chair off the small, makeshift stage. Each time he pulled those shenanigans, the kids would laugh, causing a mild roar.

This is going to be a short show, I said to myself, canceling out some of the parts I did with the owl. Gritting my teeth, I turned to the red-tail. As I picked him up from the

chair I could feel his talons sink into my glove. He glared at me, then at everyone else in the room.

At the point in the program when I allowed the birds to fly free, I would ask the kids for their cooperation, to remain as quiet as possible as the birds flew around them. I also told them not to look up (but if they did, be sure to keep their mouths shut). When I noticed that they hardly heard me, not laughing as kids usually did, I could tell this program was going to be unlike any I had ever done before (or hopefully would do again).

I tried to bring the kids to a quieter mood by expanding my talk about respect for wildlife, and almost pleaded with them to sit quietly as the hawk flew, but I think the hawk's restlessness had already infected them. They just couldn't help but squirm, chatter, and wiggle around. I couldn't put it off any longer, and slipped the leash from Hawk's jesses.

That's what I've been waiting for, he must have thought and with a sudden burst, he leaped off the glove and mounted to the ceiling. He hovered for a second, looking all around the room, then suddenly went into some of the most thrilling aerobatics I've ever seen from a hawk—even during court-ship flights. He folded his wings and dropped right into the aisles between chairs, zooming back up to the ceiling. Then he sailed around the light fixtures, and dropped again to floor level, swooping past me like a peregrine falcon, even turning to look at me as he zipped by. I thought he was going to quit any moment, but he got his speed up and began to circle the room, faster, faster and faster! I began to panic! I was afraid he might make a try for one of the windows and get killed if he struck the wire screen.

Each trip he made around the room was faster then the one before, and each time, the kids became louder and louder as their squealing, shouts, clapping, and stomping echoed off the walls. Pandemonium broke out, and I couldn't do anything about it. I knew something was going to have to give any moment, but when it did, I was aghast!

As I watched wide-eyed, Hawk twisted his tail to steer himself toward his landing place. I couldn't believe it! He was headed for the back of the room, and the only thing there was a tall man standing by the door! Oh, no! I groaned, he's never done this before . . . The hawk was going to land right where he was headed, I knew it. I wanted to shout, and warn the guy, but it was all happening too quickly. It wouldn't have done any good anyway. At the last split-second, the red-tail spread his tail, threw his big wings open, and holding both feet ahead of him, landed as gracefully as a dove on the man's head . . . then slid right off, dropping to the floor, clutching a hair piece!

The whole place came apart! Kids went wild! I wanted to leave, but they knew my name and telephone number. I was dead no matter how far or fast I ran. Hawk was on the floor for only a second as he looked down at his feet, looked up at me, and was in the air again, this time carrying his prize around the room for everyone to see. Kids shrieked with delight, adults roared with laughter. Then I looked again at the man standing in the back of the room, his bald head glowing at me!

Hawk suddenly banked. I was expecting him to land on his usual place, the towel draped chair, but not this time—oh, no—he came sailing right at me! Landing at one end of the stage, he came sliding across the floor, right to my feet! Then, as any wild hawk with its prey, he mantled the hair piece and proceeded to kill it, tearing it into small pieces. At last he had something to work out his frustration on, and he did a grand job of it! Hair started flying everywhere, and in a matter of moments, the hair-piece had been reduced to a large patch of fuzz, scattered all over the stage.

I looked up from the destruction and I truly wanted to die. The man who had been snatched bald was slowly walking toward me . . . and I thought I could hear him humming, "Fee-Fi-Fo- . . ." Every child and adult in that room had their eyes on him. I will never forget the look on his face as he closed the distance between us. With each step he got bigger and bigger. The kids couldn't see his face, but I could, and I was baffled. He was grinning at me as he reached out for the microphone.

As he turned to face the kids, a deep hush fell over the crowd. "How many of you people knew I wore that thing?" he asked slowly. A great roar went up from everyone, as they began to laugh and shout. Then he raised his hand and silence dropped like a curtain. Turning to me he said, "If you would feed your hawk more often, things like this wouldn't happen!"

Then we both started to laugh as he stooped down and picked up small tufts of hair and placed them on his balding head. I can still see the small tufts of hair sliding off his head and drifting down toward the hawk. Hawk was the model raptor after killing the hair piece. He went through the

Jim and "Owl." Owl demonstrates wingspan to a science class.

rest of the program without a hitch, even taking a bow in the form of a swoop over the crowd for his final flight, then landing on the microphone.

Of all the programs I've ever done, working with wildlife and kids, I will never forget a visit I made to a small school near Portland where I saw the real power of the world of nature. I was scheduled to do a late morning program in another school, when I received a call asking if I could bring Owl and Snake (a big rat snake I used for programs), to a school for children with social and emotional problems. This was outside my usual presentations; I had never interacted with children with obvious emotional problems. I usually worked with the other end of the spectrum: kids who were filled with natural curiosity, ready to meet every challenge, and chomping at the bit to get on with living. I thought it over and said to myself, "Why not?" then called

the school back, and told them I would be there early in the morning.

As I walked into the room, I had no idea what to expect, and I have a hunch the teachers were in the same boat. I walked in with Owl perched on my shoulder, looking at everything as we said hello. We were shown into a small room where there was a piano and chairs. I put the owl on the top of the piano, a place where he always felt safe, as he could fly off immediately if someone did something he didn't like. Snake was in his overnight carrying case, which I placed on the piano bench. In a few moments the kids started coming into the room, and my apprehension was high as all get out.

As I watched the kids slowly walking into the room I couldn't see anything different about them—no different than any of the other kids I had seen in hundreds of other programs. In fact, they were more calm, more careful, sitting quietly, and watching

The Miracle Worker: This great horned owl helped a child recover.

the owl. I took a moment to talk about the world of nature, something I always did to prepare children for the snake, who was usually first on the show. I must admit, they did act up a little as I opened the overnight case and allowed Snake to come out on his own. But as soon as the first child had the opportunity to see and feel the smooth skin of the rat snake, everyone calmed down and we got into an interesting discussion about snakes.

All the time I was talking about snakes, there was one child walking around the room (like Kipling's muskrat, always running around the walls, but afraid to come to the center of the room). I looked at my watch and saw time was flying, so I placed the snake back into his overnight case and started talking about the owl, who, right on cue—for a reason I can not understand to this day—hopped down from the top of the piano and began to walk up and down the

keyboard, playing an "owl" tune. I couldn't do anything wrong after that. Everything I said, everything Owl did, was right on target. The girl never stopped pacing around the room, all the time staring at the owl.

Time flew by much quicker than I expected, and when I glanced at my watch, I could see it was past time for me to leave. I started to finish up my talk as fast as possible, apologizing for having to leave, but the teachers nodded, understanding schedules. All the children, except the girl pacing around the room, had petted Owl, who had been unusually tolerant, and filed out, all except the pacing girl who was now standing still, her back against the wall. I gave my pal a faint little hoot, and he hopped on my shoulder like he always did when it was time to go. I picked up the overnight case, smiled at the girl, and headed for the door. Just as I got to the doorway she suddenly leaped directly in front of me, blocking my way.

We stood there, looking at each other, and I will never forget the look on that dear child's face. I could see so many things going on in those brilliant eyes that it was frightening: pain, anguish, conflict, terror, and other things I can't bear to think about today—but suddenly she smiled and lit up the room. After taking several big deep breaths, she said, "I know about owls!" That was all: "I know about owls . . ."

I'm not the most savvy person in the world, but what I had seen in that child's eyes and the way she was looking at me all amounted to something very, very important. There was just no way I was going to ask her to move and go through that door. All I could say was, "That's nice . . . what can you tell me about owls?"

That unleashed a flood of words, coming so rapidly that I couldn't keep up with her at first. She told me that owls spit up pellets that contain the remains of food that was indigestible. She also told me that owls have fourteen vertebrate in their necks—twice as many as you and I, a fact not known by everyone—so they can swing their heads about to search for prey. She also told me an owl's eyes are fixed solid in their skull, and in darkness are thirty per cent more efficient

WHOOOOO?

"Whooooo?" questioned Owl of the sea of faces
Ringing him around.
"Whooooo?" he repeated, spreading his wings
With a whirring, rippling sound.

All of the children laughed in delight
At the horned owl, and they clapped
As he ruffled up his feathers and gazed at them;
Unblinkingly at that!

"Whooooo?" he persisted over again,
Turning from left to right,
"Whooooo?" he demanded louder now,
His gold-rimmed eyes so bright.
  "Whooooooo?"

Sister M. Rose of Lima, SNJM

each other, and as she was leaving the room, she waved to Owl perched on my shoulder and said, "Goodbye Owl . . ." and smiled.

I had a good feeling about that exchange as I left the room with Owl and Snake, even though I had already missed my appointment with the other school. Several people thanked me for coming, which people always did, but this was different. The last person to thank me walked to the car with me, and as I was getting in, she took my arm and gave me a hug, saying thank you. As I looked at her I could see tears in her eyes. Oh, oh, I said to myself, what have I done this time . . .? Then, looking at her I asked, "What's wrong? Did I do something . . .?"

She took my arm again, smiled at me and said, "No . . . there's nothing wrong, in fact you did everything right. Do you remember that girl that spent so much time with you talking about owls?" I told her I did, and she knew more about owls then a great many people I ever knew. "Yes . . ." she replied, ". . . and we had no idea she knew so much. You see, that's the first time that child has spoken since she has been in this school."

That shot me clear through! Then the truth of what had happened hit me like a lightening bolt. It wasn't me who had done this, it was an owl—an animal made up of flesh, bones, blood, and feathers. An animal with no sense of right or wrong. An animal that was killed for any senseless number of reasons. An animal that wasn't worth talking about if a person didn't want it around. That owl had found a key—a path for a young girl to take that would hopefully lead her back into a world of normal activity. Ever since that day I have had a new sense of worth for the natural treasures we know as our wildlife heritage.

than yours or mine. She showed me the tiny spoilers on the leading edge of the owl's primary feathers which are designed to give them a silent flight at night—but—she told me, mice can often hear the soft sounds of an owl's wing. She went on and on, and during this time we slowly walked back to the piano where we sat on the bench while she told me about owls and petted him.

I cannot remember how long we sat on that bench, but time flew by very rapidly, of that I'm sure. Something else was happening at that time too; I noticed that several of the teachers walked by the room slowly, looking in and smiling. After a while my new friend slowed down, and as she did, a woman came into the room and asked her if she would like to leave. We said goodbye to

The Children's Zoo

One evening, as I was fumbling for the key to my office at the Children's Zoo, I was suddenly surprised by a woman shouting at me.

"Don't leave yet! Don't leave, please! I have an injured owl!"

I turned around to see who was shouting and saw a very heavy woman panting as she huffed and puffed up the asphalt path that led to my office.

"Please, wait!" she urged again. I walked into my office, leaving the door open and she came rushing in, exclaiming, "I found this poor creature on the road this morning on my way to work. You have to do something for it." With that she set a shoe box right in the middle of my desk.

"Yes, ma'am," I said. "May I have your name and the information on the bird?"

"Aren't you going to look at it . . . ?" she asked, pulling tape from the cardboard cover.

"OK," I sighed, looking into the box as she raised the lid. Of all the injured animals I'd seen—and they numbered in the hundreds—this was the saddest yet. It had not only been hit by something, it was mangled. I couldn't believe it was alive.

"Oh, I'm sorry, ma'am," I said, carefully picking up a little screech owl. "I don't think this poor thing is alive." But I was wrong.

"It moved!" she said, pointing to the one good wing the owl had left.

"By golly, you're right," I answered, not believing what we saw.

"Is it an owl? What kind?" she asked, trying to pet it.

Holding it carefully in the palm of my hand, I looked it over carefully as I said, "I think it's a screech owl."

"Oh, it's so cute," she said, ignoring all the blood and gore covering most of the owl's body, trying to pet it on the head.

"Yes, ma'am," I said, carefully placing the owl back inside the box, on a towel the woman had thoughtfully placed inside to cushion the injured bird. I set the box on top of a file cabinet and turned to the paper work, obtaining the woman's name, address, place where the owl was found and any other information she could offer. I thanked her again and ushered her out the door. I smiled as she went bouncing back down the asphalt trail, wondering how many other animals this thoughtful lady was going to rescue and bring out to us for repairs. Then I set about to tackle the business of the day, and forgot all about that poor, little owl, completely.

This all took place in the late '60s when I was the director of the Children's Zoo, a part of the Portland Zoological Gardens in Portland, Oregon. I also managed a good-sized staff of young people who operated the children's rides within the zoo and cared for the animals in the live exhibits. We also had a animal nursery and facility that cared for injured wildlife. In addition to all that, we also operated a Conservation Education department with classes in a variety of wildlife subjects for children, families, and teachers.

Four days later, while looking for something in my office, my secretary, Maxine, noticed the shoe box on the top of the file cabinet. She came over to me with a quizzical look, asking, "What's in this box?"

She would never open it herself for she had done that once and a healthy, four-foot-long, great basin gopher snake stuck his head out of the box so quickly she didn't have a chance to remember she was petrified of snakes. She just screamed and threw the box across the office. That, in itself wouldn't have been too bad, but there were three other ladies in the office signing up their children for zoological classes, and they were also petrified of snakes. As the box slammed against the wall it flew open, revealing all four feet of that beautiful reptile sailing through the air. The bedlam that followed was almost too horrifying to describe . . .

Thankfully, I wasn't in the office at the time, just reaching for the door handle. I heard the first scream, then the bang as the box hit the wall, then the next thing I thought I heard was horses galloping through my office. I knew it couldn't be horses—they wouldn't have all fit. I jumped back, fully expecting something, and I didn't want to get run over. Four women fled out the door, waving their arms, holding their skirts against their legs, and trying to run as fast as they could.

"What's going on!" I shouted, trying to stop Maxine.

"It's a snake!" she wailed, breaking away from me and dashing up the tunnel to the Birthday Party area of the Children's Zoo.

After a few moments and some smooth talking, I got all four women back to the door where they waited as I went inside to see if I could scrape the poor snake off the floor. I was sure they had stomped it to death. It took a few moments, but as I looked under my desk I caught sight of the snake's tail as it dashed for cover near the wall. I made a grab for him and lucked out, catching just enough tail to drag the rest out, and got him all gathered up. I wrapped him around my wrist (gopher snakes seem to like that warm spot) and quickly dialed up Al St. John, my herpetologist friend who cared for the reptile exhibit and gave snake lectures in the Ladybug Theater, the zoo lecture hall.

I could see Maxine and her three ladies peering at me through the window of the office, watching that snake wrapped around my arm. I pointed to the snake and smiled. They just glowered back. Al was quick that day. He appeared at the door, stepped in and slowly unwrapped the snake from my arm and started out the door for the snake exhibit area. As he went out the door the four ladies backed away, giving him plenty of room.

Al turned to them and smiled. "Don't worry, ladies," he drawled. "He's a friendly little fella."

As peace and quiet descended, Maxine asked again, "What's in the box?"

"Oh, my gosh!" I exclaimed, "I plumb forgot that poor little guy. It's a screech owl that was hit by a car—or something—it's all torn to pieces. One wing is completely gone, one leg is broken, and his head is all smashed in. To make things worse, I think he's blind as well. The poor little guy must be dead," I added, slowly removing the lid. The owl suddenly sat back on its little, frayed, tail and began thrashing at me with his only good foot, talons snapping at me. I just couldn't believe it.

"Look at this, Maxine," I said, holding the box up so she could see.

"Oh," she exclaimed. "That poor little thing." Then she took the box away from me, looked again at the owl and then gave me a withering look. "How could you forget that poor little thing?"

Of course, I didn't mean to, but the hectic pace of trying to get everything up and running for the zoo season was taking every

spare minute. The box was up above my usual line of sight, and unfortunately, I do have a terrible memory. It was only natural that I'd forget it. Like Mark Twain, I had to turn this situation around, fast.

"Shucks, Maxine," I said. "That's what I've got you for, to help me remember things like this."

She was quick on the draw. "Yes, Mr. Anderson," she said sweetly. "If you would tell me about things like this, I could help you to remember them." Then she pushed the knife the rest of the way in, "I'm not a mind reader, you know."

The truth of the matter was, she *was* a mind reader. Many times she saved my bacon by handing me a report, budget, class outline, or schedule, as I was going out the door to a meeting I had almost forgotten.

We both looked at the owl, still scrambling around in the box, acting like it would like to kill us. That's when I noticed the serious problem with the owl's lower beak. It didn't line up with the upper part of its upper beak. The lower part was way off to the side, useless. "Look at this," I said, picking the owl up carefully and placing it on the desk top.

"How can it eat anything with its beak off to the side like that?" Maxine asked.

"It can't," I said, looking more closely at the problem. "I guess the only thing is to try and set it straight. It can't eat with it like that." So I carefully pushed the lower part of the beak back into the general area it belonged and as I did I could feel a slight snap, and the little owl suddenly began clacking its beak at us.

"You did it!" Maxine said, giving me a big smile. "I'll bet it's pretty hungry. It's been in that box for several days, and maybe it was just going out for a meal when it got hit. That makes it at least five days without food!"

"I agree," I said, carefully handing her the owl. "I'll just go out and get a mouse out of the Mouse House and we'll see what he will do." I went outside to the entrance of the Children's Zoo where we had a fifty gallon aquarium set up with a huge Plaster-of-Paris loaf of bread inside, and about 200 mice. I opened the access hatch, grabbed a tail, made sure it wasn't a lactating momma mouse and headed back into the office.

Maxine had placed the owl back in its shoe box, so I held the mouse by the tail over the top. Usually I knock the poor little critter in the head and kill it before I feed it to something, but this one was lively, and it suddenly twisted out of my grip and dropped into the box. What happened next was almost as unbelievable as that little owl being alive.

The owl backed away from the mouse, tilted his head to one side to get a better view with his one good eye, then made a sudden leap, landing right on top of the mouse, grabbing it with his one good foot. All we heard was a weak little squeak and it was all over. The owl sat on top of the mouse for about three minutes, then it leaned over and slowly pecked at it, making sure it was dead. In a moment it gripped the head with the beak, flipped the mouse up and "gulp," down it went, all in one piece.

"I don't believe it . . ." Maxine whispered, gazing with wonder at that owl.

"Neither do I . . ." I murmured.

Over the next year that little owl became a favorite of everyone who came into the zoo. The story was told and retold, about how I had forgotten the poor little owl, how it had lived in spite of me, and now it was on exhibit down in the Mole Hole. We had designed a mine exhibit for one section of the mole hole where we displayed beetles, mice, shrews, spotted skunks, and in an area where he couldn't get hurt or eaten, the screech owl.

The only serious problem that little owl had, after it had recovered, was it would suddenly go spastic if someone made a sudden move or loud sound nearby. He would utter a little screech, flip over and fall on its side, looking very dead. In a few moments he would come out of shock, stand upright, blink his one good eye and go about his business as if nothing had happened.

The Mole Hole had a special rheostat that would bring the lights up slowly in each exhibit as a visitor pushed a button. As they discovered the little owl, perched on an old timber that suggested an old mine shaft,

they couldn't help but knock on the glass (even though we had placed signs asking them not to). If they did it when the owl wasn't expecting it, the results would be a sudden, death-like flip of the owl. The person who knocked on the glass usually wouldn't say anything, just try to get out of there, but more often than not, there was always someone standing close by who witnessed the owl's sudden "death." That person would come rushing into the office, announcing that they just saw someone knock on the glass of the owl exhibit and the poor thing flipped over, dead. We wouldn't waste an opportunity like that, and would nail the culprit and give he or she, a good scolding. Then I'd send one of the staff down to the mine shaft to make sure our little friend had recovered, which he always did. When I left the Children's Zoo that little owl was still doing his thing, and would often perform for visitors at feeding time.

The Ladybug Theatre was a favorite place for live animal shows at the Children's Zoo. We shared the space with live actors from a Portland company who put on some great performances throughout the summer. Of all the shows we did in the Ladybug, the one that was greeted with most enthusiasm was the snake show.

Al St. John was a natural when it came to reptile demonstrations. His Holy Cow! Gee Whiz! show about reptiles was always a hit for visitors of all ages. Al could mesmerize everyone. The Ladybug was always filled to the brim when we announced that we were doing a reptile show. In summer, it was hotter than the hinges of hell in that little building. That didn't matter, for it could be 150 degrees inside and the people would sit, sweat, and swelter, enjoying every minute of it. We got a great many zoo memberships from that reptile show, and also made many friends for other reptiles of the world. It was only natural that we would want to insure that the snake show went on before anything else, at all costs. The one thing I didn't take into full consideration was Al's dedication to the health and welfare of his charges. That came first, above all else I was soon to discover . . .

It was the right time, and I looked at my

watch again, to be sure. Yep, I was right, the snake show should have been underway, but it wasn't. I slipped into my office, picked up the public address microphone and called Al. It took two calls before he came ambling along.

"Al," I asked. "How come we're not doing a snake show?"

The snake we used for the reptile show was a big, beautiful, twelve-foot boa constrictor, "Cuddles." It had a laid-back attitude about being squeezed, rubbed, stretched out, rolled over, gazed at, and in general poked all over by visitors of all ages. "Cuddles is shedding," Al said in that slow, easy going way of his.

"Shucks, Al," I responded. "We can still do a show with him, even if he is shedding."

"No we can't," Al quickly responded. "He's at that point when his skin is real sensitive and doesn't like being handled." Then he added, "We'll have to wait for at least a week."

This was summer. The show had to go on. Shedding or no shedding, we had to take Cuddles and do a snake show. I turned to Al and explained all this to him, summing it up with, "Al, you go get Cuddles and get that show going. I was just over at the Ladybug and it's chuck full of people waiting for the show. You've got to do it."

Al just stood there, rubbing his nose and gazing at me with a defiant "Go to hell!" look in his eye. "I can't, Jim. Honest. If I try to pick up Cuddles now, there's no telling what he might do. His skin is really sensitive and his eyes are all milky colored. He's having a difficult time shedding." Then he took a step toward the door, stopped, and said, "I'll get the bull snake; it's OK."

Unfortunately, I wasn't listening, or I would have allowed him to take this way out. It was a working solution to the problem, but I was too pig-headed. "No, Al," I exclaimed. "We've got to use Cuddles. All those people are expecting a big snake . . . Cuddles is a big snake! We can't let them down."

I've known Al for over twenty-five years, and in all that time, I could count on one hand the times I've seen him angry. However when someone is pushing him against

Al St. John believes in looking reptiles right in the eye, in this case, an Eastern Oregon Leopard Lizard. They actually touched noses before the lizard scrambled off.

his professional ethic to use an animal that, in his opinion, shouldn't be used or might even be injured, that gets his fur up. This was one of those times. He just said, flat out, "No!"

That did it! I was The Boss; Al worked for me! The show had to go on, that-was-that! "Al!" I said, wearing my best, serious scowl, "You get out there and get Cuddles and get into the Ladybug and do that show! Period!" He glared at me, spun around and shot off for the Jungle Exhibit where Cuddles was kept. I turned on my heel, stomped back into my office, slammed the door and dropped into my chair, feeling defeated.

Maxine was surprised, for I was also slow to anger and she seldom saw me in this shape. "What was that all about?" she asked quietly.

I told her about the snake show, Cuddles, and Al's attitude, expecting a little sympathy from Maxine.

"Do you think that was wise?" she asked. "Al knows what he's talking about. Suppose Cuddles gets injured . . ."

I sat thinking about what had taken place. After a few moments I decided that two against one was a lesson for me. What if Al was right. Maxine was a sharp lady. She could sense something I had missed in my

Sally Carr holds a South American Boa which was used in the Ladybug Theater snake shows at the Children's Zoo.

absurd, boss-like pride. I was just getting up to go out and tell Al to do what he thought best when I ran into him at the door. He still had a very angry look on his face. If looks could kill, I was dead.

Then I noticed a young man behind him, about twelve years old, who was holding his neck, and I could see blood coming from around his fingers. At that point the snake show was forgotten. I rushed them into the office and placed the boy in a chair. Before I had an opportunity to look at what was causing the blood, I was suddenly pushed aside by a very excited lady who shouted "Is it poisonous?"

"Is what poisonous?" I asked.

"The snake!" she shrieked. "The snake that bit my son!"

I looked at Al who glared back at me with that "I told you so . . ." look, as he quietly mumbled "Cuddles bit him . . ."

"Cuddles did what?" I blurted. Then I carefully took the boy's hand away from his neck. Al and Maxine stood there, smiling at each other.

"Is it poisonous?" the woman shouted again.

I looked at Maxine, pleading with her in sign language to try and do something; everything was getting out of hand. Maxine came through, as she always did. "No, madam," she responded, taking the woman's arm and leading her to a chair close by. "The boa constrictor is not a poisonous reptile. They do have teeth, as do most snakes, but they do not have any poison. Please be seated and relax. Mr. Anderson and Mr. St. John will care for your son." Then she patted the woman's arm, adding, "All of our staff have plenty of experience in this sort of thing." I marveled how much Maxine knew about an animal that she not only loathed, but would run from as death itself.

"OK, young man," I said with my best boss authority. "Let me take you into the wash room and clean you up and take care of those scratches. You'll be good as new." I took the boy's hand and led him out of the office.

As I was going by Al, he looked at me and under his breath he mumbled, "Be sure to get all the teeth out of his neck."

I examined the boy's neck closely and sure enough, there were about ten or twelve tiny, needle-like teeth protruding from the skin above the collar of his shirt. I didn't know how I was going to get past this one.

He was a good patient. I sat him down on

the toilet bowl, took a paper towel dipped in the zoo vet's best antiseptic solution and began to wash the tiny punctures on the boy's neck. Each time I came to a tooth he would flinch and ask, "What's that?"

I always thought that the best way to deal with something like that is to tell the truth, and I did, "Well . . . umm . . . uhh, that's a tooth," I said. "You've got about twelve of them in your neck."

"Really?" he exclaimed, jumping to his feet. "Let me see." He looked into the mirror on the wall, trying to turn so he could see the back of his neck. "Is that one?" he asked, pointing to a bloody spot on his neck.

I moved closer to examine the place. "Yep, that's one," I replied. "Now come on over here and let me finish cleaning you up."

"May I have the teeth?" he asked, holding out his hand.

"OK," I said, carefully returning to the task of getting the teeth out, wiping up the blood, making certain his neck was thoroughly cleaned, and all the tiny punctures were completely washed out.

As we walked back into the office, the boy's mother jumped up, asking, "How is he? Will he have any scars? Will he get sick? Will I have to take him to the hospital?" She inspected the bandage I had placed on her son's neck, trying to peek beneath it for a closer view of his injury.

"Look, Mom!", he exclaimed proudly, holding out his hand. "Teeth from the snake. They were in my neck!"

Maxine was quicker than I was, and she caught the boy's mom before she fainted on the floor. I sputtered, "Put those things back into your pocket!" adding, "Please!" I looked over at his mom and Maxine and sighed in relief. She hadn't fainted, and Maxine was rubbing her hands. "You all right, ma'am?" I asked.

"Yes," she answered, weakly. "I'm all right." She sat there, glassy-eyed.

Just about that moment, who should come strolling through the door of the office but Dr. Matt Maberry, the zoo veterinarian. He took one look and could see that something was haywire. "What's going on, Jim?" He watched everyone as I quickly related the events, making sure I had the correct count

of the teeth. As I finished, he slowly turned to the boy's mother and without hesitation launched into the most beautiful lecture I have ever heard on the biology of the boa constrictor, the effectiveness of the cure I had used, how heroic her son had been, and then capped it all off by insuring the boy's mother that her son was going to recover without any problems, for he—Dr. Maberry—was a doctor of worth, having spent several years with the US Department of Public Health—which he had.

It worked. Maxine finished filling out all the necessary paperwork. I assured the mother again that everything would be okay. The boy knew he was a hero, and he had the snake's teeth to prove it. As the crew began to file out of the office, I quietly took Al's arm, detaining him. He looked at me with vindication written all over him as I started to open my mouth.

"It's all your fault, Jim," Al said, smiling. "If you hadn't insisted on using Cuddles for the snake show, this wouldn't have happened."

"Okay, Al," I agreed, "just tell me how that kid got so close to Cuddles to have his neck bitten."

"Well, you know how that jungle exhibit is . . ." Al began. "It's tough to get in and out of there with Cuddles, because you've got to hold him while trying to close that ----- door." I nodded my head as he went on. "Well, Cuddles was really writhing about as I was trying to lock the exhibit door. I couldn't hold him and get the door locked too, so I turned, looking for someone to help, and there stood this kid, watching me struggling with Cuddles and the door." I winced at what was coming next. "So I just handed Cuddles to him and said, 'Here, hold the snake'." He demonstrated this with his arms, and then said, "I guess the kid got to squeezing the snake too hard, trying to hold him better. The next thing I knew the kid lets out a scream, his mother lets out a scream, and there's Cuddles with his mouth wrapped around the back of the kid's neck . . . I had a heck of a time prying his mouth open."

We stood there, staring at each other, then he began to giggle. We couldn't help it. At that moment Dr. Maberry came back into the office and caught us standing there with our arms around each other, laughing our heads off.

"I thought you two would see the humor in all this," he laughed, and the day went on to its usual runamuck pace.

Education will eventually solve most of the problems facing society, I'm sure of it. This same process is also helpful in keeping a zoo operating smoothly. I had been well educated in the biology and tolerance of snakes as they're shedding their skin. Al had seen to that, and I thought Cuddles was out of the picture as a potential problem . . . but I was wrong. It was the anxious call from Dr. Maberry that got me worrying all over again.

"Jim!" he said, quickly. "This is Matt. Is Cuddles in his cage?"

"Just a minute, Matt," I answered, laying the phone down and rushing out of the office. I could tell by the timbre of Doc's voice, this was no time to joke around. I dashed up to the snake exhibits and inspected the jungle habitat. No Cuddles!

"Al!" I shouted, heading for the area behind the exhibits. "AL!" I shouted again, going through the door at a run.

"Right here," came his easy going , quiet answer. "What do you want?"

"AL!" I sputtered, "Where is Cuddles?"

"Gosh, I don't know, Jim." He answered. I almost went into shock.

"Al!" I almost shouted, grabbing him by the shoulder. "Find him! Now!" Then I ran back to the office to pass along the dreaded news to Dr. Maberry.

"Matt. Cuddles isn't in his cage and Al doesn't know where he is," I blurted out.

"Oh, oh," he said. "I was afraid of that. Jack just got a call from a lady just above the zoo, and she is scared to death. She claimed she just found a snake laying in the driveway that's as long as her car."

"Cuddles!" I moaned.

"Must be," he agreed. "Do you want to go up there with me and bring him back? I'll come right up and pick you up."

"You bet! I'll meet you out front!" I said, bumping into Al on the way out.

"I found him," he said, with a big grin. "He's up in the false ceiling above his cage." Then he looked down, adding, "I didn't think to look up there."

A great wave of relief swept over me, and I gave him a hug saying, "Get him down will you, Al. I've got to go out with Matt and see if we can catch his brother."

"Oh, shucks, Jim," Al said. "It's not necessary to go to all that trouble. He'll come down in about a week or so, when he gets hungry." He must have seen the look of death on my face as I turned to speak, for he quickly blurted out, "OK! OK! I'll get him down. Don't worry!" I didn't, not about Cuddles anyway . . .

"Ready?" Doc asked as I climbed into his car. "It's just up above the arboretum; you can see the house from here." He pointed to the steep hills above the zoo.

"Cuddles is in the jungle exhibit, Matt," I said.

"That so?" he said, glancing over at me. "Then I wonder what we've got up on the hill?"

We were both unable to answer the question as we slowly drove up the long driveway to the house of the woman who had called the zoo office. Matt got out of the car and rang the bell, saying, "Let me do the talking, Jim."

The woman who came to the door had a spooky look on her face as she asked, "You from the zoo?" As Matt nodded his head she opened the door, let us in and quickly shut it behind us. "I'm so grateful," she said, shuddering. "It was so big it scared me half to death. I was almost paralyzed."

Dr. Maberry said many comforting things and then got down to the nitty-gritty. "Could you describe the snake for us again, miss?" he asked politely.

"Oh, yes," she said, and then launched into the description of the snake she said was lying next to her car.

As her description continued I began to wonder what I was hearing. This was not a description of a boa, at least not any boa I knew about. I ran through my mental snake recognition file, trying to pick out the reptile she was describing, but failing to put it into the size perspective she claimed to have seen. The only one that had the pattern she described was the common garter snake—

but that was impossible. Dr. Maberry sat on the soft chair, waiting for the woman to finish, not saying a word. As she finished, Doc turned to me and said, "Well, Jim. Let's go on outside and see if we can find this critter." We both stood, thanked the woman and went out to the driveway.

We searched carefully, everywhere—around her Mustang, under it—behind it. In the trunk. In the engine compartment. Even inside the car; still no snake. Then we began to walk slowly in circles, each further from the car. Suddenly Doc shouted, "Here's a snake!"

I ran over to where I could see him looking on the ground, under a big rhododendron. I couldn't believe my eyes. "It's a garter snake, Doc," I declared, turning to look at him.

"Yeah," he said, looking back. "What do you think . . . ?"

I reached out quickly and grabbed the snake just behind the head, trying to keep my hand away from the thrashing tail. "Yuck!" I complained. "I sure don't like that stink they put off from those scent glands back there." I couldn't escape the thrashing tail as the snake spread that awful stink over my hands.

"What do you think?" Doc asked again.

Placing the snake in my sport coat pocket, I walked back to the house, saying over my shoulder, "I've got a hunch . . ." As I arrived at the door I pushed the doorbell and waited. In a moment I could hear the lady coming.

"Yes?" she inquired, swinging the door open.

"Umm, I think we found the snake, ma'am," I said quietly. Then I slowly took my hand out of my pocket holding the garter snake in a tight grip. "Does this look like it?" I asked.

I wasn't prepared for her reaction. No one could have been. That poor woman was as nervous as a pregnant fox in a forest fire. "That's it!!" She screamed, leaping backward and slamming the door.

"Let's go home," Doc said. On the way back down the hill to the zoo, he and I sat discussing the snake that had spooked that poor lady, and as we did, he volunteered what he thought was a solution.

"I knew a kid that was always picking up snakes and putting them in his pocket. He'd wait until he found someone who was deathly afraid of snakes, preferably smaller than he was and a girl, then he'd sneak up behind them, whip that snake out of his pocket and poke it in their faces, shouting, 'Eat it! Eat it!' over and over. I'm not afraid of snakes, but if someone did that to me, it wouldn't take long before I had some awful dreams about them."

Throughout the years that I was on the lecture circuit with my team, a red-tailed hawk, great horned owl, a beautiful gopher snake, and my big rat snake, I always remembered that poor lady and her absolute fear of snakes. I always made every attempt to never frighten someone with a snake and do everything I could to create respect for these poor, misunderstood reptiles. I would have bad dreams myself if I had been the person who created fear in anyone for such a beautiful creation as a snake.

Zoo Days Wuz Good Daze

Over the years, I've come to appreciate a saying that a friend of mine, Ray Rose, uses in his millwright trade: If it ain't broke, don't fix it. It goes with the same frame of mind that makes things look greener on the other side of the fence. I wish I had paid attention to that philosophy when I got the "grass is greener on the other side of the fence" fever

and began to look with an eager eye at the new position being created at the Portland Zoological Gardens by the Portland Zoological Society: Director of Conservation Education and Children's Zoo. That was a mouthful to say, let alone try and do it—but I decided to give it a whirl anyway.

Over the years with OMSI I cultivated a

lot of good pals—young and old alike—in both the museum and at the zoo. As the plans for the Children's Zoo's education department were beginning to take shape, several of my friends on the Zoological Society Board inquired if I would be interested in coming over and running the show. Hillman Lueddemann and Borden Beck were two movers on the Board in those days, and both were encouraging me to accept the new position.

It was easy to switch over in those days— no need for a lengthy and detailed resume to tell everyone what a wonderful person you were. What you did on the ground sort of proved what you might be capable of doing in the new place. I had helped to establish a bunch of new programs in science education at OMSI; there was no reason to believe I couldn't do the same thing at the Zoo. True enough, I didn't have Ray Barrett, Dorothy Mason, Barbara Curtis, Mike Utoff, or Loren McKinley to back me up, and I didn't know the zoo management structure very well either, but Dr. Matt Maberry was there, and he was worth his weight in gold . . . "So why not?" I asked myself.

I changed hats and went over to the Zoo to fix everything right. The first obstacle I ran into was the hard head of Jack Marx, the Director of the Portland Zoological Gardens. Jack was a darn good zoo man—a showman of showmen—and perhaps the sharpest animal trader and zoo keeper this side of the Mississippi. He had a knack for trading up for a variety of specimens, and the entire zoo was the winner.

Thanks to Jack, Morgan Berry, and Doc Maberry, the first Asian elephants to begat in captivity did so at the Portland Zoo. Although Thonglaw, the great bull elephant at the zoo had a great deal to do with the success of breeding elephants there, I think Doc probably was the man who showed him which end was which. In any event, Jack took a great deal of the credit, rightly so, for setting the stage on captive Asian elephant reproduction, and he sweated blood and tears when Rosie was about to deliver her first baby.

Jack wasn't too happy about having a Naturalist loose in the Children's Zoo, especially one who had the reputation of cutting corners and getting things accomplished quicker than many people thought it should be done. So I went into this new position with at least one person looking at me with a jaundiced eye, but I was sure the grass was greener.

My greatest ally in those days at the zoo was my old pal and co-schemer in natural science education, Dr. Maberry—officially the veterinarian for the Zoo—but unofficially possibly the best man in Portland in those days for helping teachers learn more about the wildlife with whom we share this planet. He was a pioneer in using zoo animals as tools for teaching conservation education. He and I collaborated on many, many wonderful teacher in-service workshops that involved the use of just about every part of the zoo's medical and animal facilities.

Dr. Maberry is also well known throughout the world as a wonder-worker at solving the health problems of zoo animals. He watched over all of them as my grandfather watched over his milk cows—both men thought as much of their responsibilities. I wish I had a nickel for every hour I spent helping Matt as we placed drugged cougars carefully onto the X-ray table, attended the baby hippo, clipped the wool off the infernal, spitting llamas, or watched with caution for signs of movement while working on one of the big male chimps or bears.

I always wondered how he could work so casually while trimming an elephant's feet as it balanced on three legs atop a small block about two feet off the concrete floor. I asked him about it one evening, and he just grinned at me and said, "Oh, I'm not near as nervous as they are. They don't want to fall either." He was a wonder at his trade, and a great human being to be around. We'd also go out to the Regional Primate Research Center in Beaverton often where he had several friends working in various areas of medicine. I soaked up a great deal about wildlife biology from these visits as well.

One evening an elderly woman appeared at the zoo gate holding two big sacks of veggies and fruit. "Well," she stated in a powerful bass voice, "I'm here to feed the elephants."

A typical bird-banding day in the rolling wheat country of central Oregon in the '60s. Rich Steeves arrived carrying his lunch and our water, while Carl and Grace Battjes and two students watch as other kids return with locations of new nesting sites. In the background is the old logging crummy donated to the Zoological Society for the field trips and Jim's Piper Cub parked at the edge of a wheat field where he had landed.

I looked at Doc, who had walked over to look into the sacks. As he peered into the collection of fruit and vegetables he slowly shook his head, "I'm sure sorry ma'am, but . . . well . . . the elephant house is closed for the night. We just can't let you in now."

That was the wrong thing to say. "What do you mean, I can't come in!" she almost shouted. "I've taken the bus all the way from the other end of town. I pay my taxes to keep this zoo running. Why, I've been coming up here for years feeding my babies—and now you won't let me in?" Then she puffed up like a bull frog, looked Doc right in the eye and hissed, "Well, we'll just see about that!" Doc was easy. He was a push-over for good-looking teachers, grey-haired old ladies, and hard-working naturalists. He just shrugged his shoulders and sighed, "All right. You can come on down to the elephant house and feed the elephants if you like . . ." and we all meandered down to the far end of the zoo where the elephants lived.

It's been said that elephants have a wonderful memory. I believe that. They often remember a person who has abused them and act accordingly. They also remember people who have been good to them, and they almost purred like kittens when Doc entered their domain. A scientist came to the zoo one time to do some psychological studies on the elephants, and used a cube of sugar to provide the stimulus for various responses. Each time he walked into the elephant house it was almost like one of their long-lost friends showed up. Trunks flailed the air and there was much happy trumpeting and squeals "Here comes Doctor Squires!"

It was that way when the woman stepped into the elephant house with her sacks of goodies. "Here comes the fruit lady!" the elephants squealed.

She knew every elephant by name, calling them over one at a time to get their goodies: spinach, cabbage, apples, cantaloupe, peeled bananas, grapefruit, oranges, and other 'health food'. All the time she was standing by the bars with her purse under her arm, and Doc standing right next to her—in the event something should suddenly go astray and he could quickly snatch her out of harms way, but he wasn't fast enough.

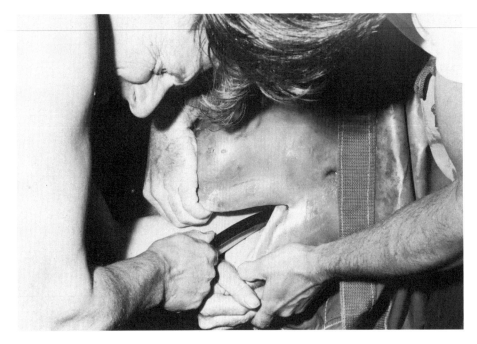

Dr. Maberry tries to save a Beluga whale by carefully force-feeding it a special formula of shrimp and vitamins.

Rosie thrust her trunk into an empty paper sack, gave a huff, and then suddenly reached over and snatched the woman's purse right out from under her arm. "Wait!" she shouted as the purse disappeared through the bars and into Rosie's mouth. "My purse!" the women shouted, thrusting herself against the bars.

That's when Doc came to life. He grabbed her quickly and we all stepped back. "My money!" she said, looking at us with wide eyes. "My keys!" she remembered, looking back at the elephants. "What will I do?" Doc looked at his watch and began to mumble some calculations to himself, then he looked up mumbling something else. "What did you say?" she asked, looking at him quizzically.

"I figure it will take about a week for your purse to get back," he said, smiling at the woman. "If you can come back then, I'll give you a rake and you can search through the elephant droppings . . ." "What?" she interrupted, frowning at him.

". . . but I doubt if you'll find any money," he concluded, and smiling at her added, "however, if you search carefully, you should find your keys."

The woman stood there, mouth gaping and not believing what she was hearing—at first. Then as comprehension dawned she

said, "All right, I'll do it. I'll be back next week."

A week later she showed up, and Doc gave her the rake. After several hours of poking around in the dung she suddenly shouted, "I found it!" Doc and I went over and looked at her discovery, and there in the heap was the clasp from her purse, and shining through the pile was a set of keys. "Doctor Maberry," she said, "Thank you!" And she scooped up her keys and left.

I also recall an event that almost cured Doc of working on wildlife. He was taking care of a small Beluga Whale that had been captured, shipped from Alaska, and was being kept in the huge salt water storage basement of the Seaside Aquarium. The little Beluga just wasn't doing very well, and Doc was having a tough time pinning down the problem.

After a long day's work he'd give me a call, and we'd make the long drive to Seaside where he'd try again to get the whale back on an even keel. The only way he could administer the medicine he was using was to force feed it into the whale's stomach by using a long piece of smooth, flexible plastic tubing. This required a great deal of teamwork on the part of the crew attending the whale—as well as the whale itself. A slurry

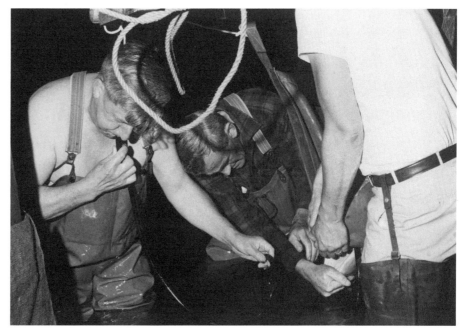

Dr. Maberry blows the formula into the whale's stomach—just before the whale burped!

of shrimp, clams, and fish was mixed with the medicine, and then poured into the tube, which was then carefully pushed into the stomach of the whale. When Doc thought it was in the right place he'd take a couple of big breaths, place the tube in his mouth and blow. It worked most of the time—but once it didn't.

After Doc had checked to be sure the tube was in the proper spot he took the usual big breaths, placed his mouth over the tube and was just about to blow when all of a sudden he suddenly threw up his arms, leaped backwards, gagging and splashing and fell into the cold saltwater. I grabbed him as quickly as I could and got him to his feet, trying to help him get his breath. He choked, gasped, and gagged for several minutes, and finally got his air passages open and then gasped, "He burped!" The odor of whale breath, slaked with rotten fish, was with Doc and me for at least two weeks after . . . it was enough to gag a maggot. As we were driving back to Portland—with the windows wide open in his Chrysler—Doc shouted over to me, with a big grin, "Why do I do this for a living?"

"Because you love it!" I shouted back. He didn't respond, just kept his eye on the treelined road ahead, but even in the dark, I could see his grin was still there.

Then there was the time he and I went out and collected hundreds of snowy owls that had drifted south because of a food shortage in the far north in the late '60s. We flew his Mooney from Portland to as far away as Pendleton and LaGrande; and drove to the Coast, picking up live and dead snowy owls. In almost every case the dead ones had starved to death. I can recall one we picked up over in Vancouver, Washington. It had been observed standing on the bank of a slough, in the same place for several days. As we talked with the woman who had reported it, she was sure it was alive, but when we walked out to pick it up, we discovered that it had been dead for quite some time, and through some freak of nature, was still standing up. That was the subject of a great deal of discussion for several days.

All in all, I personally handled over 215 snowy owls that year. In several locations along the Coast, and in the Willamette Valley, there were similarities to the landscape of the far north, and there were enough small rodents to keep the owls alive. The rolling dunes near Astoria, Newport, and even farther south were good locations. The stubble fields between Corvallis and Salem and the sand dunes along the Columbia River were good places for the owls to make a living, and they survived on voles and other rodents.

I've always wondered how many of the hundreds and hundreds that came south that year went back to breed. I wrote a story about the owls for "Northwest Magazine" of the *Oregonian*, and asked the readers for additional information on the owls. I received cards from people all over the Northwest and California who had seen owls around their places. The most surprising card I received was from a woman who had an owl appear on a cruise ship that was on a trip from San Francisco to Hawaii.

The really good times at the Children's Zoo hadn't started yet. I was still the new kid on the block, and had a great deal to learn about the politics of running the Children's Zoo and the Conservation Education department. The first thing I had to do was get an educational program underway before it was time to open the Children's Zoo for the summer season.

With the help of a whole bunch of gung-ho education majors from Portland State, we launched a pretty exciting Conservation Education program that included children from first grade all the way to high school, and we had a lot of fun conducting live-animal shows in the Lady Bug Theatre. We had weekend nature trips for families, and seasonal trips for sixth to twelfth graders that were a whale of a lot of fun too, and went a long way toward helping young people choose the trail they wanted to take in life.

It was almost like a carbon copy of what we did at OMSI, but on a much smaller scale with an emphasis on wildlife conservation. Natural history classes were held in the Birthday Party area of the Children's Zoo, the Lady Bug Theatre, and just about every place we could find that was warm, dry, and large enough to hold at least five people. We didn't make any money with the programs, but we did make friends, kept some conservation education majors from Portland State out of the poor house, and provided a great deal of understanding and appreciation of wildlife.

We had a serious handicap though, for the Portland Zoological Society didn't have a bus, not even a station wagon that we could use for our Conservation Education field trips. I had to dig one up. It had to be large enough to hold about fifteen students, and stout enough to go places that a regular bus was unable to go. (I had taken the OMSI bus to some places that Loren McKinley and I didn't ever talk about, like . . . well . . . never mind . . .)

I called on Georgia-Pacific for help and they presented the Zoological Society with an old logging crummy. A "crummy," in the event you've never been in the Northwest logging camps, is a small, bus-like vehicle that's used to haul loggers and their saws to and from the woods. It can have several shapes: a regulation bus or a one ton truck with a box on the back that the loggers sat in. No matter what the shape, however, after being in use for about a month, even a new one fits the description, "Crummy."

The one I got from G-P was nothing to brag about; it was a beat out old one-ton Ford truck with about 100,000 miles under the frame, a steel box on the back with padded seats and windows, and a wood stove, but the staff thought it was beautiful! After the first trip we took in it, even the high school kids thought it was beautiful! And thanks to G-P, it was free. My friends at OMSI didn't give me their thoughts about it—they were too polite. We charged over the hills, across the Oregon desert, down to the Coast, and around the state with that old crummy, that we named the "Zoomobile," making a great deal of conservation education headway, but poor gas mileage.

One trip I will always remember was the "Spring Safari" we took into California and Nevada over the school spring vacation in the '60s. I screened the high school applicants to be sure I had a good cross-section of society.

Of the seventeen kids that went on the weeklong trip, some were dedicated, straight "A" students, and knew who they were and where they were going. Others were kids who were doing okay in school, but not self starters and having a little trouble with their identity. A few were absolute drop outs. They scared me. I didn't know what to expect from them anymore than they knew what to expect from us or themselves. They had no idea how to behave on a trip that would take them away from their home environment, which probably wasn't too much to miss. All they did know was agitation, balking, trouble-making, bad language, distrust, a general fear of the adults who were with me, and how to stir up trouble. One of my goals was to turn them around.

The trip was planned to minimize our contact with places that made things easy for the participants. We didn't plan on using motels, but kept to campgrounds and even more primitive sites. I took along a nurse, Grace Battjes (in the event we hurt ourselves somewhere along the trail), and an old pal of mine, Clyde Miller, a man I always liked to have around in the event something really went wrong. We were a good team, capable of handling anything that came along. We thought . . .

I believe this was one of the soggiest springs recorded in Oregon/California history, or at least it appeared that way to us. From the time we left the zoo in Portland, we were in rain, and each day it got better—or worse—depending upon how much you liked sliding into soggy sleeping bags. By the time we got to Big Sur State Park on the California coast, the rain was getting really serious.

As we rolled into the campground at suppertime, we found everything afloat in six inches of muddy water with only one dry space, a covered concrete walkway between two concession stands. It was dry—and dry was like home. With a great sigh of relief, we piled our camping gear, cook stoves, and vittles onto the concrete area. The wind was howling all around us, rain pouring down in buckets and water running past us like a coastal stream in flood. As I looked up into the frame of the shelter I could see that I wasn't the only one who was thankful for a dry space—two robins were perched in the rafters.

After filling our bellies with nice hot food, darkness found us settling down for a good night's sleep. I was just drifting off into slumberland when a brilliant light suddenly flooded our campground and a bullhorn

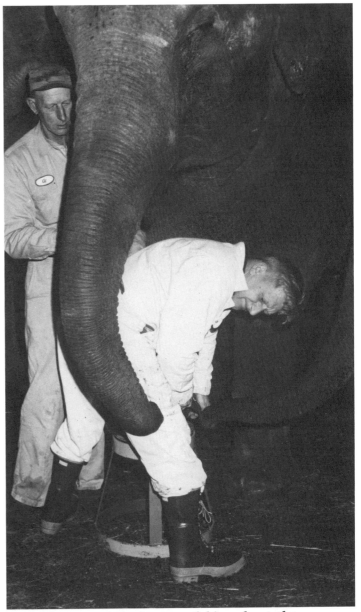

Dr. Maberry and Rosie, one of his pals at the Portland Zoo, play together. Actually, Matt is trimming her toe nails. Jim was always afraid the elephants might fall on Matt when he was trimming their nails, but Matt said that the elephants were afraid of falling as much as he was . . . so everyone was careful!

bellowed: "All right, you people . . . you can't sleep here! Come on! Get out of there!" shouted the unmistakable voice of prodigious authority. We all sat straight up in our sleeping bags, eyes squinched down, trying to see what was behind the blinding light swinging back and forth across our camp. I got into my britches as fast as I could, Clyde was stumbling into his, and Nurse Grace was staring, open mouthed as the voice hit us again.

"All right, out of there! Now!!"

After a few moments, I was dressed and blundered out onto the edge of the concrete, peering into the rain and seeing what this was all about. There sat a guy in a pickup, looking very unhappy, wearing the uniform of his authority, and requiring immediate action from his bull horn commands.

"What's going on?" I asked him.

"You hippies are camping in an unauthorized place here and got to move out," he growled back at me.

"Where?" I asked him in an exasperated voice, waving my arm toward the campground that was under at least six inches of water. It even looked as though the picnic tables might float away before morning.

"I don't care," he said, "just get going. You can't stay here."

I pointed to the kids, some of them standing at the edge of the clearing, looking miserable, and others still in their sleeping bags. Then I took a second look. My God, I said to myself, we do look like hippies. Then I remembered I had about three days of whiskers on my chin—which the park man didn't miss.

"But look at those kids, officer," I pleaded. "They'll catch a cold, maybe even die, if I try to move them to the campgrounds. Everything's under water."

"Then take them to a motel!" he growled again. "There's one that's almost empty down the road. Take them any place you damn please, I don't care; but don't give me any guff—just get goin'." Then he frowned at me and added, ". . . or I'll call the sheriff, and it's off to jail for the whole damn bunch." At that moment Clyde and Grace walked up to listen in.

"Jail!" we grumbled, giving him a dirty look.

I could see that arguing with him was like flogging a dead horse, so I said okay, and went slogging back to the camp to spread the bad news. Grace was mad, Clyde, who has a very short fuse, said some things

about the guy that he wouldn't have wanted to hear, and I wouldn't care to have repeated. The kids were groaning when I told them what the park man said was going to happen if we didn't move out.

"Where to?" Grace asked, raising her eyebrows.

"At the moment, I just don't know," I answered, all the while thinking hard to come up with a hidy-hole.

In situations like this I usually have a Grange Hall somewhere back down the trail that would get us out of trouble. I've used Grange Halls all over the Northwest to solve immediate threats to cold, wet nights for kids and adults. I have yet to meet a Grange Master who would turn me down. In fact, it has always been the opposite—we were invited to use their facilities, and almost always had the offer of hot food the next morning. One of the best was the Alfalfa Grange in Central Oregon—boy, boy, we ate high on the hog there! In our present dire circumstances, I couldn't remember a Grange Hall behind us near Big Sur, 'nor did I know of one up ahead.

Suddenly I remembered the US Navy. Not more than a mile or so back down the road from the campground was a naval base of some kind. I had seen the sign as we splashed by it earlier—Big Sur Naval Facility—and I remembered the glow from the little guard post. I asked Clyde and Grace to help the kids start packing up, then went out and asked the park superintendent if he would keep his light on and help the kids find all their gear, explaining who we were, where we were going, and what our goals were. He almost smiled when I told him we weren't 'regulation' hippies, or some bunch of religious freaks; we just looked that way. I thought his slight smile meant that he might change his mind, but the smile was for another reason: reinforcements had arrived—the sheriff was pulling up. Then I told the sheriff where I was going.

"You're nuts," they exclaimed. "They'll never listen to you. You'd better get a motel."

I went anyway, straight to the Navy gate, almost hidden in the blowing rain of Big Sur. "Good evening," I said, real friendly-like to

Although this owl lived to return to the arctic, it is just one of the hundreds of snowy owls Jim and Dr. Maberry picked up during the owls' big movement from the north in the '60s.

the young man standing watch in the gate house.

He looked out into the rain, wondering who was this rolling up to his little post at ten in the evening on such a soggy night.

"Something I can do for you, sir?" he asked.

"Yes, in fact, there is a great deal you can do for me," I responded, getting out of the car. "May I come in out of the rain?" He didn't respond immediately, just stood there, then he unsnapped the flap over his side arm and took a good, long, hard look at me.

I must admit I did feel a little uncomfortable at that point. I was wearing that three-day beard and didn't look like the "Director of Conservation Education & Children's Zoo." I had the good sense to hand him my zoo business card, which he looked at, and shrugged his shoulders. Then he opened his little door, stood next to it—with one hand on the door, the other next to his side—the gun side—and said, "Yes sir. Come on in out of the rain and tell me how I can help you."

I breathed a great sigh of relief and eased past him—with both my hands in sight—into the tiny, warm, and dry guard room. As I was getting my thoughts gathered to begin my pitch, I was reinforced by an image of

those good kids back there in the campground, packing their wet clothing, camp
gear, and soggy sleeping bags under the
watchful, and probably distrustful, eye of the
park man and the sheriff.

The guard shook the hand I offered, and
told me his name. Then we got down to the
nitty-gritty of my problem. I explained what
I had, where I was going and why, and the
current problem facing my group back at the
campground; I ended my dissertation with a
graphic illustration of what the kids were
facing if we were forced out into the cold
and wet. Then I pleaded for a place to stay
with the Navy, explaining that the kids just
didn't have the money to stay in a motel—
which was the truth—we hadn't budgeted
for such an expense.

He didn't shed a tear as I finished my tale,
but he did give me a big smile and said,
"You know, Mr. Anderson . . . I believe you,
but I can't do anything about your
problem . . ." My face must have dropped a
mile as he said that, for he quickly added,
"but I'll tell you what I will do. I'm going to
call the Skipper and ask him if he'll come
down here and listen to your story." Then
he laughed and added, "This is the best
thing that's happened to me since I've been
on this base . . ."

In about twenty minutes a car pulled up
in front of the guard post and a very neat,
trim, tall man dressed in the uniform of a
naval officer got out and leaped across the
puddles and into the room.

"Good evening!" he said, closing the door
against the blowing rain, "You Mr.
Anderson?" he asked, giving me a wide grin.

"I sure am," I answered, shaking hands
and returning the friendly beginning.

"Well, I've heard your story from our
guard," he stated. "Now, if you don't mind,
I'd like to hear what your problem is, in
person, sir."

I didn't hesitate, but launched into the
night's dilemma for the second time, adding
additional soggy details that I might have
overlooked during the first rendition. I also
made sure that he knew I was an "Old Navy
Man," having served my four years on sub-
chasers in the Atlantic theater. He listened
with what appeared to be a sympathetic ear,

and even looked thoroughly impressed.
Perhaps enough to do something, I thought.

As I finished my tale, he sat down on the
edge of the desk that was against one wall
of the crowded little room, gave me a
quizzical look and said, "Mr. Anderson, if
what you tell me is true, you do have a
problem. But before I make a decision, let
me tell you what my problem is." I thought
for sure I was going to get a negative reply
when I heard he had a "problem."

"You spent time in the Navy," he added
quickly. "And you know what an Operational Inspection is."

"Yes, sir, I do." I answered quickly.

"Well, Mr. Anderson, at the moment this
base is under an Operational Inspection.
This morning we had some "fires" in our
radio facilities, then at lunch time we had a
strange vehicle suddenly appear at the gate
and before the man on watch could stop it,
it drove right onto the base."

He glanced at me sideways with a look of
suspicion. "Now, here it is ten thirty on a
night not fit for ducks, and you appear at
our doorstep with this tale about a bunch of
kids out there in the rain and wind, trying
to pick up their gear, and facing the possibility of going off to a motel they can't
afford—or to jail, which they can't afford
either."

He looked me right in the eye and said,
"Frankly, Mr. Anderson, I think you're
another part of this Operational Inspection."
I started to say something, but he held up
his hand and added, "No, please let me
finish. I'll tell you what—if you do have
seventeen kids out there, and they're as wet
as you say they are, and you're trying to do
all that you say you're going to do, I would
say you have a bigger problem than I have.
Go get your people Mr. Anderson. I'll wait
here for you."

"Yes, sir!" I said with a jump, and headed
out the door.

As I sloshed into the campground I could
see by the park man's body language that
things weren't too good. The sheriff had got
out of his car and was standing under the
breeze-way, writing in his little black book.
Oh, blast! I thought, he's getting ready to
haul us off . . . I ran up to them and put my

arms around Clyde and Grace and said, "Hey, guess what? We're going to be the guests of the US Navy!"

The sheriff let out a great sigh, placed his book under his arm, turned to me smiling, and said, "Thanks, thanks a lot!" Then he grumbled something to the park man, and got in his patrol car and splashed away into the night.

I didn't give the park guy another look; we just finished loading all the gear and kids into the crummy, turned it around, and headed back down the trail for the Navy base.

As we turned into the gate, the kids were peering through the rain-streaked windows and grinned at the guard. The skipper came out of the guard house and called out, "Welcome to Big Sur Naval Facility!" then stood there shaking his head, mumbling to himself, "Now I've seen everything!" After a moment he walked out into the rain to stand next to the cab of the crummy and pointed down the road, "Stop by the gymnasium, Mr. Anderson, and you'll see one of my men who will show you where the boys will sleep; across the road is the mess hall. Put your ladies in the far end; there's a shower and bunks there." Then he waved at the grinning kids and shouted, "We'll see you at the crack of dawn for breakfast."

During breakfast of those good old navy pancakes—crash mats they call them—an officer sat down next to me at the table and whispered, "I'm with the Operational Inspection team. In about three minutes there's going to be a great deal of smoke coming out of the galley. Would you mind leaping up and shouting 'Fire!! Fire!!' We'd like to see how the crew and your kids, respond to this one."

True to his word, just as I was finishing my coffee, a great pall of black smoke erupted from the galley, and as instructed I leaped to my feet, yelling, "Fire! Fire!" Then he and I eased out of the mess hall, carrying our coffee cups, to watch the fun.

The kids were having such a good time with their meal that I wasn't surprised when they casually got to their feet and walked calmly to "safety." It really impressed the Inspection Team and Navy personnel, but then, I didn't tell him that I had already told the kids the night before about the Operational Inspection.

Thanks to the US Navy, and the warm friendliness of the base commanding officer, we spent a warm, dry, comfortable night under cover, provided with a great breakfast and entertainment. I wrote a thank-you letter to the Pacific Fleet Headquarters, giving a glowing account of how kind and considerate our Navy hosts had been on that awful night. Clyde, Grace, and the kids also sent along a note of their own.

We rolled into San Francisco two days later and one of the girls asked if I would stop at a store as we headed toward the California Academy of Science. A little later, a get-well card caught up with me for a signature. I signed it and asked one of the kids who it was going to, "The Big Sur Park guy," she replied.

The best ending I can give to this tale is to tell what happened when I met two members of the expedition a few years later. I met one of the honor students from the trip in Ashland, and we hugged each other as we recalled some of the great times of that trip. She was going to college, studying to be a teacher. However, it was one of the so-called drop-outs, that gave me the biggest thrill. He was dressed in the uniform of the US Navy, and headed for his graduation from ROTC at OSU. Sometimes we do win one . . .

Outdoor School

The concept behind Outdoor School is to bring about a sense of appreciation and respect in young people for the Nature of the world they live in. This is accomplished as they're introduced to the interrelation-ships of soil, water, animals, and plants in an outdoor setting. A lot more than that goes on though.

I got involved in the Multnomah County IED's Outdoor School program when I was the resident director of Camp Colton, back in the '60s, right after things didn't happen at the Portland Zoo like I would like to have seen them happen. That was sort of like jumping out of the frying pan into the fire.

The head honcho that was running the program had his ideas on how things should go, and I had mine. Oh, sure, we both wanted the kids to get acquainted with the World of Nature. On that we agreed 100%. We just didn't agree on how they were going to get acquainted. This came about because of what I thought was his failure to understand what was really going on in the camps. What we were doing to introduce the kids to nature was nothing when compared to what we were doing to introduce them to what it takes to get along in the world. They were learning to get along with their fellow man, to be tolerant of others who have a different skin color. They were learning to tolerate others who didn't think like they did, acted differently, found different foods more to their liking, wore different clothes, and looked at the world they live in much differently. Notice I didn't say "accept" but rather "tolerate." In my opinion, that's the beginning to understanding, respect, and acceptance—tolerating, then acceptance.

Outdoor School, in the Multnomah County IED was—and may still be—one of the greatest places to make things happen when it comes to people getting along with people, as well as learning about the Natural Sciences.

Stop and think about what will happen when you mix sixth graders from four different racial, sociological, and economical backgrounds. Suddenly they're shoved into very close contact for a week in the out-of-doors. On Monday, they all get on their respective busses and travel half the day out to the land of the big trees and open spaces. They go camping in the "wilderness" (which is what it was to many kids who had never gone camping or been outdoors in their whole life—wilderness). The kids from each class are separated out, with about five from each school sleeping in the same cabin with kids they've never met, and will probably never meet again. (In some cases that's like sharing your life with someone from another world.) The camping accommodations are like a Boy Scout Camp, but without the swimming and canoeing. Each cabin has a high school student who is the live-in housemother or father. Oh, these kids were not just any old high school student, but some of the best of the breed.

These young men and women were the ones who really enjoyed being with younger kids, and could afford academically to leave school for a week and come out to camp with "their" little sixth graders. They were the big brother, or sister, mother, father, teacher, and Father Confessor—all rolled up into one. I will never live long enough or find the right way, to express my appreciation for every one of those high school kids who volunteered to be live-in counselors in Outdoor School. They never let me down, and they never let the kids down. Yep, they were (are) The Best.

In Outdoor School no one is supposed to know your real name; you've got a camp name. Our water studies man, whose real name was Murray Miller, an eighty-year-old naturalist in real life, was known as "Flood," while the soils man was "Rocky" and the plant man was "Mossy." The songleader, one of the most energetic and caring ladies I've ever known, was "Skeeter." I was "Mr. Owl." However, the staff called me "George" every once in a while, as sometimes the kids would sing, "George of the Jungle", and I'd swing into the dining hall on a rope, right over the kids' heads and try to grab one with my legs as I went by. I knew my boss would never have approved of that one . . .

We also had a nurse on call at camp who had retired from nursing, but not from caring. "Nursey" always had plenty to do putting band-aids on scraped elbows and knees, but she was even better at helping people to think about the other guy, and to understand a little more about themselves. I enjoyed watching her work that magic of hers on kids who were homesick, angry at their campmate, angry at their parents, or lost in the world. Thanks to Nursey, a great many kids left Camp Colton with better tolerance of people who were different, greater understanding about themselves, and how they can (should) interact with their fellow man.

Now this was back in the '60s, when Martin Luther King was trying to get us WASPS (White, Anglo-Saxon, Protestants) to see a little of what it was like on his side of the fence. We hadn't learned very much, or grown very much, or advanced very much toward tolerating, or understanding what black, white, yellow, or brown people had to put up with to make a living, or to just get along. Black kids from an economically depressed section of Multnomah County were not too happy to find themselves living for a week with white kids who lived in big houses on big hills—or at least that's the way a lot of black kids saw it. The white kids were just as uncomfortable, but when you added in those wonderful high school kids who camped in the cabins with this mixture of younger kids, you've got the makings of a Great Sociological Experiment. That, in my opinion, is what Outdoor School was (is) all about. That too is what nature is all about: a marvelous tool to help us learn and grow.

My boss wanted me to wake the kids up every morning with tape recordings of a Boy Scout trumpet doing reveille. Then I was supposed to have each kid change stations from soil to plants, from water to animals, and around again, with further blasts from a trumpet. That might work well in a Boy Scout camp, but I didn't think it was appropriate in outdoor school. Not that there's anything wrong with Boy Scout Camp, don't get me wrong. The Boy Scouts of America have one of the greatest programs there is for young men on the face of this good earth. I would, and often have, trusted my life to men who were once Eagle Scouts. At the Outdoor School, I thought roosters crowing, and/or Oliver's "Good Morning Star Shine" were more appropriate as wake-up "songs" than a trumpet blowing reveille. During the day, instead of the trumpet blast, I used the theme from the movie 2001, and various bird calls to signal the kids it was time to move from place to place.

You've got to have a feel for kids and older people in order to run an outdoor school. You also have to be ready to shift gears, change direction, even change the program, if you're going to meet the needs of the kids, that is, without sacrificing the objectives of the program. That's the way I will always see the Multnomah County IED Outdoor School program at its best.

We started out each day with a rousing good time in the dining hall. But as it must be in any society, we too had rules to live by, some that were unbreakable. For example, you had to be at your table at 7:00 am for breakfast and announcements, no exceptions. That rule applied not only to the sixth graders, but to the high school counselors and the adult staff as well.

Skeeter, our songleader, was not a person who enjoyed getting up in the morning. She'd rather sit around the campfire, after the kids left for bed in the evening, and sing songs, laugh at stories, look at the stars, dream of the future, and squeeze a little more out of life rather than go to bed and get up early. "Early" to her was any time before one in the afternoon. There were several mornings when she would come bouncing through the dining hall door a little late, or at times a little too late. However, she was the best songleader anyone could ask for, so I was inclined to be a little lenient. No one could get the kids singing that fun-filled, so-called, "eskimo" song, "Ukky-Yukky-Yunga," like Skeeter could. Rules are rules, though, and that's the way it has to be. If a person was late they had to roll a peanut down the middle of the dining hall with their nose, for all to see and enjoy. Skeeter lived in mortal fear of that peanut.

Well, one night she stayed up a little later than she should have, and when rooster burst forth, Skeeter was lost to the world. In fact, if I had put that trumpet reveille and a live rooster in her cabin, she probably wouldn't have heard them either. The little kids were all at their respective seats, along with the high school counselors and the staff. Everyone was ready and waiting for the moment of silence we always had before each morning meal—but no Skeeter.

Every person in the dining hall knew Skeeter was sleeping in, so we waited. It was customary to have announcements every morning before breakfast so that each kid knew where he was supposed to be, when, where, and why. Everyone loved to sing that little ditty, "Announcements, announce-ments, announnnnce—ments," which then would be followed by one of the staff using Johnny Carson's way of being introduced, "And h-e-r-e's Owl." Then we'd discuss the day's activities with teachers, students, and staff. This time I told everyone to ignore Skeeter when she came in, then when I gave the signal, they'd all shout, "GOOD MORNING SKEETER!" So we sat and quietly waited. Two minutes went by. Five minutes went by. Ten minutes went by. Still no Skeeter. So we made a plan. We had our moment of silence, then I told everyone to go on with their breakfast, but keep an eye out for Skeeter. She'd do anything to escape the peanut.

Sure enough, almost twenty minutes late, she tried to sneak into the dining hall by crawling under the tables. One of my high school counselors near the door began to wave his hands at me, pointing under his table. I knew who he was pointing to, so we all acted like we didn't know what she was doing and continued to stuff down the wonderful hot cakes, eggs, and home-made syrup. Then Flood raised his hand and pointed under his table. Unbelievably, Skeeter made it to the table where she was supposed to be sitting without stirring up the kids too much, but she didn't know quite how to suddenly appear without someone noticing her. I gave the high-sign to four high school boys and we all tip-toed to each corner of the table Skeeter was under and at the count of three, all the kids sat back quickly and we lifted the table into the air and across the room.

There was Skeeter, all hunched over, her hands over of head, looking like a squirrel suddenly exposed to a swooping Goshawk. Everyone in the room, including the cooks, shouted, "GOOD MORNING SKEETER!" Then pandemonium broke out as the chant rose like a tidal wave through the hall: "Roll the Peanut! Roll the peanut! Roll the peanut!" Feet banged on the floor until I thought the roof was going to collapse. The price for being late had to be paid, and Skeeter knew it. She slowly stood up, and silence settled

over the room; you could have heard a pin drop as she whispered "Do I have to . . .?" in a tiny falsetto voice. The kids' response was an overwhelming. "YES!" they all screamed. Skeeter rolled the peanut the full length of the dining hall and became a champion to every person in the room, including me . . . and she was never late again.

I mentioned that Outdoor School was a wonderful place to create new thoughts about living with people who didn't think like you did, a place to make things happen. One incident I'll never forget took place when we had classes from Martin Luther King School, West Sylvan School, another from way out Rose City way, and the other from the St. Johns area. We couldn't have mixed those kids better if they'd been placed in a blender.

I had gone to see the teacher and class at Martin Luther King School earlier in the year, as I did with all schools, so they became better acquainted with what Out-door School was all about, what the school could expect from us, and what we expected from the school. That's when we'd also try to answer everyone's questions, and to have everyone look forward to going.

I'll never forget the teacher who was in charge of the class at Martin Luther King School. She was a second generation black teacher, a woman who knew what she was doing, knew her kids, and loved every one of them, but knew almost nothing about the out-of-doors. I was scheduled for the last part of her class that day, so afterwards we went out to have a beer, and to pin down a few more things she was curious about. We had been discussing the Outdoor School program so intently it took at least fifteen minutes before it suddenly dawned on me I was the only white face in the place. For the first time in my life I suddenly felt—well—out of place. Not apprehensive, not uncom-fortable, but out of place.

Then, a big, black man came strolling over to our table, laid his hands right along side of mine, looked Harriet right in the face and said "What are you doing, Hattie, slumming?" The shoe was on the other foot for Whitey. Looking back over that moment

Erin Decane holds a juvenile saw-whet owl that dropped in her fireplace flue near Portland.

today I'm filled with remorse and regret for all the ethnic garbage that I've put up with over my lifetime, some of which I joined in while a young man. I can remember looking at that big guy looming over the table, wondering what to say.

Obviously I had to say something. I reached over, shoved a chair out for him to use, and asked him to join us. But he didn't. He didn't even look at me, he just walked away. I wish I could have reached out and found a way to have him tolerate me, perhaps to know me, but it was probably too late for him. Maybe he hated too much, like so many white people I've known. Perhaps he had a child, or knew one, who was in that awful blast that killed those beautiful children in that Alabama Baptist Church. Maybe he had been subjected to so much race hatred by his parents, friends, or white trash, that he'd had enough. In any event, my school teacher friend apologized for his attitude, which wasn't necessary, as she knew what I was saying and feeling.

When her class arrived at Outdoor School I could sense and hear the friction coming from many of the kids from the other

schools, as many of the white—and black—kids cast angry looks at each other. That's when I got to know Horace.

Horace was one of those people who comes along that makes you happy that you're alive and interacting with your fellow man. Horace was a sixth grader from Martin Luther King School, an exceptional sixth grader. He took to the whole program just the way Multnomah County IED hoped every kid would. He learned about soil. He learned about water. He learned about plants, and he loved learning about animals. However, he was carrying a load all week long that many people would have been incapable of carrying for a moment, myself included.

It was just after dinner on Tuesday that he suddenly appeared at my side and asked quietly, "Mr. Owl, can I talk to you for a moment." I looked down into that beautiful face and saw something that many people will never have the pleasure or pain of seeing. In an instant I saw a world I will never experience. He had the face of a sixth grader, but the eyes of a college professor or a grandfather, a man who has lived a long time and understands what the world is all about.

"Sure, Horace," I said, suddenly finding it difficult to read the name tag tied on the string around his neck.

At first glance you'd take Horace for the kind of boy that blended into the woodwork. You wouldn't notice him in a crowd. He didn't stand out until you got to know him, then he was six feet tall, four axe handles wide, and you saw a kid that you knew would grow into a giant of a person.

"I don't know how to tell you this, Mr. Owl . . ." he began, looking down at his feet. "But I've got a problem I don't know how to handle." Then he looked at me, and again I saw his world in his eyes. "There's someone here who keeps calling me names," he said softly.

"What kind of names?" I asked.

"Nigger and others I don't want to repeat." he replied, quietly.

We stood there looking at each other for a long time. I thought I knew immediately where the name was coming from but not who. I also knew how Horace felt, but I knew too he was ready to endure this torment, if he had to. He just wanted me to know what he was living with, and see if there wasn't something I might be able to do about it.

I'm a person who has to make physical contact in order to get my feelings across to people. I hug people because I love them. In some segments of our society you can go to jail for doing that, but I still do it anyway. I did it that day. I can remember the warmth, and love we both felt as I put my arms around that kid and hugged him to my chest—apologizing for the cruelty that man inflicts on his fellow man.

"Oh, it ain't your fault, Mr. Owl," Horace mumbled, as he hugged me back, and then went on. "It's just that my classmates think I should smash the kid who's doing it, but I can't. I just feel sorry for him."

The next day I set the entire camp staff to the task of finding the person who sneaked around calling names. At least three times a day one of my staff would come in, furious. "I heard it too, Owl," Mossy said one day after lunch. "But I can't find him. He's just too damn sneaky about it."

"I don't know how he does it without my seeing him," another exclaimed. I circulated among the various stations, hovering in the background, trying to spot the individual. I even heard it once, but when I turned, all I could see was Horace looking at me with that expression of resignation and hurt. It went on that way all week long. Then, on Friday morning, the kids were getting ready to leave camp as their busses returned. Each school was reassembling next to their loading place, and the staff was circulating among them, hugging, crying, laughing, slapping backs, sharing last minute memories, promising to keep in contact—all of the things that kids and adults do when they've shared an intense, emotional, and great learning week together.

Then I heard it. "Black-assed nigger," the voice said, right behind me. I spun and reached out at the same instant. I had him! Right there in my hand I had a kid that suddenly looked up at me with an expression on his face that was almost frightening. I saw the gut-wrenching hatred and fear that was ruining his life and that of others. The tragedy of it was that Horace was over fifty feet away from him this time, and couldn't have heard him over the din if the kid had used a megaphone. In his frustration, the boy had just blurted it out to himself.

"So you're the one . . .'" I said, looking him right in the face.

"No!" he whined. "I didn't say anything!" Then, the most remarkable thing happened: like one person, almost his entire class groaned and turned their faces from him.

I didn't even ask permission of his teacher, I just hauled him by the collar over to where the kids from Martin Luther King School were getting ready to board their bus. As I dragged the unwilling boy with me I saw Horace turn, and I called out to him. "Here he is Horace! He's yours!" I said. Almost groaning myself, from the inner conflicts I felt, I let go of the boy's collar. They stood looking at each other, the white boy shaking, not knowing what was going to happen (nor me either for that matter). Then, with that kindness that I saw in Horace when we first met several days before and the pity that he had for the kid, he reached out and gently touched the boy's face with his palm, then turned to me and said "Awh, Mr. Owl, I'm sorry, but it ain't worth it," and walked away. I'm not ashamed to say I had tears in my eyes as that young man boarded the bus for Portland.

That was the year Martin Luther King was assassinated. My family and I attended the first documentary film about Reverend King, shown in Portland. It was the first time I remember really seeing what Martin Luther King had to live with and up to, and what he means to our society. The memory of the hatred on the faces of the white men and women who confronted King's group as they strolled, arm-in-arm, down the sidewalks of the white community in Chicago still gives me the shudders. Like many Americans, I will always have his speech, "I have a Dream . . ." in my heart. This is what I saw, Martin Luther King's philosophy, alive and well, demonstrated by Horace, a sixth grader.

The film was a great experience for us all, and afterwards, as the lights came up in the theater, a buzz of voices sounded throughout the place. As I looked around I saw black people, yellow people, white people, brown people, all talking to each other—not just "talking," but feeling, listening, exchanging, and most of all sharing what was in their hearts. I think that's the legacy of Martin Luther King.

I was caught up in the beauty of the moment when suddenly a voice rang out, "Hey! Mr. Owl! Mr. Owl!" I turned around to see who was calling that silly name from Outdoor School, and there, about twenty rows down toward the screen was Horace.

"Hi Horace!" I shouted back, as he came leaping over the seats toward us.

"I want you to meet my parents!" he exclaimed as he got closer.

I jumped over a couple of seats to meet him, and then we stood there hugging each other. "Gee, it's sure good to see you again!" he said, looking at me with that wise, old-man gaze. Then, tugging on my hand, he added, "Come on and meet my parents."

When I met Horace's parents, I knew why Horace was the boy he was. They were those kind of people that you find throughout the world who want nothing more in their lives than to provide the best for their children, live a good life for themselves if possible, and then to leave the world a better place for all of us when the time comes for them to go out among the stars. They were nothing more or less than Good People who loved their children. That may sound oversimplified or even trite to some, but that's what I remember.

I don't know where Horace is today; I've never seen him since that time in Portland, but I know that wherever he is, the world is a better place from his being there. If it hadn't been for Outdoor School, our trails might never have crossed, and I might have missed him—and that would have been my loss.

4 | FIGHTING THE GOOD FIGHT

The Coyote Wins—Again

The State of Missouri (and I) have been long-time advocates for the removal of individual predators causing livestock damages. This is a wise action from several viewpoints, especially economically and ecologically. I have always wondered at the wisdom of an agency that goes far-afield in their efforts to destroy predators—coyotes in particular—that are at best, perhaps connected to a possible threat to livestock. In the west, "predator control" was carried out for years in a manner that did very little to "control" predators, but went a long way to benefit the trappers themselves. (I prefer to think in terms of management of wildlife, rather than "control.")

Over the years, wildlife researchers have proved that the more indiscriminate the destruction of coyotes, the more available food there is for the survivors. So called "control" techniques that removed a coyote from an area indiscriminately and where there was no threat to livestock, meant females would come into breeding season earlier and males began taking up a harem of several females. Rather than having one pair which established a hunting and breeding territory, which is the normal condition, a male could be found running with several females, and the females having bigger litters than normal. If that's not job security for a trapper, I'd like to know what is!

Another factor has surfaced over the 100 plus years that we've been molesting the coyote. When we first started pursuing this wily "adversary," he was pretty much limited to the wide-open spaces of the Great Plains and other western areas. Most biologist now agree that because of this indiscriminate and relentless pressure on the coyote, he has responded by increasing his numbers and increasing his range. The latter response staggered most wildlife experts as they saw the dispersal. We can now find the coyote throughout the Continental United States, and even in parts of Alaska and Canada where he had never appeared before. Fishermen on the coast of Maine can hear the same species of coyote singing to him as the orange farmer in Florida, and the land developer in California. The coyote is at home in the suburbs of Los Angeles (where they dine on our throw-away stuff in land-fills, rats, stray cats, and dogs), as he is in the rim-rock wilderness of the Oregon desert.

Many people interested in wise use of monies budgeted to solve wildlife damage problems kept asking the question: why spend enormous sums of money chasing all over the desert, most of which is Public Land—yours and mine—killing animals that don't or probably wouldn't cause problems? Why not, asked many wildlife experts, focus the control attempts to those individual animals that were actually causing the problems.

There are a few individuals within our society that cause problems for others. They rob, molest, kill, and in general cause a great deal of trouble for our society. We try to solve the problem by removing the individuals causing the problem (or try to—some quirks in our judicial systems often defeat us). We don't go around on a witch hunt, knocking off people because they look like they might cause a problem some day. It may sound laughable, but I couldn't help but equate that with what the government trappers were doing with coyotes back in the '50s and '60s.

Sure, a coyote will kill a sheep. Why not? They're easy to catch if there are hundreds of them all around, and you're stumbling over them—why not eat one or two? After all, a predator is an opportunist, ready to take advantage of any food supply that's easy to get, but that's not justification for spending piles of money trying to kill a coyote wherever you find one, just because it might do livestock damage.

Contrary to a statement I heard from a trapper who called a coyote a "murderer" for killing sheep, coyotes can do no wrong or right in the eyes of nature. They are governed by a set of rules that most people do not understand, and probably never will, or want to. But you know, from the standpoint of man's use of the land, a coyote is doing "good" most of the time: eating mice and other rodents and rabbits that compete with livestock for forage. That's on the plus side for a rancher. However, it's that small percentage of coyotes that destroy our livestock, ten percent of the time, that we can't live with. Looking at it that way, coyotes are pretty much like some of my friends; it's difficult to live with that ten percent figure. Come to think of it, some of my friends say the same thing about me . . .

In the world of nature, it's (usually) the role of a predator to remove the sick, injured, and young of a given area. Coyotes are known to remove ("recycle" if you will) fawns, pronghorn kids, old, winter-weak elk, mule deer, gophers, mice, ground squirrels, ground-nesting birds, tons of grasshoppers, a wide variety of beetles, and other insects, as well as an even wider variety of plants. A sheep rancher who throws his still-born lambs over the fence (out of sight, out of mind?) is inviting the coyote to come and get the ones that are still alive. A cow man who does the same thing with dead calves is going to have the coyotes down his throat like a whirlwind in Texas. A coyote who discovers or is presented with an easy prey (food) source can get to be quite a problem for anyone trying to raise livestock on public land or even a place with fences. It's just the way a coyote makes a living.

Missouri figured that out in 1948. They could see that the government trapper wasn't doing very much to solve the livestock losses due to wild predators, so they eliminated the cooperative financial base from the government trapper program and set out on their own. The concept of dealing with the animal causing specific damages was, in reality, a relatively simple one. A wise old trapper was recruited to teach the farmer and rancher how to remove the coyote that was causing livestock damages. It was almost as easy as that. In the first year that Missouri had their program going, livestock losses to coyotes were reduced eighty-two percent. At last the farmer was getting something for his money—and he was solving his own problem.

The steel trap, used wisely in the hands of a responsible person, can remove an animal very quickly that has been causing specific livestock damages. I've even done it . . .

When I was a kid on the farm in Connecticut back in the '30s, my grandfather taught me how to trap skunks who raided our chicken house regularly. In that era, skunk pelts were bringing fifty cents each, and to a high school kid whose dad wouldn't buy him any more shoes because he wouldn't stay out of the muddy pond, that kind of money couldn't be passed up.

Each evening, after my paper route was finished, I'd put my traps in the old, soggy, burlap sack and head off to the chicken houses to set them out for skunks. Each morning, before daylight, I'd go out on my trap line and bring in the night's catch. My grandfather taught me how to skin a skunk without puncturing the scent sack—or at least he gave me a powerful lesson on what happens when you do.

One morning he was in a hurry to get to the Post Office where he worked, and got a little too close to the ammunition sack with his sharp, skinning knife. "Poof!" The yellowish liquid gushed forth, dribbled down onto his hands and then permeated everything within 100 yards—including me. I can recall the comments when I got to school that day. My mother had assured me that tomato juice would remove all the scent, so we poured several jars of canned tomatoes from our winter stores into the big, copper tub and I bathed in the stuff. We soaked our clothing in tomatoes too—but all to no avail. It might work for some people, but for the rest of my years in high school I was known as the kid from the "Skunk Works." It would be many years later that I'd use the steel trap again . . .

In the late '60s, and into the early '70s, I was employed as the Naturalist for one of Oregon's most environmentally-conscious land development schemes, Sunriver Properties, located along the winding Deschutes River in central Oregon. Don McCallum, and John Gray and his family were among the moving forces behind Sunriver, and John had some very specific concepts on how the lodgepole forests and open meadows bordering the Deschutes River would be developed. He hired a man to do the master plan who, in my opinion, was one of the most responsible land planners in the world: Bob Royston of Royston, Homomoto, Beck & Abbey, out of San Francisco.

His plan demonstrated what a developer can do who respects the nature of the land he is working with. Bob's plan called for a great deal of open space, a nature center, ponds, and winding roads. But most importantly, it required a wide separation between the development structures and the Deschutes River. The original master plan of Sunriver was, in my opinion, a living example of the conservation ethic described by Aldo Leopold in his book, *A Sand County Almanac*, published by Sierra Club Books.

My chief responsibility as Naturalist for Sunriver was to maintain an ecological concern within the development, assist in all on-the-ground activities to insure harmony between the contractors and the land, and to work with the residents and guests of Sunriver. That was a pretty big bite to chew, but we did OK—most of the time. John also gave me a great deal of latitude to move around, state-wide, in my attempts to bring about communication between what Sunriver was doing and the conservation and education communities. He allowed me to continue doing school programs, conduct my studies of Osprey and other raptors, and encouraged me to remain an active lobbyist for environmental concerns in the Oregon legislature, and especially in my attempts to try to reform the predator management programs within Oregon.

It took me a few years of losing battles before I began to realize that the wars were won—or lost—in Salem, the state capitol. It just so happened that in the early '70s I had the time and the corporate permission to travel to Salem and do battle. It was also the time that a great many people were questioning the wisdom of the old approach of indiscriminate poison stations as efficient agents to remove predators from the livestock community on public land. President Nixon had banned the use of 1080, a very effective poison that killed a great many carnivores, perhaps even raptors. (1080 is a poison that has no known antidote.)

The fallacy of this strategy was beginning to surface, and responsible people within the government agencies charged with the removal of predators destroying livestock were caught with only the steel trap and the "getter," a device that fired a cyanide capsule into an animal's mouth when it touched a baited trigger. Many of the more enlightened wildlife managers saw that it was time for a change—but for some of the old timer rat-chokers, there was no other way but to shoot, trap, poison, and kill every coyote on sight!

It all came to a head in Salem one hot May afternoon in '71. I was at the witness table presenting the Missouri method of removing predators causing damage, and at the other end was the state supervisor for the federal government trapper program. He and I had been at opposite ends of the table for over twenty years, and unfortunately, neither of us was able see what the other was trying to achieve. I still can't understand or agree to what happened to a great deal of Oregon's desert wildlife in those years. That also came to a head that day.

I knew the Natural Resource Committee of the legislature was on my side—it probably would have been unwise not to be—this was when environmental awareness was a politically wise thing to practice. The Earth Movement was in high gear. People who didn't have the remotest understanding of what "ecology" really meant were using the term in their every day language. Environmentalists have often been accused by the livestock raisers of being too "emotional" when discussing native wildlife. However, stockmen can also get a little carried away. I recall one fellow from Madras who while testifying, hunched up to the microphone, and slamming his fist on the table, shouted, "What we've got to do is get this damned emotion-al-ism out of this coyote issue!" After the hearing the head of Oregon's wildlife department and the state supervisor stopped me on the stairs of the senate building and threatened me with legal action if I didn't stop meddling in their business. I knew then I was very close to getting the job done.

Several years earlier, I had presented a paper at a National Audubon Convention that had been held in Tucson, Arizona. That was when I met Mary Hazel Harris, the woman who started the Defender of Wildlife, an organization dedicated to bringing about understanding and respect between man and wildlife. I was scared to death. This was the first time I had ever addressed such a gathering, and I knew the subject was controversial—at best. Just as I was about to step up to the podium, Sandy Sprunt, the Audubon Society's great naturalist and preserve manager from Florida, stopped me and said, "See those guys along the back of the auditorium?"

I nodded my head, looking to where he was pointing. "Well," he continued, "they're attorneys from the government trappers office, and they've come all this way to hear what you've got to say."

I looked at him with my eyes wide and a big lump in my throat. Then he grabbed my shoulder and squeezed it. "Go on up there and give them an earful!" he said. Which I did.

Sam Johnson, a wonderful statesman from Central Oregon, was the legislator from our area who listened to my argument as to how the government trapper had mismanaged the reduction of livestock losses from coyotes. He understood very quickly how the Missouri method had worked, and—with slight variations—might work in Oregon. I told Sam about Bob Smith, an old coyote trapper and wildlife manager from Missouri. He had taught hundreds of residents all over the state how to trap coyotes and solve their

own livestock loss problems. I asked if Sam would sponsor him to come to Salem and testify. Sam financed my scheme out of his own pocket, and I met Bob at the Portland airport when he flew into Oregon.

On the way to Redmond, where we were to meet with Sam at his office, Bob gave me one of the most impressive lessons I ever received in how important it is to know your work well, if you want to be successful. We were driving through lava and grasslands on the Warm Springs Indian Reservation, along Highway 26, when Bob pointed toward some shallow gullies about 100 yards from the road.

"There's a coyote over there," he stated quite clearly and confidently.

I looked toward the direction he was pointing, but couldn't see the coyote. "Where?" I asked, searching the lavas.

"Right in that little dip," Bob replied.

"I can't see him," I murmured, slowing the car down and pulling over toward the shoulder for a better look.

"Oh," he said, grinning at me, "I can't either. But I know he's there."

I pulled the car over on the shoulder and stopped. "Now wait a minute!" I exclaimed. "You can't see the coyote—but you know it's there." I gave him a funny look. "I don't believe it."

Bob just sat there, smiling at me and then said, "OK, if you don't believe it, get out and walk over and look. He's there all right."

"OK," I replied, easing the door open. I jumped over the ditch, landed among the bunchgrass and lavas, and started hopping over the sagebrush and wildflowers. I headed for the little depression that was supposed to have a coyote in it. I hadn't gone more than twenty feet when suddenly a coyote jumped out of the depression, about 300 yards away, and took off like a smart coyote should when he's got someone behind him.

"I'll be dinked!" I mumbled, heading back for the car.

"Well! Did you see him?" Bob asked as I slid behind the steering wheel.

"Yep, I sure did," I replied, shaking my head. From there all the way to Redmond, a distance of about fifty miles, he did that to me again and again.

Cautiously, the coyote watches Jim.

As we rolled up to Sam's office, he greeted me with a rush. "Jim," he exclaimed. "One of my constituents called me today and said he had a coyote getting into his lambing pens, and could I do something about it. I told him about you and Mr. Smith and what we're trying to do in Salem, and he was pretty excited. He said to have you come over and catch that blankity-blank coyote that's been getting his lambs."

I asked Bob if he'd have a go at it and he just smiled at me and said, "No, Jim I won't, but I'll teach you how to."

And that's just what he did, from the ground up.

We went to the hardware store and purchased three Number 2 steel traps, brand-new, right out of the greasy sack they came in. Then we went over to the rancher's place outside of Redmond to look the

ground over. Bob walked around, and in a moment or two he turned to the rancher and said, "Yep, you sure got a coyote here; it appears you've got a bitch with pups raiding your pens."

Then he pointed toward the fence. "See, that's where she's been gettin' in, right at the end of that little gully there." We all looked in the direction he was pointing; sure enough there was a shallow spot from some old washout, and it was plain to see where the coyote was sliding under the fence. "Now, Jimmy," Bob said. "You just take them three traps up along that little gully and set 'em just the way I show in my little book."

I was just heading off to the house, asking the rancher if I could boil the traps to get the grease off, when Bob stopped me.

"Oh, shucks," he exclaimed. "You don't

have to go to all that bother. Just set 'em out the way I got in that little booklet I gave you—grease and all."

So I turned around, took the traps back, and turned to page one. The first thing I needed, according to Mr. Smith's directions, was a six inch square piece of denim. At my request for material, the rancher went to the house and brought back an old pair of his jeans which I cut to obtain my six inch piece of denim.

"Is that six inches?" Bob asked as I finished cutting the first one.

"Sure," I replied

"I don't think it is," he said, taking the cloth out of my hand and reaching into his pocket. A small tape measure suddenly appeared in his hand and he measured the piece. "That's what I thought," he grumbled, handing the cloth back to me. "It's only five and three quarters that way, and five and seven eighths the other."

"Now wait a minute," I started to say.

"Look! Do you want to catch that coyote or don't you?" Bob asked, putting his hands in his pockets.

"Sure he does!" Sam and the rancher both answered.

"OK, then make that chunk of denim to six inches, like it says in that little book," Bob said, taking the first piece of cloth and putting it into his back pocket, and giving me a dirty look.

Well, I did everything I was told to after that. I cut the cloth the correct size, placed the traps at exactly the depth under the surface of the ground they were supposed to be, and spaced them exactly as they should be according to Mr. Smith and his little how-to manual.

The next morning I got a call from Sam. "You caught the coyote!" he exclaimed, sounding happy as a kid with a new toy. One thing Sam really liked to do was please his constituents, not only because it was politically wise, but because he believed that was why he was called to that office: to make things better for the people of central Oregon.

We all drove out to see our quarry and arrived to find that the rancher had already killed it. "You were right," he said, shaking

An all-too-common sight on the Oregon desert: a dead coyote draped over a fence post. People are slowly learning that not all coyotes are bad.

Bob's hand. "It was a bitch all right, and she was nursing pups." Then he said something that has been a lesson for me over the years. "Yeah, too bad I had to kill her. You know, I sure don't like the idea of them little guys starving to death. It's no wonder she turned to getting after my lambs; there ain't any jackrabbits left around here anymore. Every weekend I have to chase off a bunch of people who come roaring by here on their motorcycles, rifles in the scabbard, out killing anything that moves. I haven't seen a jackrabbit in these parts since them guys started coming around."

Well, Sam and I took Mr. Smith to the legislature where he testified about how much his Missouri program had cut the costs and reduced losses of livestock by removing the specific animal(s) causing the damage. The director of Oregon's wildlife department back in those days appeared (to me) to be a coyote hater from the word 'go'. His department and the feds had a pork barrel going that was costing more money than the results could justify.

When Sam and I brought the old Missouri trapper into the legislature, we really rocked the boat. We didn't know just how much we had it rocking until I received a phone call one night from the head of the Cooperative Wildlife Research Unit at OSU (a joint state/federal research program). He asked me if I could come to the Wildlife Society meeting on the Oregon coast, which was to be held that coming weekend. He was pretty dejected as we sat in his room, drinking his good scotch whiskey. He explained that his department might lose the federal Pitman/Robertson funds—if I didn't back off in my attempts to reform the federal strangle-hold on predators in the state.

This was something that I hadn't anticipated, but if it did happen, the results would be devastating to the students of the wildlife school at OSU. Sam and I discussed this possibility and both agreed that we were licked. I can recall how low I was when I went back to Sunriver with my tail between my legs. All the effort, time, and money we had spent was all for naught. We'd apparently been licked by the same political skullduggery that seems to win more often than it should. The real losers, though, were going to be the livestock ranchers and Oregon's wildlife.

Then, a couple of weeks later, at about ten in the evening, I got a phone call at home I'll never forget.

"This the big mouth trouble-maker Jim Anderson who loves coyotes?" a grouchy voice asked.

What can you say to a question like that? I was caught off guard, but then jumped back and asked my caller who he was and what was going on. He went on to say he knew what Sam and I had tried to do over in Salem, and it was ". . . too damn bad you didn't win . . ." Then he told me he was the new federal trapper in our area—an unusual one, I was shortly to discover. He said he agreed with everything Sam and I had tried to do. He also saw money wasted by

trapping and poisoning animals that were far from any livestock or agricultural community, in other words, animals not causing damages.

Then he sprung the good news on me. He was going to use a helicopter to kill predators in the places where they caused damages—around the calving and lambing grounds. He invited me to go to Silver Lake and observe the first hunt of that type to be carried out in central Oregon. The most surprising thing about this was that he was doing it over the head of his supervisor in Portland, the man whom Sam and I had been fighting! The trapper had made all the arrangements on his own, without department approval. He had drawn up a cooperative agreement with the ranchers who would pay part of the costs and the feds would pay the other.

I went to Silver Lake and observed the pilot project and watched as twenty-three coyotes were killed adjacent to the sprawling calving grounds on a big cattle ranch. That winter, calving losses due to coyotes was reduced by better than eighty-five percent throughout the central Oregon area! I remember what the trapper said when I asked him what he'd be doing as he flew between ranches.

"Oh, I promise that I won't kill a coyote, Jim," he said. Then added, "When I get to a ranch I yell out the window: OK you coyotes, the one that ain't been killin' calves raise his hand! Well, not one raised a hand so I got them all!" The trapper then went one step further: he got the buckaroos to burn and bury the still-born calves, instead of just throwing them over the fence. He also carried the coyote carcasses in to skin them, and sell the pelts to help defray the expenses.

That's exactly what Sam and I had tried to get going in Oregon, a program designed to remove the individual animal(s) causing livestock damages and to educate the rancher on methods to reduce losses. Thanks to Sam's efforts in Salem to introduce the Missouri system for predator removal and a responsible trapper who took the time to undertake a more ecologically sound method in the reduction of livestock damages caused by coyotes, the helicopter program that removes predators killing livestock is standard procedure in the west today. The balance of the predator population is left alone to carry out the ecological interactions that nature designed them to do.

We had lost a battle, but by golly, we didn't lose the war. The coyote wasn't the only winner; ranchers came out ahead too. Ecosystems dependent upon nature's efforts to establish equilibrium between habitat, predator, and prey have been left to operate without our interference. In addition, livestock raisers and environmentalists have come a little closer to understanding each other.

5 | ARIZONA LIVING

National Geographic Calling

One of the things I used to dream about was receiving a call from the National Geographic, requesting a photograph of a specific subject from nature. I was sure it would never happen to me; I'm not in that league. But while I was working for The Nature Conservancy (TNC) as the preserve manager of Ramsey Canyon Preserve in southeast Arizona, I was standing in the right place at the right time when my dream came true.

It may have been like that the time Reub Long, an old time horseman from the Fort Rock Valley of Oregon, received the Grass Man Of The Year Award for the third consecutive year from the Range and Wildlife Society back in the early '60s. When he was interviewed on TV by a very flamboyant reporter who lavishly introduced Reub, saying, "Please tell all our television viewers what you had to do to win this coveted award, Mr. Long." Reub just smiled and answered, "I guess I was just standing in the right place when the judges looked up."

That's the way it was when the National Geographic called me looking for a photograph of a hog-nosed skunk.

Ramsey Canyon Preserve, also known as the "Hummingbird Capital of the World," has twelve species of hummingbirds that utilize the feeders and adjacent habitat. Some nest in the oaks, juniper, apple trees, and sycamore along Ramsey Creek. The beautiful, blue-throated hummingbird seems to prefer the old buildings in the upper parts of the preserve built by Dr. Bledsoe, the first white resident of the canyon. (We had the first successful nest in the US of the Beryline hummingbird on the preserve. This colorful Mexican species fledged three young from a tiny, spider web and lichen nest located adjacent to Ramsey Creek.)

The manager's residence was located in the upper parts of the preserve, at the end of an old road. This road was actually a rutted track that washed out every winter and summer during the heavy rains, and was once thought to belong to Cochise County.

One part of the upper preserve used by visitors coming to view the wildlife and plants was once part of a thriving orchard that supplied a wide variety of fruit (pears, peaches, apricots, and apples) for the local community back in the '20s. Only the hardy apple trees had survived the extreme heat of summer and the occasional below-zero weather of winter.

Even though the Mexican border was only a few miles away, the preserve enjoyed a uniquely mild climate for Arizona because of the altitude and rainfall. Our house was located at 5,500 feet above sea level, while the lower rental cottages, known as "Mile-Hi" and operated by TNC, were at about 5,000 feet.

When my wife Sue, my son Dean, and I arrived in March of 1979, we found the manager's residence in tough shape. The Arizona TNC Chapter was operating the preserve at the time and voted to supply all the materials we would need to rebuild the old house. It was during the remodeling project that I was reintroduced to the spotted skunk (*Spilogale gracilis*), the smallest member of the skunk tribe. In some places it is known as the "civet cat," a misnomer if there ever was one. The true civet cat (*Civettictis ciceta*), lives half a world away in Africa.

Our first night in the house was a noisy one, not so much because I snored too loudly or because I couldn't sleep, but for the prancing and stomping around of the resident spotted skunk. The place had been empty about two months before we moved in, just long enough for the skunk to stake it out as its own. As everyone knows, it's a dangerous business to argue squatter's rights with a skunk, no matter what size it may be.

"Jim," Sue whispered. "I think I hear something rummaging around in the kitchen."

It was a very dark night and I was leery about blundering about with all of the open walls and lumber in the dark. I was sure I would knock over something (as I usually did) and make a terrible mess.

"What do you think it is?" I asked.

"How do I know?" she answered. "You're the naturalist."

As I turned over, making the bed squeak, I could hear a series of staccato thumps emitted from across the room. I fumbled around and finally found the flashlight, taking aim at where the sounds were coming from and hit the switch. A shaft of light split the darkness and sent back two tiny red spotlights, surrounded by shades of white and black.

"It's a skunk," I whispered.

"A small one though," Sue added. "Hold the light still so I can see it better."

As we watched, the small skunk stared back at us, slowly stomping its front feet on the old, wood floor. It was a Mexican standoff: I wasn't going to get out of bed, and it didn't appear the skunk was going to leave.

"It looks friendly," I said. "Let's go back to sleep."

That was agreeable to Sue, but Dean woke about that time and started to muddy the water.

"Dad," he whispered. "I think there's a skunk in here."

I whispered back that he was right, I could see it, but we were all going back to sleep and let it be. I didn't hear anything from him for several minutes, then he whispered, "that's a great idea," and silence settled over the house.

Field guides show southeast Arizona as a place where all four species of skunks found in North America overlap. The field guides are correct. In the first year we lived in Ramsey Canyon and hiked the Huachuca

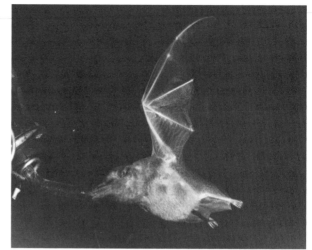
Mexican long-tongued bat slurps at hummingbird feeder at the Ramsey Canyon Preserve.

Peccary. It is not really a swine—it just resembles one.

The Coatimundi, a relative of the raccoon, strays into southeastern Arizona and part of New Mexico.

An Anderson houseguest ("pet") at Ramsey Canyon Preserve.

Ramsey Canyon Preserve is the only place in America where all four species of skunk native to North America are found. The hognosed skunk is the most unusual of the four.

Mountains, I saw all four of them: spotted, hooded, striped, and hog-nosed.

In addition to the skunks we also had coatimundi, ring-tailed cats (the latter bowled up in the attic, making frequent strikes, and also ran races), peccary, Mexican gray squirrels, rice rats, and a host of other mammals, including the sleepy, old, Mexican black bear (who used to peep in the bathroom window when Sue was bathing . . . we had a "peeping bear").

There were three major problems confronting us when we moved into Ramsey Canyon. One was the overabundance of daily visitors who had discovered the preserve and wanted to soak it all up in one day. People would travel down from Tucson on weekends and join the others from the US Army facility adjoining the preserve, plus the residents from Sierra Vista, and guided, birding tours. Most of the year, visitor numbers would be almost unmanageable, causing a severe strain on the preserve.

Along with Rick and Connie Hewett, the managers of the Mile-Hi rental cabins, we established definite hours and limited the numbers of visitors within the preserve at any specific time, and offered guided tours. This helped to reduce the strain on the flora and fauna of the canyon.

Another problem was the snake poachers. There is an ilk that is always ready to fatten their bankroll by sneaking around stealing wildlife and selling it to the highest bidders: the rarer (or endangered) the species, the higher the prices. Unfortunately, there will always be a market for things that are rare. The ivory from elephants today and the plumes from the egrets back at the turn of the century are just two examples.

The Huachuca Mountains are noted for having rare and endangered snakes, among them the twin-spotted, green-rock, and (Willard's) ridge-nosed rattlesnakes. It was the latter that tempted a number of crooks to try and steal them. There was—and still is—a market for rare rattlesnakes, and the ridge-nosed leads the list, taking top dollar.

The Arizona Fish and Game officers don't treat snake crooks any better than they do any other thief. Pat O'Brien was the wildlife officer who worked in the Huachucas, and he and I often teamed up to catch snake snatchers in the preserve and the Forest Service lands adjacent to us. I would call him when the crooks were either going up,

This is the first known successful nest of the Beryline hummingbird in the United States (Ramsey Canyon, 1978).

Dean Anderson fills hummingbird feeders while patrons wait impatiently.

or coming down the canyon, and we'd go after them, one of us at the top and the other at the bottom. We were also very fortunate to have a sympathetic judge in Sierra Vista who thought the wildlife laws should be upheld, and fined snake crooks all the law would allow. The pressure we put on the snake poachers went a long way in solving the threat to the rare and endangered ridge-nosed rattlesnakes.

Another big problem we suffered was the overabundance of stray house cats that were feeding on the ground-nesting birds and other animals of the preserve. When I arrived, I had been told that there were no problems with cats. But after a week of hiking around getting acquainted with the flora and fauna, I spotted six tough-looking, feral house cats stalking birds and small lizards.

Pat O'Brien loaned me a dog-sized, live-trap that I baited with sardines. The first night I set it out, I caught a big male feral house cat that was about the toughest feline I have ever seen. As I walked up to the trap, it slammed against the wire, clawing and coughing at me like a captive cougar. I'm not ashamed to say I had a real sense of fear as I watched that huge animal tearing at the trap. Because we were located very close to civilization, I developed a policy for all the cats caught on the preserve. I'd run an advertisement in the local paper, giving details of the cat and asking the owners to come and get it. They never did, not for all twenty of them. Did you know that tomatoes do exceptionally well on a cat graveyard . . .?

The California Sister (a relative of the Red Admiral which is found in the Northwest) is just one of the many beautiful butterflies found in the Ramsey Canyon Preserve.

Jim and son Dean Anderson band great horned owls near Sierra Vista, Arizona.

When the National Geographic called asking for a photo of the hog-nosed skunk, I flew into the project head-on with substantial vigor! I knew this would be my first and probably the last time, to ever receive such a request, and I wanted to fill that order. Night after night, I prowled around the preserve, trying to find a hog-nosed skunk. Weeks before they were underfoot at our house every night. Now, true to the way this sort of thing works out, I couldn't find a hog-nose anywhere. Too bad they didn't want a photo of a spotted skunk; it was like a puppy dog, waiting under the kitchen table every evening at dinner, looking for table scraps.

One dark and moonless night, while I was slowly making my way through the old apple orchard along Ramsey Creek, I thought I heard a hog-nose snuffling along in the leaves ahead of me. The closer I got to the sound ahead, the more I was sure it was a hog-nose, and I slowly raised my Pentax, equipped with the 135 mm lens and switched on the strobe. I eased around several big, dark boulders as I slipped silently through the trees, putting each foot down with the care and stealth of an Apache warrior.

As I slipped by the tenth large boulder, a thought hit me like a flash of lightening: there are no boulders in this orchard! I stopped in my tracks, suddenly aware of additional snuffling sounds—ahead, behind, left, and right. Oh, no! I thought, they're peccaries! I knew how poor their eyesight was, and I also knew how long their canines were! I didn't know what to do. I just stood there.

As if on an unspoken signal the whole troop suddenly grunted in unison and bolted. I don't know what made me do it, but I just jumped and spread my legs apart, standing stiff as a statue. I'm not sure to this day, but I believe at least three of them ran between my legs as the group thundered off into the oaks surrounding the orchard. I was shaking like a leaf for several minutes, then as quiet descended again among the apple trees I thought to myself, I guess that wasn't a hog-nosed skunk . . .

Several days later I did get the photo National Geographic wanted, thanks to a neighbor down the canyon who had chickens (we purchased eggs from him often). He trapped the skunk in his chicken house in a big Havahart, live-trap and asked me to come down and get it. I turned the skunk loose in the upper parts of the preserve and with the help of my son Dean and my wife Sue, we herded that beautiful, animal around until he finally turned his face to me for a photo. I was amazed at the patience of that skunk; it tolerated us for over twenty minutes as we kept it contained in a small area. Only once did we get a hint of the awful weapon skunks are capable of using when they finally do run out of patience. I would have preferred to have obtained the photo in a more "natural" way—but at times you have to accept what Mother Nature gives you, regardless of the circumstances. The Society published the photo, which pleased us all.

6 | A CLOSER LOOK

Eagles Fly High

One of the objectives I had when I was given the opportunity to teach soaring was to fly with eagles. That's what I told Dean Johnson, the owner of Eagle Soaring Center, in Hillsboro, Oregon, back in the '70s, when he asked me if I wanted to fly gliders with his group. They operated out of a little strip near North Plains, Oregon, between a wheat field and the Tillamook highway. Dean had five Schweitzer sailplanes: three 2-33 trainers, a single place, 1-26, and a sleek, new single place high performance 1-34. He used an Aeronca Champion with a 150 HP engine for a tug.

I took my first glider flight with one of my OMSI students, Frank Archibald, who had gone on to get his Private License in gliders when he was seventeen. His dad was his first passenger, and I was his second. I was hooked! Every spare moment I drove out to the gliderport and took another lesson. Finally it became pretty obvious that I was serious about flying gliders, and one day Dean walked up to me and said, "Jim, why don't you stop by my office this afternoon after the crew puts the gliders to bed." After a day of flying, I always went out to the Helvatia Tavern with the glider crew, but that day I passed it up to go and see Dean.

As I walked into his office, where he was deep into his computer—something he was always doing—Dean got right down to what he had in mind. "Jim," he said, waving to a chair. "How would you like to go for a Glider Instructor Rating?"

I looked at him in astonishment. "Gee, Dean," I responded, sitting down, "that would be great, but I'm in no shape to pay for anything like that. I'm about flat busted."

He stopped typing on his keyboard for a moment, gave me a serious look and said, "I didn't say anything about money. I asked if you were interested in getting an Instructor Rating."

"Sure!" I replied.

"OK. That's the answer I need," he said, concentrating on the computer keyboard again. "Why don't you and Tim come in before you go out to the gliderport tomorrow and we'll set it up."

Tim Tilton was his Chief Pilot at the gliderport, and a guy that I enjoyed—most of the time. He had a nasty habit of not getting too much sleep from time-to-time, or perhaps not enough blood sugar, I never did know, but at times he acted so nasty I thought he could chew nails and spit rust. When he got into that mood our tow pilot, Jack Smith, called him LBS (Low Blood Sugar). In the years I've flown with Timmy though, I've come to love him as my brother. He and I did the first back slide in a sailplane that either of us had ever done. It was the day we were flying the Blanik, a European sailplane designed for aerobatics. We were doing hammer-head stalls and didn't get quite enough speed up to bring the nose over as the sailplane stopped moving at right angles to the horizon—so it just went backwards—until the nose flipped over and we started flying again.

"I've never done that before, Tim," I exclaimed when I got my voice back.

"Neither have I," Tim whispered.

After we did a couple of smooth wingovers on the way down, we landed and inspected the sailplane very carefully.

I progressed up to my Commercial Rating, took the FAA exam for Instructor, passed it, took my check ride with the FAA Designee, and got my ticket to teach. What a thrill that was!

One of the things I enjoyed most about flying the Schweitzer trainer was that it's a real sailplane—not just a glider. We got along very well together. I learned about thermals from books, from others, and soaring in them. After a lot of practice on my own, that 2-33 and I could blow the wings off other sailplanes when she got into a good thermal. Those long wings could carry us up at 800 to 1,000 feet per minute, and I'd often be looking down on everyone else before they knew it.

One time while taking an auto tow off the Alvord Desert over by Steens Mountain, in southeast Oregon, Bob Moore and I took that sturdy training sailplane to almost 16,000 feet above sea level. We got into a big thermal in mid-afternoon that was a real boomer. At one point the sailplane was shaking like a stray farm cat in the jaws of a coyote. The thermal tried to toss us out, but we kept our nose into it like a bulldog. Bob turned and said, "You know, I'm happy that Bill Schweitzer designed that 60% safety factor into this old bird." The guys in the high-performance sailplanes were doing good, chatting to each other over the radios about how strong the lift was and how great the soaring was. As we broke the 15,000 feet mark, which was as high as we wanted to go, Bob got on the radio and said, "Ahhh, this is three six Sierra going through fifteen thousand."

"Who's three six Sierra?" someone asked over the radio.

"Why that's the Schweitzer trainer," an astonished voice exclaimed.

Just two weeks before that flight we had all been in the high altitude chamber at the Whidby Island Naval Air Station, up near Seattle, and I discovered that my altitude threshold was about 19,000 feet above sea level. Anything above that, and my brains turned to peanut butter.

Bob turned to me grinning, and said, "We'd better go on back down, Jim. I'm beginning to feel like I need a breath of oxygen." I agreed with him. His lips were beginning to get a little blue, and I was happy I couldn't see mine—but I did glance at my fingernails for the tell-tale blue tint of a lack of oxygen.

As we slowly descended back toward the sprawling Alvord desert I was overpowered by the sights that spread out before us. I felt as though we could see forever. Idaho was spread out under us to the east, Nevada to the south, Washington to the north, and the Oregon Cascades poked up to the west. "What do you say we fly down Wild Horse Canyon?" I asked him as we soared above the summit of the Steens.

"You bet!" he answered.

As we glided down the canyon, I suddenly spotted a long gash of white and yellowish white-wash that streaked the canyon wall. "That looks like a falcon aerie," I said, pointing to the spot on the cliff face. As we sailed by, a falcon flew out from the cliff, right on cue, screaming at us loudly. As it flashed by us I was astonished to see that it was a Peregrine Falcon. "This was another reason I took up flying gliders," I said to Bob. "To go birdwatching."

Another thing I wanted to do was duplicate the experience I'd read about when glider pilots in Africa have pulled into a gaggle of soaring vultures and flown with them. However, every time I tried to get close to the turkey vultures in this country they'd only tolerate me up to a certain point, then in a flash, they'd do what looked like a split-'S' and vanish from the sky, and swallows were even quicker.

I was teaching a student to ride thermals one summer day when the Willamette Valley was really pumping them out—something that was rare. One of the things I tried to teach with the 2-33 was to approach the thermal aggressively. As soon as I was sure which side of it we were on, I'd have the student stick the nose of the glider into that rising column of air, and as soon as we were in the middle—the core—I'd have he or she roll up into a steep bank and try to stay on the core. That's when that 2-33 would really go up. One way to find these powerful thermals is to watch for birds. That day I spotted a huge flight of swallows going up on a thermal; it appeared they were feeding on a big mating swarm of gnats. "See those swallows?" I exclaimed to my student. "Go after them. That's where the thermal is."

"Where?" he asked, twisting his head this way and that, trying to spot them.

"Right there!" I said, pointing over his shoulder, to show him the spot.

Frank Archibald hooked Jim on gliders.

"I can't see them," he said in an exasperated voice, peering intently ahead.

"I've got the glider," I said, taking over the controls and heading for the birds. In a few seconds we were right under them.

"Now I see them!" my student said, looking up into the flight of swallows. "Are they feeding on insects?" he added in wonder.

He had never seen swallows pursuing insects this way, but then neither had I—in a glider. "Yeah, I think they are. OK, go get 'em." I said to the student, turning the controls over to him again. We slowly climbed while I coached him on how to find the center of the thermal, while at the same time he had to not only fly the glider, but keep watching out for other sailplanes. He had to keep his eyes on the swallows and on the variometer that recorded our vertical ascent or descent. "You're gaining on 'em," I said, trying to make the glider go higher by pulling up the seat under me with my hands. I couldn't stand the wait; I knew how excited he'd be when we caught up with them. Suddenly I began to sink into the back seat cushion. "You've got it!" I shouted. "Steepen your bank! You're in the core!" In an instant we were right into the swallows. But for only a few seconds.

I think one of them must have looked over his shoulder and spotted us closing in. Perhaps he shouted to the others, "Holy Cats, guys! Look what's coming up behind us. It's a BIG hawk, and he's already eaten two people!"

With an audible splutter, the entire windshield was suddenly covered with a solid sheet of white paste—swallow poop—and the birds swooped away from us. "I can't see a thing!" the student exclaimed, trying to rub the stuff away, but he couldn't, of course.

Jim Anderson became an instructor at the Eagle Soaring Center, North Plains, Oregon.

Soaring over Steens Mountain

I dropped down the window by the left rear seat of the glider, and stuck my head out. "I've got the glider," I said, and headed back for the gliderport. It was the first—and last—time I ever got in among a bunch of swallows, or when I had to land a glider from the back seat while looking out the side window.

As we rolled to a stop my student opened the canopy, turned in his seat and gave me a big grin, exclaiming, "Hey. That was great . . . but I got cheated. You flew the glider back—can we go again?" I assured him he could, if he cleaned the windshield, and we went back up to do more birdwatching, and thermal hunting.

While my wife and I were operating our commercial glider operation in Central Oregon, we used the Bend Airport most of the time. One day when business was slow I decided to take a flight and try for my five-hour badge. That required me to stay in the air for five hours and fly at least twenty-five miles out, and then land.

We had purchased a two-place, WWII Schweitzer trainer—the TG-2—to do our instructing with. Like the 2-33, it too was a great soaring machine, but not nearly as fast. In fact, it was slower than molasses in January. Red-line speed for the TG-2 was eighty miles per hour, but it would float along on the weakest thermals.

One day I took a tow to 2,000 feet above the terrain, dropped down to notch the barograph that recorded the flight, and set off for Brothers, about forty miles east of Bend. It was about 1 pm when I left Bend, so I had to hustle to get out there and stay up for the required five hours, as the thermals started dying in the afternoon.

When I passed Millican, about twenty miles out, I got into a big patch of blue sky with big sink, and began to drop toward the desert below me at an alarming rate. I was in hot water. The ground was coming up too fast, and I couldn't get out of that sinking air mass. The book says to fly the best L/over/D (Lift over Drag) when you're in sink, so I just kept the nose down and faced what was coming.

Then I saw that Golden Eagle. It was just a little below me and turning in a thermal. "Hot Dog!" I shouted and headed right for him. When I arrived at the thermal I was just at the point of no return, where the lift is usually never strong enough to allow you to gain altitude.

"Come on old girl," I coaxed the glider. As we penetrated the thermal I felt the right wing go up. "It's over there," I almost shouted, banking hard right to try and hit the core. "Clunk-clank" the right wing oil-canned as I hit the thermal again, and I felt the pressure on the seat of my pants.

A juvenile golden eagle soars above the glider at 12,000 feet.

"Yahoo!" I shouted as we began to go back up. I looked for the eagle, and there it was, now way above me, circling in the sky and a big cloud slowly growing above him. "I'll get up there with you, hold on," I called out to the eagle, as I watched the vario go from down, to 300 feet, then 500 feet, then 800 feet per minute—UP! It took me almost a half hour to work my way up to him, but when I caught up with him we were both right up against that big, flat-bottomed cloud, at 12,500 feet, and the air was so cold I began to shudder to try and keep warm.

I'll never forget the way that eagle looked at me as I pulled along side of him. He was a magnificent, full adult, probably over ten years old by the abundant golden sheen of feathers on his nape, and the brilliant gold along the leading edge, and topside of his wings. He was just off my left wing, both of us heading for Brothers, when I guess he decided it was time to leave. He never flapped his wings once; he just pulled them in slightly toward his body and in a few seconds he was a mere speck ahead of me— and he never lost a foot of altitude as he vanished. I tried to catch up with him, but as I pushed the nose down to gain speed, my altitude began to fall off dramatically— and I needed a lot of that stuff. So I just let him go.

During the winter of that same year we changed our operation from Bend to Sunriver for the Thanksgiving/Christmas Holiday—the only time we ever actually made money. But from my standpoint, this was the best time I ever had, because it was the first—and only—time I had the opportunity to fly with a Bald Eagle.

We had people lined up, waiting to go on a flight most of the time, especially holidays. Airplane traffic was also busy, so at times I'd enter our traffic pattern, opposite that of the powered aircraft, and I'd make a full 360 degree turn to look for other aircraft traffic in preparation for landing. The turn was directly over the golf course sandtrap near the Sunriver Lodge.

As I was making the slow circle, waiting for a twin to land that was on final, I looked down and spotted a man trying to hit his ball out of the sand. He made about three swings at it, splattering sand in all directions without the ball making any headway. I could almost hear what he was saying to himself—if not to his golfing partners. So I opened the side window and shouted down to him, "Watch—your—language!" He jerked his head up to see where that voice was coming from and I waved to him from the glider. Then he picked up his ball and threw it at me! An hour later he went flying with me in the glider.

A couple of days later, we were busier than a cat on a hot tin roof. Up and down, up and down. In late afternoon I took off with a man who was so excited that he could hardly contain himself. He was a long-time power pilot who had never been in a sailplane, so we were both going to have a good time. I usually took a tow to 2500 feet above the surface, released, and then slowly glided back to the airport. That day there was no lift to go after, so I knew we'd be back on the ground in a few moments, but we'd be in the air long enough to allow my passenger a chance to fly the glider himself—something I always encouraged everyone to do. I had coached my passenger on what was required to keep the glider flying, and had turned the controls over to him after release from the tug.

"Oh boy," he sighed, turning to grin at me from the front seat, "This is grr—reee—ate."

On the way back to the airport I had explained the principals of flying a glider and turned the controls over to him. We were gliding along, doing gentle banks and turns, when I looked out my side window, searching for other traffic; we had traffic all right—so close I could almost touch it!

"Look at that!" I said softly to my passenger, but with a sense of excitement in my voice. At that moment he was concentrating so hard on flying that he was staring straight ahead.

"What?" he said, breaking out of his reverie. "What is it?"

"Off the left wing," I said, placing my hand close to the stick and my feet gently on the rudder pedals in the event he freaked out.

"Oh! My God!" he blurted. "I don't believe it!"

We had a full-grown adult female Bald Eagle gliding along with us—it had to be a female, it was so large—and she was watching us intently, perhaps with disdain. At times she'd slowly let herself drift toward us, even to a point where she was actually beneath our wing. We could see her bright, yellow eyes as she gave us the once over.

"I've never seen anything like this," my passenger whispered.

"Me either," I replied, staring at that magnificent bird.

At that moment she suddenly looked ahead and like the golden eagle of the desert flight, she just pulled her wings in slightly and began to pull ahead of us. In a matter of a few seconds, all we could see was that white tail barely visible against the green of the trees. Then, without warning she suddenly began to dive, and out of nowhere another eagle suddenly swooped by her and then they both pulled up into a chandelle that was a sight to behold. As we glided by they ignored us and began to grasp each other with their talons, and then slowly spin down toward the ground, and out of sight.

"Wow! That was fantastic!" my passenger exclaimed in awe. Then he suddenly jerked upright in his seat and almost shouted. "Who's flying?"

In all truth I didn't know myself. We were both so transfixed by the eagles that everything else we were doing—like flying the glider—was automatic. I looked down at my hand which was just lightly touching the stick. I felt where my feet were, and they weren't touching the rudder pedals. "You are," I said, patting him on the shoulder.

"I am?" he said, slowly moving the stick and rudder to rock the wings in a Dutch Roll. "I am," he said again, as we approached the traffic pattern for a landing.

I coached him through the landing, which he accomplished very well, considering that it was his first flight in a sailplane. As we were rolling to a stop he suddenly said, "Oh, no!" and I felt him let go of the controls. Squirming around a little he got his hand into the side-pocket of his jacket. "I forgot I had this," he groaned, raising his camera for us both to see.

As we walked away from the glider, we both looked up into the sky and there, in the cold December afternoon, were the two eagles soaring on what I thought could never be a thermal, their wings 'feeling' every ripple of the air they soared in. Eagles have always known a great deal more about soaring than I ever will.

Hawks and Eagles

If there's one thing I've enjoyed in my life, it's climbing into trees and hanging off cliff faces looking into the private lives of raptors. It began when I was on the farm in Connecticut and still goes on today. Having a life-long love affair with birds of prey has taught me a great deal.

For example, it makes a lot of sense to watch what's happening to "hawks," a term used by science to describe the families *Accipitridae*, *Pandionidae* (Osprey), and *Falconidae*, all the diurnal birds of prey in North America. The health of raptors in any given area is an indication of the overall health of their habitat—and yours and mine. I've had so many wonderful times with so many of the hawks, eagles, and falcons that I think I could probably do a whole series of tales on raptors (pun intended).

Falcons have always been a great love for me. In my youth I wanted to be a falconer. What kid didn't who loved birds—especially hawks? I can recall reading about Genghis Khan flying the Imperial Eagles that soared over the steppes of Asia. I thrilled at the stories about the great men who flew Golden Eagles in Scotland, the kings and other nobles who flew the Peregrine Falcons, and the royal Gyrfalcon from the Arctic. I can also remember the first time I did a serious literature search on the subject of falconry.

I had gone to the Deschutes County Public Library in Bend and asked Marion Grover if she'd help me. Marion was one of the finest ladies I've ever had the pleasure of knowing. She was at her best whether it was in the library, at a horse camp at Taylor Burn campground in the Cascades, or hand-tinting photographs. She got me going in the right direction, and as the list grew, the books piled up. I took them all home and devoured one after the other. Then I received a call from Marion that she had stumbled upon a work she missed on her first run through the index: *The Art of Falconry, De Arte Venandi Cum Avibus* (The Art of Hunting With Birds), written in the year 1210 by King Frederick II, Emperor of the Holy Roman Empire of what would some day be Germany and published by C.T. Branford & Co. in 1943. This has been the best work I've ever found on the subject of birds of prey and falconry.

A great deal of what was written between 1194 and 1250 by King Frederick, and his son, Manfred, can be applied today to the studies and management of hawks, eagles, and falcons. Those men not only studied, knew, and flew their birds, they loved what they did. They built their entire castle around the mews, the place where they kept their hunting birds. Without a doubt, the dedication of those men is unequaled in the world of birds today.

My first in-depth work on falcons was in the Fort Rock country, in northern Lake County, Oregon. The first time I saw Fort Rock, an ancient mud volcano standing erect in the sprawling sagebrush basin, I fell in love with the country. Ares Rock in Australia has nothing on Fort Rock, believe-you-me. It's a rugged, but beautiful land. The people who live there are tough—they have to be. In summer it gets hotter than the hinges of hades during the day, but blankets feel good at night. In winter you could freeze to death walking the ten yards from your pickup to the post office. You'd wonder why folks would want to live there, but long-time native Reub Long often told stories about the legendary beauty of the area.

During the early '50s, there were as many as eighteen active prairie falcon nests on the cliffs of Fort Rock, perhaps more. They swooped around like the White-throated Swifts that nest on the cliffs today. One day, while slowly birding around the north side of the cliffs I looked up to see the male falcon emerge from the nest, apparently going out on a hunting trip. At the same moment a mourning dove came sailing by, intent on going elsewhere. The falcon spotted the dove, mounted up with about ten swift wing-beats, then dropped like a bullet in the direction of the dove. The speed that bird attained so quickly was almost unimaginable. It sped downward like a bullet, smashing into the dove with a sledge-hammer blow, sending it cart-wheeling through the air. Then the falcon zoomed up again, and caught the dove before it hit the ground. It began making the falcon's 'kacking' sound, and the female came out of the nest as the male went flashing by, dropping the dove. She caught the dove in mid-air and wheeled back into her nest with it, where she presented it to the screaming, squawking youngsters. I stood transfixed. This whole incident took longer to tell than the actual event. The feathers that were knocked from the dove on impact by the falcon hadn't reached the ground when the dove was deposited in front of the young falcons for a meal. What a bird the prairie falcon is! And yet, it rarely can compete with ravens that usurp their nests.

When you don't have a rope, you have to do it the hard way: banding red-tails in central Oregon.

Unfortunately, Fort Rock became known as a breeding site for falcons. People from all over the US—and probably the world—came to Fort Rock to steal them. Falconry was, and always will be, a sport that attracts the very best, and the very worst in people. Some people are very responsible as they go out to remove a falcon from the wild to use in the practice of falconry. Others could care less: all they want is the bird, regardless of what harm they may cause to the species. Probably, most of those people are "keepers," or perhaps in the business of selling birds—not very nice people to have impacting the falcon resources. I ran into a whole van load of them one day when I stopped to call on Reub at his ranch in Fort Rock.

"You should have been here a while back, Jimmy," he said as we shook hands.

"How come, Reub?"

"There was a whole bunch of guys here who band those bullet hawks that you like, and they were looking for nests. So I sent them over to Butte Well. You know there's a falcon nest out there on the butte behind it."

"Thanks, Reub," I replied. "I'll be back in a little while and we'll sit and chat." I jumped back into my old Jeep and headed out along the road to Butte Well. As I got to the old site of Fremont, a small town that flourished in the early 1900s with families who thought they could turn the desert into a garden paradise, I slowed down so my dust wouldn't show, and eased along to the corral at Butte Well.

Sure enough, about a quarter of the way down the old desert track I could see a van parked. As I walked up to it I noticed that it had California plates. Looking up at the butte, I could see the Prairie Falcons, and hear their protesting cries. I took out my

Golden Eagle

Prairie Falcon

binoculars and scanned the steep, lava ridges on the butte and spotted three men slowly climbing toward the nest. As I watched I spotted another a little lower down, a heavy-set guy huffing and puffing to catch up with his partners.

It only took a moment to hot-trot it up to the van and I poked my head into the window. It was full of falconry furniture. A brand-new falcon hood hung down from the rear-view mirror, and in the back, under a blanket, I saw a bunch of small cages used to transport the birds. That was enough for me. I removed the cores from the valve stems and let the air out of all four tires, and then went out a ways in the sagebrush to wait.

I watched them with my binoculars as they crawled about slowly, trying this-and-that route to the nest, but perseverance won out and they got to the nestlings. Soon they

were heading back, each one carrying a bird. As they walked up toward the van I could overhear their conversation.

"I'll get at least a hundred bucks for this one," one fellow was saying, holding the kacking bird up for all to see.

"Oh, I'll bet we can get more," another said, as they started down the track toward their van.

"What the hell . . ." one of them exclaimed, as he spotted the van sitting on flat tires.

They ran over to their rig and began to really cuss. "The)(*&#@! tires are flat over here too," one of them shouted.

")(*&#@!, they're all flat," another exclaimed, kicking the dust high into the air.

"What the hell's goin' on?" the fat guy shouted, looking around him.

An animated, arm waving, cussing conversation got underway, with other gestures that discussed everything from hanging the person who did this to them, to other actions that aren't worth talking about. I was sure I was out of pistol range, but I waited prudently until they simmered down a bit, then stood so they could see me.

"Hi, guys!" I shouted. They spun around to see where the voice was coming from, and from where I was standing I could see by their body language they were ready to do mayhem. I knew I could outrun them and get to my rig before they could, so I felt pretty safe. "I'm the guy who let the air out of your tires," I said, staring them down.

"Who the hell do you think you are?" one guy shouted back.

"I live here," I said.

"Why the hell did you let the air out of our tires?" the leader growled, glaring at me and handing the bird that he was still holding to his partner.

"Because you're stealing our falcons," I answered, getting ready to run.

He started to bull his way toward me, cussing and shouting evil threats. The sagebrush in that country is about seven feet tall, and tougher than oak. He had to fight that, plus the tall rabbit brush that blocked his way, so he wasn't making much progress.

"That won't do you any good," I shouted as he blustered through the brush. "Even if

Jim's Piper Cub was tied behind a trailer, but a big wind broke it loose and almost wrecked it.

A very old golden eagle nests on a cliff in central Oregon.

A young golden eagle, about to fledge, stands on the edge of a tree nest.

Looking down the mouth of a baby golden eagle, you can see the trachea.

you caught me, you'd still have four flat tires, and the man in blue is already on his way."

He stopped dead in his tracks, and stood there giving me a look that would have curdled milk. Then his tactics changed so quickly I could hardly believe it. "OK," he sighed. "You win. But listen, we're only taking the surplus. There's lots of falcons around here. We won't hurt the population by taking these. Besides, we left two back there in the nest."

"That's a bunch of hog wash," I said. "You took the best of the birds to begin with. You wouldn't have left a healthy bird and taken a runt. In fact, I think you've got every bird that was in the nest. I've been watching that nest for years, and they rarely produce over

While banding golden eagles, Dean enjoys a good laugh while his brother Ross cleans up the mess in his lap left by the eagle.

three birds. You've got four now." When I finished, he didn't say anything, just stood there looking at me. I kept a sharp eye on his partners, but they were just standing there, holding the squawking falcons, trying to hear what was going on.

"We'll pay you," the fat guy said, looking back at his partners.

"Yeah," one of them responded heartily, shaking his head up and down and smiling at me.

"No deal," I said, emphatically.

"You, *&#$#@!" the leader shouted again, "I'll bust your *&##@!"

"I'll make you a deal," I shouted over his voice.

"What kind of deal?" he shouted back.

"You put the birds back and I'll get you a tire pump."

"You can go straight to hell!" The leader shouted, waving his fist at me.

"So long," I said, and started to back away from them.

I hadn't got more than ten feet away and could hear their conversation, rife with angry responses, and more cussing. "All right!" one of them shouted angrily, "you win, you, *&#@!. We'll put the birds back, you get the tire pump."

Dick Loper holds a huge golden eagle pellet.

Jim picks up an electrocuted golden eagle. Electrocution is still one of the primary causes of death for eagles.

"It's a deal," I said, adding, "But after you leave I'm going up there to count the birds and see if they're OK. If anything is wrong, you'll never get out of Oregon without seeing the inside of the nearest jail."

"All right! All right!" the leader exploded, "Don't give us any more of your *&#$#@! lectures. Just go get the tire pump!"

I put some sagebrush between us, trotted back to the Jeep, and drove over to Reub's place. As I pulled into the yard, he asked, "Did you find those bird banders?"

"Sure did," I replied, and then asked him if he had a tire pump.

"What do you need that for?" he asked, stepping back to look at the tires on the Jeep. I told him why I needed the pump, and what the guys had been up to. He

grinned at me and said, "Well, I got two tire pumps, Jimmy, one's an old, worn out one, and the other's pretty new. Which one do you want?" He and I both knew what the answer would be.

When I got back to the falcon crook's rig I could see three of them still climbing toward the nest. One was waiting alongside the van. "Have you got the pump?" he asked, giving me a sullen look.

"Right here," I said, throwing him the tired, old pump that Reub had given me.

"Are you sure it'll work?" the guy said, giving me another dirty look.

"If you want air in those tires, it'll work," I said, adding, "If I were you I'd get going. It won't be long before that State Policeman gets here, then your life will get very interesting." Then I remembered the valve cores. "Oh," I added, "you'll need these." I tossed the cores to him, one at a time.

He let out another stream of cussing, but screwed the cores in, attached the end of the air hose onto the stem of the tire, and began to pump.

It took a long time to get enough air into all four tires so they could move the van safely, but after a lot of sweating, cussing, pleading, and baloney as to why they wanted those falcons, the crooks finally got on their way. To this day, I don't know if it was coincidence, divine justice, or what, but as I followed them out to the county road I noticed a blue pickup coming down the road from Fort Rock. Sure enough, it was a State Policeman. The van stopped for the stop sign at the county road, and must have seen the pickup coming, but they didn't know the significance of the moment. I had suggested to them that they turn left and head back for California when they got to Highway 97. As they pulled out, the blue State Police pickup followed, closing the distance between them rapidly, and I could see Avon Mayfield driving it.

A few days later I happened to meet up with Avon, and I asked him about the van— if he had stopped it, or what. "That was a funny thing, Jim," he said, "I followed that van all the way to 97, and they acted like they were driving over fresh eggs. But they didn't check out as bad guys, so I let them

The blacktail jackrabbit is the most important prey item for golden eagles.

Ground squirrels are also important in an eagle's diet.

The yellow-bellied marmot is another favorite of the eagle.

go on when they turned left and headed back for California." After I told him what they had been up to, he took out his big notebook, pointed at a vehicle description and license number and asked, "Is this them?"

Unfortunately, that wasn't an isolated incident. Time and time again, the falcon crooks would come into Oregon from California, Nevada, Washington, and other states. They knew that Oregon was the breeding basket for falcons, and there just wasn't enough policemen to keep an eye on all of them. For a while I conducted training seminars for the Oregon State Police on how to recognize falcon crooks. That information

helped in apprehending a lot of bad guys later on.

I can recall one officer I met later on who told me about a man he stopped who had a whole station wagonful of bird's eggs that had been collected illegally from Alaska to Oregon. He also chased a vanful of falcon crooks into Washington but they got away from him when they dashed across the bridge that crossed the Columbia at Walla Walla. Even with Oregon's falconry laws, and the federal government's safeguards, I fear it's still going on today.

One spring day in the '60s, while conducting an aerial nest census on Golden Eagles, I had to leave my Piper Cub at Reub's place when one of those unpredictable wind storms suddenly came

Osprey build their nests in the tops of trees, a trait that makes them pretty safe from their enemies—and bird banders like Jim Anderson. (Crane Prairie Reservoir, Deschutes National Forest)

This juvenile Osprey has been tagged with a colored leg band that will help to identify it if—and when—it returns to the area it was banded.

After falling out of the Ponderosa pine and into the water, Jim decided to climb to get his courage back.

Sometimes it was necessary to use the old, "Ladder-in-the-canoe" trick to climb the old trees to band Osprey. Everything was OK until the canoe moved!

In an effort to help Osprey raise more young successfully, the USFS placed hundreds of these steel platforms on the tops of the dead lodgepole pine in Crane Prairie Reservoir. They were very successful.

The bright yellow eye identifies this Osprey as an adult.

Osprey are especially adapted to soar over water and have the ability to look into the water to spot their chief source of food—fish. This male one is doing a one-foot carry, bringing food back to the nest for his mate and a hungry nestling.

whistling out of the southwest. The buttes and rims were sending sledge-hammer winds at me, and the turbulence was so bad it was all I could to keep the plane heading toward the ranch. Finally I could see the bold outline of Fort Rock sticking up through the dust that was screaming across the desert floor, and out beyond it, Reub's big crested-wheat field on the west side of the house. "Oh, boy!" I said, sitting up high for a better look. "Does that look good to me!" Fortunately I was able to land straight into the wind and get behind a shed where I could jump out and tie the plane to an old loading dock.

Reub came out with his usual happy grin and helped me tie the plane down. I mentioned the fact that we were having a pretty good wind, and he promptly replied, "Oh, we don't *have* very much, there's just an awful lot passing through."

He did that to me all the time. He even did that to me when I pulled up to his house the morning after his house had burned down. I can recall the many nights I stayed with him during winters in the '50s,

One of the ways a nestling Ferruginous Hawk can scare off an enemy is to open its mouth wide, stare at the intruder, and flash the nictating membrane across its eyes. Sometimes just breathing on a bander will do the trick . . . the breath of a young hawk is enough to gag a maggot!

There can be up to five Ferruginous Hawk nestlings in the nest on a year when food is plentiful. These youngsters were well-fed on gophers and ground squirrels that were abundant in the alfalfa fields that surround the town of Fort Rock.

Jim found this Ferruginous nest in the Fort Rock Basin at the time when the young birds should have been feathered out. Instead he found these eggs hatching, took one photo and left.

and in the morning he'd fire up that old wood stove that rested at one end of the living room with the stack running across to the hole at the other end. He'd load it up with pitchwood, stick a match inside, then stand back and watch the old stove as it started to huff and puff. It would shudder and shake the whole stove pipe, going, "Woof! Woof! Woof" sending black smoke into the frigid morning air like a steam engine getting ready to haul a load of coal over the Rockies. I'd always tell him that some day he was going to burn his house down. His reply was almost always the same, "Aint nothin' worse than a kid on a ranch." Well, he finally did burn the house down, and if my memory is correct, he did it with an electric frying pan.

Anyway, he rolled into the yard that morning as I was standing there looking at the smoking ruins with the horrifying thought he had burned up in the fire. I was so happy to see him I ran over and gave him a big hug, and then said how sorry I was that his house had burned down.

"Oh, it 'aint so bad, Jimmy," he immediately replied. "This is the first time I ever had a fire in my house, and look, I'm a complete success. I burned it to the ground first time!" Then he pointed into the ruins and said, "Besides, I needed a new horse trough, and that bath tub will make a great one." I started to say something, but he cut me off and said, "And you know how Eleanor is always getting after me with, 'What'd you do with this—or what'd you do with that?' Well, now I have a perfect excuse: I'll just tell her it burned up in the fire." He was like that.

One of the most important elements in the reproduction of Ferruginous Hawks is a safe place to nest. The old junipers found near Brothers, Oregon are ideal nesting habitat.

Well, we tied the Cub down good and tight and I asked Reub if he would keep an eye on it. "Oh, sure, Jimmy," he said, "You don't worry about it one little bit. I'll watch it for you."

Well, about three weeks later I had the opportunity to fly down to Fort Rock with a friend who was going to California, so we landed on the road out in front of the ranch and got out to fly my J-3 back to Portland. Reub wasn't home, so I untied the plane, cleaned about a ton of sand out of the inside, polished the scratches out of the windshield, cranked her up and took off for home. Over a week later, at about two in the morning the phone rang. It was Reub. "Jimmy!" he shouted. "I've got terrible news! Somebody has stole your airplane!"

"Why you old horned toad!" I shouted back at him, "I came down and got that airplane over a week ago! A heck of a pal you are. I thought you said you'd watch out for it . . ." As I stopped talking I could hear him laughing on the other end of the line.

"Yeah, I knew you'd come and got it that day," he laughed. "I just wanted to call and

say hello, and tell you how the book is selling."

Then there was the time I landed at Shorty and Echo Gustafson's place at Christmas Valley to get out of another of those spring winds, and was forced to spend the night. We were sitting at the table that evening eating elk steak when all of a sudden a great bang sounded on the side of the house.

"What the devil was that?" I exclaimed, looking from Shorty to Echo.

"That was the wind!" Shorty answered.

"If that was the wind I just lost an airplane," I said, jumping to my feet and heading for the door.

I had left the J-3 parked on the lee side of the trailer house, out of the wind, wheels chocked, and a rope tied from the wings to the steps of the trailer house. When that gust hit, it swirled around and carried the little Piper Cub backwards, breaking the ropes, and stuffing the fuselage under the tongue of a big flat-bed trailer parked nearby. If it hadn't been for that, the plane would have gone off across the desert and

The Ferruginous Hawk on the wing is perhaps one of the most beautiful birds of prey in the West. They are, without a doubt, one of the most beneficial hawk, known to prey almost exclusively on rodents that cause crop damage and carry diseases that are communicable to man.

rolled up in a ball. There she was, her backbone stuffed under the neck of the trailer and both feet off the ground, bouncing in the wind.

"Oh, no!" I groaned.

Shorty, Echo, and their daughter, Judy, helped me slide the plane out from under the trailer neck and we rolled it back against the trailer house where we tied one wing to Shorty's pickup, the other to his car, and the tail to a big roll of cable that was left over from a high-line crew that had gone through. The right wing-tip had been crushed, almost to the aileron, there was a wrinkle in the fuselage, and a couple of holes were visible in the horizontal stabilizer. Other than that, she was fine, but I didn't get a good night's sleep that night.

The next morning Echo gave me some of her best feed sacks that I taped to the gash on the wing tip and patched the tears in the horizontal stabilizer. I then painted it over with some silver paint left over from a roofing operation. Then Shorty took a big strap, wrapped it around the fuselage, and tied it to a long jill-poke.

"OK," he said. "You get down there at the end and sight down the tail. When I get it twisted back give me a yell." I did as he instructed and watched as he pulled on the long pole. The wrinkles came out of the fabric nice as you please, and when I could see every thing was plumb again, I shouted "Good, Shorty!" He waved back, and then gave it one more twist. When he released the pole you couldn't see a wrinkle anywhere. I cranked up the old 65 Continental and headed for Bend.

I was expecting the plane to behave differently with all the patches and about a foot gone from the right wing, but she flew along like there was nothing wrong, so I took some additional time to look at a couple of eagle nests on the way back to Bend. As I landed at the airport, I pulled up to the big hanger that Pat Gibson used for a shop. I noticed a big man standing by the gas pumps giving me the eyeball. I shut the Cub down and let her roll up to the shop doors, then got out and placed a chock behind each wheel. As I looked up I saw the big fellow walking toward me with a grin, "I

When Leslie Thompson was a young lady, she couldn't wait to go on bird-banding trips. Then one day she discovered what a young raven had done to her hair and clothing. In spite of it, she went on many more OMSI science trips to learn more about birds, and the world she lived in.

know who you are," he said, glancing at the silver patches over the right wing-tip. "You're Jim Anderson."

"Now how do you know that?" I inquired. I'd never seen this man in my entire life.

"That's easy," he replied, pointing to all the patch-work. "I can see an eagle got you, and I don't know of anyone else who spies on eagles with a J-3." When we shook hands, he said his name was Dean Johnson. It's funny how people's trails will cross; many years later I flew for him as a glider flight instructor.

Then there's the time I landed at Reub's place and his horse tried to eat my airplane—but that's another tale for another time . . .

Even the golden eagles used to fall prey to

would-be falconers. More than once I ended up with eagles that were taken from people in Portland who had them illegally. The new federal regulations prohibiting anyone from taking eagles has almost put a stop to it, though.

An eagle is a difficult bird to keep hidden away—not like a little Kestrel who can be kept in the basement, or garage—an eagle requires a lot of room. If people were aware of what is required to keep an eagle in captivity, they wouldn't be so eager to have them. I can recall one that I had that was as gentle as a lamb, but one day I got sloppy and as it flew back to me it grasped the unprotected portion of my arm. The talons sunk into my arm and penetrated all the way to the bone. I was almost unconscious

The dark eyes of the flammulated owls aid in distinguishing them from their look-alike relative, the screech owl. "Flams" are the travelers of the little owl family, spending their winters in Central America and nesting in the Northwest. Unlike other owls, the "flams" are known to prey upon insects as their principal food source.

with the excruciating pain that put me to my knees.

Unfortunately, the killing of eagles for feathers and talons is still going on.

The Warm Springs Indian Reservation was the site of a recent flagrant disregard for the welfare of a species that the Indians are supposed to hold in religious respect. While some Indians will kill an eagle with respect, and utilize the feathers for legitimate religious and cultural reasons, apparently there is an ilk who have no regard for the eagle's role in Indian lore, and think of them only as a source of immediate revenue.

A small group of people were killing eagles and making Indian religious paraphernalia to be sold to collectors throughout the world. This lucrative market has led many a good Indian astray because of the dollar signs dancing in his eyes. In the spring of 1991, an Indian from Warm Springs was apprehended in Burns where he had illegally killed a deer.

Further investigation uncovered several parts of golden eagles as well. When the Indian realized he was caught red-handed, he confessed to the killing, and then took the officers to the site where he had killed and buried the bodies. Apparently, the killing had been done at night, in the light of a full moon. As the eagles came to roost for the night in the high power transmission towers, the killers would use binoculars to pick out the birds they wanted, shoot them out of the towers in the bright moonlight, remove feathers and talons, and bury the rest.

It will take many years for the eagles to recover from these losses. Then too, many of the birds killed this way might have been carrying US Fish & Wildlife bands, and researchers like myself wonder why we don't receive more data from the banded eagles.

My family and Joseph Jones (one of my old students from the OMSI days) make an annual trip to the King Ranch to band the eagles that nest there on a high, lava cliff. These eagles depend on the ground squirrels and jackrabbits that live on, and adjacent to, the ranch. Each year this nest produces two eagles, thanks to an abundant and dependable food supply. It wouldn't be that way unless Peter and Sondra King, third-generation owners of the ranch stood their ground and said, "No Hunting of ground squirrels and rabbits on this land. Period!" That's what it takes, just a little cooperation with Mother Nature and things smooth themselves out.

It's the same way with the Lazy 'Z' Ranch near Sisters. There's an active nest on the Forest Service Land that's within spitting distance of the ranch fenceline that marks the line between the respective properties. The owners of the ranch know the eagle is there, so they keep the gate closed and the cattle out while the birds are young and vulnerable. Private land owners are a vital element to the survival of a host of wildlife species, eagles included.

Of all the Buteos—the soaring hawks—the red-tailed is enjoying a new lease on life. Forest lands that once were dense with trees have been clear-cut: scalped. This has allowed shrubs and grasses to grow in places where they have never been before, which has given rise to rodent populations that were never there either. Red-tails, like any other creature of the wild, will never let a food supply (or niche) go by without taking advantage of it. The trees along the edges of the clear-cuts are perfect sites for nests. The rodent supply within the clear-cut is prefect as a prey base—so why not use it all.

These factors, coupled with additional protection and wonderful support from people who are well-informed about the needs of hawks, have given red-tails a new lease on life. We can find them nesting in places they've never been found before, and in the historical nesting areas they're in greater numbers. Of all the hawks that migrate each year, red-tails make up the largest percentage. The red-tails I've banded in Oregon over the years have turned up in California, New Mexico, Arizona, Washington, Idaho, and Texas. It's helpful to wildlife managers to know the Oregon birds are such travelers.

The rolling wheat country of Wasco County that borders on the big Columbia River has produced some interesting questions about Red-tails. It's not possible for me to say for sure, but I have a hunch the chemicals used in the wheat business may have a negative impact on the nesting success of the red-tails that settle near those rolling fields of grain. On several occasions we've found complete red-tail clutches nests adjacent to the wheat fields that failed.

Johnny Simpkins, an OMSI student from the '60s, had climbed into a big cottonwood one afternoon to check a Red-tail nest on an old plantation surrounded by wheat fields, and as he reached the nest, he called down. "Hey, Jim! There are four eggs in the nest." It was very late to find eggs in the nest, so I climbed up to take a look.

"Look out for some of those limbs," Johnny shouted as I began to climb. "They're pretty rotten in places."

I was thinking about Red-tails when I should have been thinking about climbing as I went up limb-to-limb. As I pulled myself up to the nest, Johnny stepped to the lower branches to make room for me at the nest. I

Sometimes it was necessary to use an airplane to return young owls to their parents. Jim and Jeff Cooney flew these young owls back to LaGrande from Bend. They were returned to their nest with the help of the Oregon State Police and the USFS.

glanced up at the adult hawks who were putting on a luke-warm display of protecting their nest site and dismissed them as a threat. I reached out and picked up an egg, placed it next to my ear, and gently gave it a shake. I could hear the remains sloshing around that indicated an addled egg. "Looks like they're . . ." I started to say when I was interrupted by a loud crack. It was the limb I was leaning against. As the limb broke I dropped the egg back into the nest and then went falling through the tree. It was pretty

Jim talked his friend, Larry Langley (a Bend fireman) into climbing the biggest Ponderosa pine around to get to the nest of the golden eagle.

Saw-whet owls come by their name because of their call that sounds like someone "whetting", or filing a saw to sharpen the teeth. These little owls are very noisy at times, and can be heard up to a mile away in dense forests. Saw-whets are cavity nesters and depend on woodpeckers to hollow out their homes for them. However, they have also been known to use wood duck nesting boxes when available. This juvenile was raised in a duck box on Sauvie Island Wildlife Management Area close to Portland.

exciting—to say the least. I can't recall everything that was happening, but I do remember the big limb I crashed into that caught me across my legs. I made a grab for it, and as luck would have it I got a good hold and stopped, about thirty feet from the ground, and fifteen feet below the nest.

As anyone will tell you who has climbed up and down trees, if you fall, and don't climb again, you're sunk. I looked up for a hand hold and went back up to the nest. As I pulled up to Johnny he put out a hand and helped me back up to where I had been a few minutes before. "You sure had a funny look on your face when you went by me," he said, checking my hands and face for cuts.

The biggest clutch of Red-tail eggs I ever found was in a nest built in a juniper tree in the Fort Rock Basin. I sent my son Ross up to check the young, and he counted six downy youngsters.

Red-tails can be fearsome at protecting their nesting territory. I was perched in a blind one time on a rimrock in the Fort Rock Basin watching some Mountain Bluebirds when I heard the familiar scream of an angry red-tail that wasn't too far away. I lifted a flap on the side of the blind and saw a pair of red-tailed Hawks chasing two golden eagles. As the hawks swooped on the eagles, the latter would suddenly flip over and try to grab a hawk as it flashed by.

The result of this was the eagles lost altitude each time they rolled over. It only took about ten or so dives from the hawks before the eagles were beating along just over the tops of the sagebrush, but the hawks didn't give an inch. Both birds mounted up and made one final dive toward the eagles. There was nothing the larger adversary could do; they went crashing into the sagebrush in an effort to escape the hawks.

It's a ignoble thing to be an eagle and get smashed to the ground by a couple of "mere" hawks. The eagles ended up on the ground, running around the sagebrush, trying to hide, or get out of the way of the pestiferous, antagonistic hawks. Suddenly, as if they turned off the attack switch, the hawks quit. It was as though they had chased the eagles across an invisible line. They had done it. They had removed the threat from their nestlings, and out of the nesting territory—and that's all that mattered. The last I saw of the eagles, they were heading for a small lava outcropping where they ultimately launched themselves into the sky and raced away—in the opposite direction of the hawks.

One bird that seems to travel about without too much notice these days is the northern harrier, known as the marsh hawk for a long time. Oh, some duck hunters seem to think that these beautiful birds are responsible for destroying the ducks that they like to shoot—and rarely eat—but that's not really the case. Of course a harrier will

Owls have a small row of feathers along the leading edge of their wing that help to silence their flight, as visible on this barn owl.

take a duck; that's the way they have to make their living. Nature designed them that way, but the impact of a harrier on ducks is nothing when compared to what draining a wetland can do—or when a hunter takes more than his legal limit. It's a shame that more people don't take that into consideration. Ducks Unlimited can do more for the waterfowl by saving wetlands than shooting a hundred harriers.

I can recall the time my family and I were slowly driving down the Bull Dike road on the Summer Lake Wildlife Management area operated by the Oregon Department of Fish & Wildlife in Lake County. We spotted a harrier standing in the water alongside the road and didn't think anything of it—for a moment.

"Wait a minute!" my wife said. "That marsh hawk shouldn't be standing there like that; the water's too deep."

"You're right," I said, shifting to reverse and slowly backing up.

As we pulled up alongside the hawk it began to fidget, looking this way and that, preparing for instant flight, but appearing reluctant to fly.

"Now, what do you suppose is going on?" Sue asked, as she scrambled after my old 300 Novaflex attached to the even older Pentax.

"Beats me," I said raising the binoculars for a closer look.

Suddenly my wife shouted, "There he goes!"

We didn't have time for a picture, and I had just gotten the binocs to my face when the hawk jumped out of the water and sailed away. "Pop!" up came an adult coot.

"Did you see that?" I said, astonished.

We sat there wondering what in the world this was all about, then as the truth hit us, I turned to her (not really believing that was possible), "I think that harrier was trying to drown that coot!"

The coot began to swim around and preen its feathers, like there was nothing to worry about in the world, seemingly oblivious to the fact that it had escaped death. That's the way nature operates: there are no "good guys" or "bad guys," just a great deal of ecological interaction.

Fishermen and Osprey interact a great deal at Crane Prairie, a big storage reservoir on the Deschutes River system south of Bend. The area immediately surrounding the reservoir was set aside in the '60s as an Osprey Management Area. Less responsible fishermen would tie up to a tree with an Osprey nest in the top, and the young would suffer from weather, or starve to death as the adults deserted the nest. A great deal of effort to educate people has helped to eliminate this problem, as well as help from the Oregon State Police Game Officers.

If I had a nickel for every scraggly pine tree I climbed on Crane Prairie, I'd be rolling in money. Each summer I'd go out on the water and scramble among the trees, climbing to nests and banding Osprey nestlings. Hadley Roberts, the Forest Service Biologist that helped set Crane Prairie up as an Osprey Management area, and his son, went out with me a great deal in the early days. We often used the "Ladder-in-the-

The oval shaped face, and the binocular vision of the barn owl are a wonderful asset when it comes to listening, seeing, and catching their favorite prey items—rats and mice.

canoe" trick to expedite climbing the trees that had lost their limbs, or were too fragile to climb on. All too often I'd get into the top of the tree only to come crashing back into the water as the fragile limbs gave way. It was a good way to cool off on a hot summer day, but frustrating when Osprey banding was the objective.

I can recall one time when I was on Crane Prairie with Gordy Lind, an OSU wildlife student who was studying Osprey as part of his Master's Thesis. We were working in an area that was popular with the fishermen as well as Osprey, and had talked to several people about getting too close to the nests. Most of them were agreeable, and moved on to find another fishing hole. As we were

Barn owls will often use nesting boxes set out for wood ducks. This adult owl was photographed as it left a box that was being checked for such use.

The young owls in the box are all different sizes, from tiny to large. This is Nature's way of insuring the survival of at least one chick. If food becomes scarce the bigger one will sometimes devour the little one, or take what food there is. It's very evident that these little owls have been dining well on rodents, as can be seen by the great mass of pellets that carpet the floor of their box home.

pulling up to a nesting tree in our boat, we noticed an elderly couple fishing about fifty yards away—far enough that they offered no threat to the birds.

I had just climbed up to the nest and Gordy was in the boat when we heard someone shouting across the water. "You there! You men! Get out of that tree! Those birds are protected!" I looked out over the water and could see a frail-looking, older lady standing up in her boat shaking her finger at me. "Yes, you!" she shouted again, waving at me, "Get out of that tree and leave those birds alone!"

I looked down at Gordy and said, "Oh, oh."

"Don't worry, Jim," Gordy said, reaching out to untie the boat from the tree. "I'll take care of it."

I watched as he putted over to where the couple was anchored, and across the water I could hear Gordy explaining what we were doing and why. Every once in a while I could hear the response from the irate lady, "Yes, I understand . . . yes . . . thank you . . . oh? Yes . . . thank you . . . that's fine, young man . . . goodbye young man," and Gordy came putting back with a big smile on has face.

"Ok, Jim," he shouted up to me. "She knows what we're doing. No problem."

I looked over across the water just in time to hear her say, "All right Henry, drive on," and in a moment the outboard on the back of their little boat putted to life and they chugged away in the direction of Gales Landing.

We had finished that nest and I was just tying us up to the next one when we spotted the Forest Service patrol boat roaring toward us over the water. Gordy looked up. "Now what . . .?"

The boat came to a halt in a splash of spray, rocking alongside us. Jack Smith, the Forest Service biologist, looked at us severely. "OK, you guys," he shouted, with tongue-in-cheek. "You've been reported by a very angry lady who says you guys are out here molesting the Osprey. You can come peaceably or I'll have to use force."

I looked at Gordy and laughed, "Well, so much for your clear and concise explanation of what we're doing!"

You know, we were both happy that the woman didn't believe Gordy. We were depending on the public to help us protect the Osprey. People like that were vital to the total management efforts.

I can still remember one tree I fell out of that summer. It was a shaky old lodgepole, severely weakened by rot that had set in over the long years it had been standing in the water. Jack Smith was with me that day, and I asked him to untie the boat and wait a little way from the tree in the event it fell into the water—or I did. I tested the lower limbs that were, at best, not worth talking about, and slowly inched up, keeping my feet tight against the trunk where the limbs would be strongest. Finally I got to the nest, which was one of those artificial nests the Forest Service put up, and placed in such a manner that reaching over the top to grasp a young Osprey was difficult or at times next to impossible. Anyway, I had an Osprey in my hand and was just about to lower it down in a sack to the boat below to be banded when a loud, "Crack!" sounded right under my butt. I quickly threw the Osprey out as far as I could, and in an instant I was crashing down the tree, cleaning all the limbs on the way to the water. As I hit and went under I felt the stub of a small tree that had broken off long ago brush my side. I popped to the surface, treading water and looked around. Jack was already on his way to rescue the Osprey. After recuperating and banding the bird, I had to strap on the climbing irons to get back up the tree and

Mothers aren't the only ones who seem to have eyes in the back of their head! This pygmy owl looks as though it has, but they are really just colored feathers that resemble eye spots, and might make an enemy believe the owl's really looking at them.

put the bird back into the nest, and the idea of falling into the water with those on really gave me the creeps.

"Do you want to quit for the day?" Jack asked as we were heading across the reservoir.

I was almost ready to reply with a "Yes," when I looked over and saw a big, dead, Ponderosa leaner towering seventy feet into the air near the shoreline, and it had an Osprey nest perched in the very top. "N-o-o-o . . ." I said slowly, sizing up the tree and wondering about going up again. "I've got to go up that one," I continued, pointing toward the big pine. "If I don't, I'll never climb anything again."

Jim's old 1947 Piper Cub was the perfect airplane for looking into eagles' nests. The dusty old roads on the desert also made perfect landing strips for refueling from a drum of gas in Larry Langley's pickup.
Courtesy of Larry Langley

Well, we tied up to that punky old buckskin. The base of the tree had been smashed away by the winter ice beating against it, leaving about two thirds of solid wood in the trunk. I gave it a good push and it seemed to, sort-of, stand still. I put on the climbing irons again, stepped out of the boat, thumped the irons into the tree and went up. In all honesty, I was shaking pretty badly when I reached the top. Both adult Osprey were a little more aggressive than most of them are usually, and kept swooping over my head, screaming at me in that wild, high whistling call. It wasn't until I reached the nest and found it was big enough to step into that I relaxed and enjoyed the view. It only took me about five minutes to place the USF&WL band on one leg and the special color-band I was using on the other of the two nestlings. By that time I was feeling confident that all was well, and descended to the boat. As I stepped in I noticed a big grin on Jack's face. "You look a lot better, Jim," he said, giving me a slap on the back as he moved past me to start the motor. I felt a lot better too.

That fall I received a special note from the Bird Banding Lab that contained a Polaroid photo of a man holding a dead Osprey in his hands and a note on the back describing how he shot the Osprey that had an aluminum band on one leg, and a colored band on the other. It was one of the birds from that big pine—and the picture came from Volcan, Costa Rica. To date, this has been the farthest away the Osprey from the Deschutes Forest have ever been found.

I would be remiss if I didn't share a few moments with you about another favorite bird, the Ferruginous Hawk. This beautiful buteo is found throughout Central Oregon nesting in solitary junipers between Fort Rock and Hampton, and on low rock outcrops farther north in the wheat country along the Columbia River. Unlike most raptors, they rarely raise a fuss when people climb into their nests to band the nestlings. Their whistling cry is unhawk-like, almost a musical and gentle call, even when they're agitated by human visitors.

There are a few nests in the Fort Rock Basin that I've been banding for almost thirty years, and the birds rarely miss a season. I can recall one spring when we had a cold rain, and several of the nests failed, probably due to the excessive cold. I usually

Nine-and-a-half pounds of feathered fury! This young golden eagle was full of fight as Jim climbed into the tree to band it and its nest mate.

band the young in late May or early June. I climbed into a nest once on June 4 and found a newly hatched young and the others just pipping. This was a very uncomfortable situation for me. I knew that interference during hatching might cause serious problems, so I shot one photo and withdrew immediately. I came back four weeks later to find all the eggs had hatched; four healthy hawks glowered, hissed, and gaped at me as I peeked over the edge of their nest. A notice from the Bird Banding Lab reported that one of the young from that nest was shot in Concord, California in October of that year. Not a long time to live for such a beautiful bird.

One time I found a Goshawk nest high up in the forests above the small town of Sisters, Oregon. I had heard that Goshawks can go bear hunting with buggy-whip and come home with the bear, and it was best to give them a wide berth, but I wanted to photograph the nest, so I dragged my blind out and set it up—at night—quietly. The next morning, just as the sun peeked over the ridge, the Goshawk was alert and kacking at the strange apparition on a hillside close to her nest. I worried as she fretted about, staring at the blind—and at me, I was sure. My hair crawled up on the back of my neck every time she glared my way.

Jim holds a Ferruginous Hawk that a rancher saved after it fell from a nest.

As the sun moved up I slowly placed the 500 mm lens in the hole cut in the blind and began to focus on the nest. Just as I was getting everything in focus I was aware of something heading right down the barrel of the lens like a cannon ball. I couldn't believe it—it was the Goshawk! Before I could move she came crashing into the blind! Her wild kacking and screeching was enough to scare the daylights out of anyone with any sense, Suddenly she crashed into the blind and knocked my tripod over, which in turn fell

against me. We all came tumbling out of the back of the burlap blind: hawk, camera and human. Before I could protect myself she was on my head, back, shoulders, and arms, screaming and grabbing.

That was enough for me! I jumped to my feet, hands over my head and face, and went dashing for cover. It took her a few minutes to calm down once I was gone. She stood her ground, gazing in defiance at the tripod, camera, and the small stool I had been sitting on. Then, with a shudder, she fluffed her feathers, turned and let go with a big slice of mutes that landed on the camera and tripod, and flew back to her nest. Each time I tried to get close to my equipment she would scream at me in such a way that I knew what would happen if I went any closer. So I just wandered off down to my rig, got out a good book and waited 'til sundown. Even then, under cover of darkness, I was as nervous as a pregnant fox in a forest fire as I retrieved my equipment and got out of the hawk's territory.

As I mentioned earlier, my love affair with hawks, eagles, and falcons spans a lifetime. I could go on for a long time about my adventures with them. I'm sure many of my old friends who read this will say, 'Yeah, but what about the time . . .?' Some of those tales have already slipped into oblivion for me. It will take another campfire, an old friend, or a visit to a tree or cliff, to remind me of them, to bring them back to life . . . Like the time I was showing off while repelling down a cliff, doing long free-falls, when suddenly I got twisted around and slammed back into the cliff . . .

If you would like to get involved in the fun of raptor research call your local wildlife management agency and ask if you can help. You will be happy you did—and take the kids with you—they'll be happy you did too.

Butterflies are Beautiful

"Hey, Dad!" my youngest son, Caleb, shouted from the back seat, "They're mating!"

"I do believe they are," my wife said,

surprised. "But I wonder why they're doing it here? There's nothing here for them to eat."

It was a beautiful hot day with a clear,

Miriam Anderson peers at the caterpillar of the monarch butterfly that is almost ready to pupate. Monarchs feed on milkweed which is poisonous, making the caterpillar almost immune to predators.

A monarch caterpillar sheds its final skin.

It prepares to become a chrysalis which will then metamorphose into an adult.

bright blue sky and we were slowly driving along the tour route watching birds on the Tule Lake National Wildlife Refuge in northern California.

"Do you see what I see?" I asked my wife, as we slowed down.

By the time we came to a complete stop, everyone in the old Chevy was looking out the side window. "No question about it," Reuben, Caleb's older brother, said, leaning out for a closer look. "They are mating all right."

"Look!" Caleb suddenly shouted, as he bolted for the door of the car. "Over there— on the other side of the road! I see cater-pillars!" Like most boys, when they see

caterpillars there's no holding them back. He's the fastest eight-year-old I know when it comes to chasing creepy-crawly critters, and that includes insects, lizards, and snakes. He was out of the car and into the patch of shrubs so quick I couldn't stop him. "Mom!" he shouted again. "Look, there's a bunch of chrysalides too!"

That did it! We all bailed out of the car to see if what he was saying was really true. Sure enough, right there, alongside a road that I've been driving over for better than twenty years, we discovered a tiny patch of

The final chrysalis.

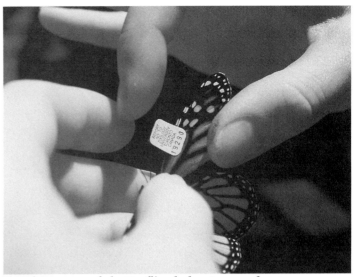

Tagging monarch butterflies helps to reveal more information about their travels as they migrate from the Northwest to their winter quarters in California. Sue Anderson carefully places the tag on the butterfly's wing membrane.

The adult monarch emerging from the chrysalis.

milkweed, and with it the eggs, caterpillars, chrysalides, and adult Monarch Butterflies. "Well, can you beat that!" I said, scratching my head.

This was quite a surprise. To begin with I had never seen milkweed like those tiny, dried-out looking plants that appeared to be struggling for life alongside the road. They didn't look as though they had enough leaf on them to generate photosynthesis, let along support the hundreds of Monarch larvae crawling about the plants. As we got down for a closer look it became obvious that you can't judge a book by its cover or a plant by its leaves. Those little caterpillars were chomping away on that stuff like one of those 40/60 cows (a beef cow on the western range that has a forty-feet-wide mouth and has to graze at sixty miles per hour to get enough to eat).

"Get your camera . . ." my wife prompted me as we carefully poked around the tiny milkweed plants, peering at all the life stages of the butterflies.

Of all the butterflies in North America, I don't think there's another that has a more beautiful chrysalis than that of the Monarch. The jewel-like case with golden spots on the surface becomes transparent, as the adult butterfly slowly evolves, and one can observe the changes. My little son, Caleb took the thoughts right out of my mind . . . "Let's take a few of the chrysalides home, Dad," he pleaded.

We talked it over and decided that it would be OK to bring home a couple of chrysalides, if we were very careful. We had seen monarchs flying past our home near Bend as well, so we carefully brought two of the delicate chrysalides back with us and placed them under almost a twenty-four-hour watch. The kids gave us hourly updates, starting at 6 am each day. When the chrysalid's skin turned transparent, revealing the orange, black, and white wing patterns, we knew emergence was imminent. It was Caleb who gave us the good news. "It's happening!" he shouted one morning at 6 am. "It's happening!"

We all bounced out of bed and ran out onto the back porch where the chrysalids were hanging in one of our butterfly rearing cages. Sure enough, the chrysalis had split and the adult monarch was slowly pulling itself out of the case and into the warm, morning sunlight. Although the struggling insect took more than an hour to fully pump up its wings and ready itself for flight, we dared not leave, not even for breakfast, afraid we might miss a single detail of the whole process. Finally, with its wings dried and stiff, and after posing for photographs, the monarch tested its wings for the first time, fluttered about the garden for a few minutes, and then said goodbye. Another day—another miracle.

Tagging monarchs is a great family adventure. The wonderful enthusiasm and energy of children is a powerful energy resource that can be unleashed—and guided—to capture the elusive monarchs. All my children seem to have an abundance of that stuff. I'm sure George Barnard Shaw was being facetious when he said that youth was such a wonderful thing, it was a shame it was wasted on children. They don't waste a bit of it. Anyone who has watched them charge off across the fields, dodging rocks, trees, and leaping over obstacles in pursuit of a butterfly must agree. We channelled all that energy into capturing and tagging monarchs.

We receive our monarch tags from Professor Urquhart of the University of Toronto and made our annual pilgrimage to Tule Lake and the Lava Beds National Monument each summer to tag monarchs and keep an eye on the breeding habitat. That's the scary part—habitat. It would only take one sweep of herbicide to obliterate the breeding habitat of the monarchs in that part of northern California. Even though both government agencies are aware of the tiny milkweed plants on their respective lands, I fear for the welfare of the butterflies. It's just too easy after a change in leadership, habitat emphasis, native and introduced plant management philosophy, or some other unknown factors, to destroy the ecological conditions that support the species.

My wife refuses to collect while in the field. Most entomologists will often kill their quarry, and then carefully place it in their collecting envelope for future study, and later in their collections. My wife will collect her specimens only on film. At first this technique was greeted with skepticism by a few of her associates, but as it is with anyone who has the respect for Nature, they never made any disparaging remarks about her methods, and I have often observed them to do their collecting in such a manner as to not offend her. Respect for Nature, and the feelings of others, comes in all sizes and ways.

As my children became more involved with the whole world of butterflies, I began to recall when I was a kid on the farm and watched monarchs sailing over my head as I hoed corn, hauled glacial rocks out of the fields, and rode the hay wagon back to the barn in late summer. We had a great deal of the classic milkweed, *Asclepias speciosa*, all over the pasture, and along the fence rows. It just never occurred to me as a kid to get excited as I am today about butterflies.

Oh, sure the insect world of my youth had its attractions. The fireflies were always a source of enjoyment as we captured them by the hundreds and placed them in a big jar to use as a lantern on the dark, moonless, summer nights. What kid didn't know about fireflies in Connecticut? The huge, predacious water bugs and beetles in the pond outback were better to watch than the Saturday Tarzan movies, and we had a bout with bed bugs once, and I'll never forget them! My Uncle Ben had a collection of butterflies and moths, but the real excitement of butterflies was a long time a-coming.

Thinking back, I now believe that in my subconscious I've always had a strong attraction to butterflies. In the early '60s I was browsing through a book store in Portland and chanced upon two ancient editions of *The Moth Book* and *The Butterfly Book*, both by W.J. Holland (published by Doubleday, Page & Co. in 1904), and had the brains to purchase them. When I think about the printing equipment available at the time, I consider the color plates to be remarkable, especially compared to the technology of today's laser printing and the other gadgets. Another outstanding feature becomes clear as one reads through the books: they were a labor of love.

In my talks about insects, it always seems natural to me to draw the analogy between the metamorphosis of the butterfly and what I believe man goes through when mortal death closes our eyes. The butterfly larva—the caterpillar—will "die" as it enters the chrysalis stage, then will reappear as a beautiful, flying insect. I prefer to believe that when I die, I will reappear again, changed, as another—hopefully more beautiful—being, capable of "flight."

There is one thing that is constant in Nature, and that's change. Talking with lepidopertist friends about the biological mechanics involved in metamorphosis, the transformation becomes, to me, even more miraculous. As the larva settles into the chrysalis stage, the respiratory, digestive, circulatory, and locomotion organs within its body apparently dissolve into a primordial, green, biological soup. Then all the genetic codes rearrange the soup into that of the adult butterfly who will have not only a completely different method of moving, eating, and breathing, but the capacity to

reproduce as well. As if that wasn't enough to try and comprehend, Mother Nature has other miracles working too. There are several species of parasitic wasps who take advantage of metamorphosis, and will often cause the process to not become a butterfly, but a brood chamber for the wasps. The female wasp will lay her eggs in the caterpillar during the last stages of its growth, and then as it goes into the chrysalis stage, the eggs hatch and the wasp larvae slowly eat their host, protected from predation and diseases by the hard shell of the chrysalis.

The results of this is what my son, Reuben, saw in some California Tortoiseshell butterflies my wife was rearing in her cages at home. "Dad," he shouted one afternoon. "There's tiny insects coming out of the butterfly chrysalids." We all dashed to see what was going on, and sure enough, tiny, brilliant gold-colored, adult wasps were emerging from the butterfly chrysalids. It would be easy for someone to believe this to be "cruel," but in Nature, no one is cruel, mean, or a murderer. It's just the way balance and checks are established. Nature is always trying to reach an equilibrium between habitat and users: what is, is.

As I ponder over insects, I really believe that entomologists are one of the most remarkable ecologists in science. The web of life that affects insects is so complicated that I wonder if it's possible for one man to fully understand the intricate relationships of insects, even if they stayed with it for a lifetime.

What a beautiful gift we have from Nature in the form of butterflies and moths. Here are insects to study that are almost endless in variety and form. Children can not only learn about the biology of these beautiful creatures, but also have the doors to engineering, ecology, zoology, art, and perhaps most importantly—appreciation and respect for the diversity of nature—opened to them for a lifetime. It's been that way for me!

A Final Word

Dear Mr. Owl,

You were very funny. I liked when you flew. I liked when you made us laugh. I like you very much too, Mr. Anderson.

Love, Soraya Meza,
Grade 2, Our Lady of the Lake,
December 2, 1968.

There are hundreds more of those lovely letters, drawings, essays, and poems that children have given me over the years, that I wish I could share with you. I've saved them all because they're so real, they speak from the heart. A child will often tell you what's really going on with him or her, if you'll take but a moment to listen. Children tell it how it is.

I can remember the thank-you note I got from Art Tatum when he was in the sixth grade. He was one of the eager ones who went on every OMSI field trip we offered. After we got back from a wonderful day of digging fossils in the Coast Range, west of Portland, he wrote:

Don Spiegel photographed a beautiful gopher snake discovered as Jim and he were hiking across the sand and sagebrush near Madras, Oregon.

Bruce Welton and Steve Oppenheimer were two of the boys who showed up for every science trip Jim took during the wonderful OMSI days. Here, they're showing us a group of mushrooms that can kill a person very quickly: the colorful—but deadly—Amanitos.

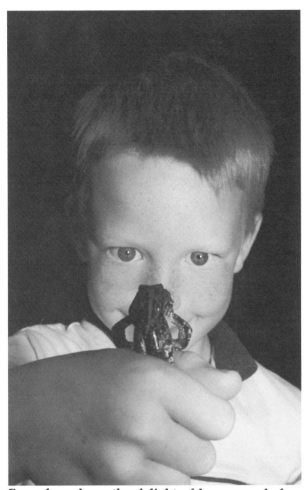

Frogs have been the delight of boys even before Tom Sawyer. Reuben, Jim's son also finds them fun to study and play with.

If there's one owl that will go down in history as one of the most important species of wildlife to affect man, it will surely be the northern spotted owl.

Dear Jim,

I had a wonderful time digging fossils and concretions, but I lost them all when I fell off the cliff in Vernonia.

The last I heard of Art he was teaching chemistry in a mid-western university, and I still miss him.

Among those boxes of letters and drawings are some that contain intimate thoughts on how much Nature means to a child. Most of the beautiful messages and drawings reflect an original thought. Sometimes, however, their new knowledge conflicted with what they had learned from their parents. I've seen a change of attitude in the eyes of a child who was told all his life that snakes are slimy and evil, something to avoid or destroy, but when he or she got the courage to touch one, they found what they had been told wasn't true at all.

I've seen that glow of comprehension in the face of a child who was raised to fear spiders, but when my old "pet" tarantula walked over their hands, the only thing that happened was that their eyes got wide in wonder, and sometimes they laughed because the spider's feet tickled.

I've seen how the wonder of Nature brought peace to a young woman I was asked to help; she was hiding from the world because she was pregnant—with no husband. We talked about the birth of bats and their fantastic natural history, and she

A place for healing. Sparks Lake was one of Ray Atkeson's favorite places for photographs.

became so interested in these beautiful creatures that she forgot to be embarrassed, to think badly of herself, or to suffer with guilt.

I've also known how Nature can cure many of the ills brought on by the horrors of war. An example of this came to me one night several years ago when the phone rang and a hollow voice asked, "This Jim Anderson of the OMSI days?"

As I replied that it was, the voice interrupted, "Well, I was out with you a lot of times before I went to Vietnam," he coughed and went on. "I was a prisoner there for a long time. They had me in a bamboo cage where people threw ---- (feces) at me, poked at me with sharp sticks, and spit on me. I was about to go nuts when, for some reason, I remembered something you said a long time ago about finding something in Nature

to occupy your mind when you were bored—when things weren't going too good—or found yourself in a lousy situation. That's what saved me, you know, those little bugs, spiders, fleas, beetles, spring-tails, and other things that lived with me in the cage. I was able to shut out the stuff outside my prison and study the world that lived in my filth."

I couldn't say anything, except mumble a thanks—the tears in my eyes and the lump in my throat were too much. After a minute he quietly added, "You know . . . I'd like to come and see you sometime if I can get my act together . . . but . . . well . . . I don't know when that'll be . . . I'm still pretty well screwed up." I started to say something, but he cut me off. ". . . Thanks, Jim . . ." and hung up.

I've yet to shake his hand or have him sit by my fire. I sure hope he made it.

Out of sight—out of mind. Only small portion of the chemicals that have been buried in the sprawling alkali basin of northern Lake County. Will it all come back to haunt us someday as chemicals have in other parts of the world? Only time will tell . . .

Don Spiegel used to be afraid of snakes, but once he got that behind him, other fears—and defeat—were easier to face. I believe our OMSI trips together gave him an opportunity to expand, and express what he learned from his parents at home in other ways too. He brought me up short one time as we were hiking out of an enormous shale talus in Wyoming that contained some of the most beautiful fossil Ordovician fish I've ever seen. We were standing on the top of an eight thousand foot high ridge that overlooked western Wyoming, and as he gazed at the beautiful fossils in his hand, and then out at that majestic scenic splendor all around us, he glanced up at me and said, "You know something Jim . . . If a guy doesn't believe in God now, he never will."

In my opinion, there are two laws that we have to help us on this earth. One is the Law of Nature. We must follow this one. If we don't, we'll perish; it's really as simple as that in the long run. If we louse up our air, water, and soil, we just won't be able to live here—and that's that.

The other law is the Law of God, the one that asks us to be kind to one another, and to practice stewardship of our Earth. It's our choice whether we follow this one or not. For me, I think we'd be better off if we took both laws into account for our actions, for they are inextricably linked together.

No one will ever be able to tell me that there isn't power in mountains, glowing sunsets, owls, flowers, beetles, whales, little children, and you and me. Margaret Murie found the power to save mountains when she and her husband studied the wildlife of Alaska; she spent most of her life working for wilderness areas. Rachel Carson found that power as she shared so much of her knowledge of Nature with children and adults. She tried to warn us in her great work, *Silent Spring*, about the loss of that power as a consequence of our irresponsible actions. Either we didn't listen or we've still got a long way to go.

I can recall a phone call I received one

evening back in the '70s: "This is an anonymous phone call," it began. "I cited a truck driver today who was leaking some stinking goop from a tank trunk on the highway between Bend and Burns. I was curious where he was taking that stuff, so I followed him. We turned south from Highway 20 at the Riley Junction, onto highway 135, and then out onto Alkali Flat. I saw the biggest dump of drums I've ever seen in my life. A whole bunch of them had ruptured and were leaking evil-smelling stuff all over the old lake bed—just thought you might like to know about it . . ." and he hung up.

I went out to the site with my family the next day and discovered it was worse than he described. There were hundreds and hundreds of decaying drums from a variety of chemical firms from all over the Northwest, leaking and stinking up "my" Oregon Country. The fury I felt was only secondary compared to my sorrow at seeing the Land insulted and defamed. Oregon's northern Lake County had become a chemical dump—at a time when we had the strongest environmental governor of our history, Tom McCall. What's going to happen to the water table under that old alkali flat? I wondered. I asked a great many people for the answer, and got as many viewpoints and opinions as there were people—no one had a definite answer that I was satisfied with—just opinions. The bottom line was that no one really did know; perhaps the chemicals "might" leach into the water table, "someday." This in itself should have been enough to stop anyone in their tracks who depended on the water for their livelihood in that part of the country. Perhaps "someday" could be tomorrow.

The wisdom of our government leaders found what they thought was a perfect solution to the problem at Alkali Flat: they buried it. "Out of sight, out of mind." In time, we may forget that chemical time bomb lying under the blowing sand and dust of the alkali basin—but will Nature forget it? I think not. It may come back some day to haunt us all. Maybe ten miles away from Alkali Flat a rancher (as in Carson's book) will discover his sick and dying cattle poisoned by the water from his

Jim once had a man say that looking into the eyes of an owl was like looking into the eyes of God. Ross, Jim's son, stares with our smallest owl, the pygmy owl, found in Ramsey Canyon in southeastern Arizona, and other areas of the Southwest.

wells. In addition to the insult to the Land, it was the Oregon taxpayers who had to pay the bill to "clean up" the irresponsible actions of people in our free enterprise system who think only in terms of financial profit and loss. There are Responsibilities that go with our Rights. I hope we will listen to the future Rachel Carsons before it's too late.

I've also seen the confusion of some people who don't understand that all life is important to the Earth. I can recall a woman who, having been bitten several times by mosquitoes, angrily asked, "What good are they?" I could have told her how important

A portion of the 700 plus pronghorn antelope that wander around the Fort Rock Basin in northern Lake County, Oregon. Shorty Gustafson, a long-time resident of the old lake basin country, was asked how that many pronghorn affected his hay fields in winter. His reply was, "Oh, it ain't so bad, Jimmy. That's the way I pay my rent."

they are in the web of life that revolves around the marshes and swamps, but she was so upset with her bites that she didn't want to—or couldn't have—heard me anyway.

Then there was the woman who thought it was so "cute" the way her little poodle played with the coyotes out on the golf course near her home. I tried to tell her that coyotes don't play the same games or have the same rules as her poodle, but she was convinced that it was all in "fun"—until the coyotes ate her poodle. Then Nature was the villain—again; she went around telling everyone how terrible those "murdering" coyotes were. There is no "right" or "wrong" in Nature. It just "is."

What I know to be the truth, what I know to be the way we must look at our Earth, the way we must consider every part of our ecosystem before we tinker with things, has been written by better writers than I. The science of ecological thinking has been with us long enough that it should convince even the most hard-hearted exploiter of Nature that if we interrupt or damage, any part of

the Earth and the ecosystem without considering what we do to the whole, we're in a heap of trouble. It's going to be up to you and me to bring this truth to those who share this wonderful home (away from home) with us.

It's not enough to discuss the welfare of the spotted owl when we address the Ancient Forests that remain in North America. We must look at an old-growth forest as a complete ecosystem unique to itself, but also interacting with other biological and social communities surrounding it. That not only includes plants and wildlife, but the economic and sociological interactions of our own culture as well. In the summer of 1990, I designed and implemented a full-blown interpretive program for the Bend District of the Deschutes National Forest. At campfire programs I used a crippled juvenile great horned owl to get across my philosophy of the conservation ethic and show-and-tell for the kids. I could tell when a logger or someone in the timber industry asked questions, for the first one was, "Is that one of those damned spotted

If there was ever a bird that was the true herald of spring, it's the Western Meadowlark, the Oregon State Bird. Even if it's snowing crosswise—as it often does in the Northwest—the song of the meadowlark promises that the warmth of summer is on the way.

owls?" As we progressed from the antagonism and past the old-growth syndrome, I'd take up the subjects of shipping raw logs overseas for someone else to saw into lumber, and automation in the mills in the Northwest. In a moment the owls were forgotten, as the individual slammed his fist into his palm and growled, "You're damn right!" The rules of the discussion, or debate, changed too. The science of ecology isn't limited to just the world of nature. We live here too . . .

Years ago, I was out birding along the Columbia River with Roland Clement, who at the time was the Vice-President of the National Audubon Society, and Bob Zeke, a logger-turned conservationist. As we were looking at the remains of a gigantic Sitka Spruce that had been felled with an active

bald eagle nest in it, Roland remarked, "We can come up with a suitable substitute for wood any time we want to, but we'll never find a substitute for a tree or a forest."

". . . or an eagle", Bob added. It's best we think in terms of whole communities, rather than individual species.

Joseph Jones was a mild-mannered kid filled with incessant questions when he walked onto the OMSI bus back in the '60s. He wasn't satisfied with a pat answer, he always wanted more, a storehouse that had to be filled. When he learned that owls, hawks, falcons, eagles, and several other bird species were brought up on oral pellets that contained the undigested remains of their prey, he wanted to know why and how it worked. If we went out to dig fossils at Beaverly Beach on the Oregon Coast he wanted to learn everything he could about the conditions when the fossils were laid down. If we went to see birds on the Coast or in the desert marshes, or if we chased lizards and snakes on the desert, he wanted to know about the life history of the animals and their association within their respective niches, habitat, and other environmental conditions. He gleaned every scrap of natural history knowledge I had—and then some. Now he's the director of OMSI's Hancock Field Station, a position he has occupied for the past twelve years.

He called me the other day, as he has in the past, for a little help. "Hello, Jim? Joseph here. I'm taking a group of students to Fort Rock and the surrounding area next week. How would you and your family like to join me?" I hesitated only a moment, then agreed to rendezvous at the Cabin Lake Campground, nestled among the giant, old-growth Ponderosa Pine on the very south end of the Deschutes National Forest.

As the big yellow bus pulled into the campground, I heard the familiar sounds of teenagers having a good time. Sleeping bags were tossed out onto the ground, cooking gear clanked out onto the picnic tables, the outhouses and water faucets were investigated, and the business of setting up camp got under way with the final touch—the smokey campfire. The sights, sounds, and smells filled me with memories of the many trips I had led myself over the years. Despite the neon shoelaces, computer watches, and "cool dude" talk, the kids seemed pretty much the same. When we boarded the bus for a moonlight road hunt and to set out the Sherman live-traps, I walked up the steps and back in time nearly thirty years.

The next morning Joseph gathered everyone, and we sat in a cross-legged circle to review what we had learned so far, and what we wanted to learn tomorrow. As I listened I saw a young boy sitting in my circle long ago, always asking questions, never satisfied with the pat answers. The circle was complete. The mantle was passed. My heart was full.

It's time to call it a day. I didn't even get a chance to tell you about Australia, and the fun I had with the kids, kangaroos, and aborigines there—or the time I dumped a dead bald eagle on the desk of the Vice President of Georgia Pacific because his outfit had cut a big, old-growth Sitka Spruce with an active nest in it—we'll just have to save those for another campfire. I really could go on and on about the wonderful times I've had with hawks, owls, snakes, fossils, and kids.

That's the way it is when you've been at the Nature business as long as I have . . . Like the time I went to be the speaker for a group of engineers at the Weyerhauser plant in Longview, Washington, with a four foot Gopher Snake tucked inside my shirt. Right in the middle of dinner the snake decided he had been in there long enough, stuck his head out from under my tie and flicked his tongue at my host's wife. That started a very stimulating conversation. Then there was the time . . . oh, shucks, the fire's burning out, there's smoke in my eyes, and it's time to turn in. As my little girl, Miriam, says when I tuck her in for the night, "See you when the sun comes up."